Writing the History of Memory

WRITING HISTORY

Published:

Writing History, Heiko Feldner, Kevin Passmore and Stefan Berger (2003)
Writing Medieval History (2005)
Writing Early Modern History (2005)
Writing Contemporary History, Robert Gildea and Anne Simonin (2008)
Writing History (Second Edition), Heiko Feldner, Kevin
  Passmore and Stefan Berger (2010)
Writing Postcolonial History, Rochona Majumdar (2010)
Writing Gender History (Second Edition), Laura Lee Downs (2010)
Writing the Holocaust, Jean-Marc Dreyfus and Daniel Langton (2011)

Forthcoming:

Writing the History of Crime, Paul Knepper (2014)
Writing the History of Material Culture, Giorgio
  Riello & Anne Gerritsen (2014)
Writing the History of Empire, Alexei Miller (2015)

Writing the History of Memory

EDITED BY
STEFAN BERGER
AND BILL NIVEN

B L O O M S B U R Y
LONDON • NEW DELHI • NEW YORK • SYDNEY

Bloomsbury Academic

An imprint of Bloomsbury Publishing Plc

50 Bedford Square	1385 Broadway
London	New York
WC1B 3DP	NY 10018
UK	USA

www.bloomsbury.com

Bloomsbury is a registered trade mark of Bloomsbury Publishing Plc

First published 2014

British Library Cataloguing-in-Publication Data
A catalogue record for this book is available from the British Library.

ISBN: PB: 978-0-3409-9188-6
ePDF: 978-1-8496-6674-9
ePub: 978-1-8496-6673-2

Library of Congress Cataloging-in-Publication Data
A catalog record for this book is available from the Library of Congress.

Typeset by Deanta Global Publishing Services, Chennai, India
Printed and bound in India

CONTENTS

NOTES ON CONTRIBUTORS

Lynn Abrams is professor of Gender History at the University of Glasgow. She has published extensively in women's, gender and oral history and her books include *The Making of Modern Woman: Europe 1789–1918* (Longman, 2002) and *Oral History Theory* (Routledge, 2010). Her current research centres on the liberation of the female self in women of the post-war generation.

Stefan Berger is professor of Social History at Ruhr-Universität Bochum, where he also directs the Institute for Social Movements and is executive director of the Foundation Library of the Ruhr. Between 2000 and 2005 and from 2005 to 2011, he held chairs at the Universities of Glamorgan and Manchester, respectively. He has published widely on comparative labour history, nationalism, history of historiography and historical theory. His last monograph was Friendly Enemies: Britain and the GDR, 1949–1990 (with Norman LaPorte, Berghahn, 2010).

Peter Carrier is a fellow at the Georg Eckert Institute for International Textbook Research in Braunschweig, Germany. He has published widely on the impact of language and contemporary arts on collective memory and historical identities, including *Holocaust Monuments and National Memory Cultures in France and Germany* (Berghahn, 2005).

Rick Crownshaw is a senior lecturer in the Department of English and Comparative Literature at Goldsmiths, University of London. His recent publications include *The Afterlife of Holocaust Memory in Contemporary Literature and Culture* (Palgrave Macmillan, 2010) and a guest-edited issue of the journal *parallax* on the topic of transcultural memory. He is currently working on a book project provisionally entitled *The Natural History of Memory*.

Mary Fulbrook, FBA, is professor of German History at UCL. She has held many professional roles, including chair of the Modern History Section of the British Academy, and chair of the German History Society. She serves on the Academic Advisory Board of the Foundation for the former Nazi Concentration Camps at Buchenwald and Mittelbau-Dora, and on the International Advisory Board of the Chancellor Willy Brandt Foundation. Her current research is on 'Reverberations of Nazi Persecution', and she is directing an AHRC-funded collaborative project on *Reverberations of War in Germany and Europe since 1945*. Author or editor of more than 20 books, Fulbrook's recent publications include *Dissonant Lives: Generations and Violence through the German Dictatorships* (OUP, 2011) and *A Small Town near Auschwitz: Ordinary Nazis and the Holocaust* (OUP, 2012).

Wulf Kansteiner is associate professor of European History at Binghamton University (SUNY). He has published widely in the fields of media history, memory studies and historical theory. He is the author of *In Pursuit of German Memory: History, Television, and Politics after Auschwitz* (Ohio UP, 2006); co-editor of *The Politics of Memory in Postwar Europe* (Duke UP, 2006), *Historical Representation and Historical Truth* (Oxford Blackwell, 2009); and *Den Holocaust erzählen: Historiographie zwischen wissenschaftlicher Empirie und narrativer Kreativität* (Wallstein, 2013). He is also co-founder of the Sage-Journal *Memory Studies* (published since 2008).

Benoît Majerus is associate professor of European History at the University of Luxembourg. He has recently co-published *Inventing Luxembourg. Representations of the Past, Space and Language from the Nineteenth to the Twenty-first Century* (Brill Academic, 2010).

Bill Niven is professor of Contemporary German History at Nottingham Trent University, UK. He has published widely on aspects of Germany's attempts to come to terms with its, e.g. *Facing the Nazi Past* (Routledge, 2001) and *The Buchenwald Child* (Camden House, 2007). He is currently completing a book on representations in East German literature of the flight and expulsion of Germans from central-eastern Europe at the end of World War II.

Attila Pók is deputy director of the Institute of History at the Research Centre for Humanities of the Hungarian Academy of Sciences in Budapest, general secretary of the Hungarian Historical Association, member of the Presidium of the Hungarian Academy of Sciences, recurring visiting professor of History at Columbia University in New York. His publications and courses cover three major fields: Nineteenth to twentieth-century European political and intellectual history, history of modern European historiography with special regard to political uses of history and theory and methodology of history.

Kimberly Rivers is professor of History at the University of Wisconsin Oshkosh. She has published articles on the use of memory techniques in preaching and religious life and has recently published a monograph, *Preaching the Memory of Virtue and Vice: Memory, Images and Mendicant Preaching in the Late Middle Ages* (Brepols, 2010).

Gordon Spencer Shrimpton is Professor Emeritus of Classics at the University of Victoria. He has authored many articles and reviews on Greek history and historical writing, edited a festschrift on Greek History in honour of Malcolm McGregor and authored two books: *Theopompus the Historian* (McGill-Queen's, 1991) and *History and Memory in Ancient Greece.* (McGill-Queen's, 1997). He is currently preparing a book on the human memory and how it preserves and distorts the past.

Introduction

Bill Niven and Stefan Berger

The relationship between history and memory

In Classical antiquity, and indeed right into the medieval period, memory and history were not imagined as opposites. In Plato's Socratic dialogue *Meno* (380 BCE), Socrates explains that the immortal soul, through its various peregrinations, has acquired a knowledge of all things; all learning is but recollection (anamnesis).[1] On this reading, memory is an all-encompassing and accessible storage system, not the unreliable witness to past events as which it is often understood today. In a world strongly dependent on oral transmission, it is perhaps unsurprising that memory's powers and abilities should have been admired and cultivated[2]: the ancient arts of rhetoric and dialectic are unthinkable without it. Moreover, the ancients imagined writing as a process of recording experiences already stored in the mind. As Mary Carruthers puts it: 'from this viewpoint, the symbolic representations that we call writing are no more than cues or triggers for the memorial representations, also symbolic, upon which human cognition is based'.[3] The *ars memorativa* or system of mnemonic principles upon which pre-modern memory was based ('mnemotechnics') deployed a wide range of associative skills to implant impressions in memory. Well-known is the story of Simonides, whom Cicero credits with being the first to introduce the art of memory. According to Cicero's account, Simonides was able to identify the crushed bodies in a collapsed banquet hall because he could remember where each of the guests 'had been reclining at table'.[4] The pre-modern age conceived of the mind as a building with rooms to which mental images and experiences, reimagined in the form of symbols, were allocated for ease of recall. In those days, one might say, people felt at home in memory, they truly inhabited it, and from it they took all they needed to interpret, describe and define the world – and to narrate its history.

If the mechanization of printing and bookmaking, at least according to Benedict Anderson, led among other things to the decline of Latin, the rise of 'print capitalism' and the emergence of the nation,[5] it also may have introduced a cleavage between memory and history: increasingly, history came to be identified with the written source and with the growing discipline of historiography, the *writing* of history, while memory, which prior to then had largely been the very medium, indeed substance of history, became associated with imprecision and distortion. Certainly, Nietzsche's critique in *Untimely Meditations* of the unhealthy impact of memory was fundamentally a critique of what he termed monumental and antiquarian history, which was marked in his eyes by a tendentious or obsessive relationship to the past. But Nietzsche's warning against memory becoming the 'gravedigger of the present' reflected a growing scepticism towards it.[6] Generally, the nineteenth century saw the onward march of positivism, with history writing too falling under the sway of influence of empirical science; attention was directed towards observation as the source of true knowledge. The 'inward' gaze – towards intuition, or indeed memory – was eschewed in favour of the principles of scientism. The scientific and psychoanalytic study of memory in the late nineteenth and early twentieth centuries did little to restore the enormous reputation it had enjoyed in pre-modern times. Hermann Ebbinghaus may have pioneered investigation into memory retention (and the 'learning curve'), but in some ways he reduced memory to a question of mechanics.[7] Freud's writings on memory, for all their importance for later generations of psychoanalysts and memory theorists (especially trauma theory), could be seen as contributing to understanding memory as something deeply suspect, even pathological. The concept of 'screen memory',[8] i.e. the retention of the seemingly unimportant and concomitant repression of significant experiences, suggests at the very least that memory operates within a complex web of psychological scars and defence mechanisms. It is hardly the sovereign repository imagined in pre-modern times.

In the 1920s, Maurice Halbwachs further problematized the issue by developing his theory of collective memory as a product of social frameworks. We discuss this at length below and elsewhere in the volume. For now, it seems important to highlight Halbwachs' view of the relationship between memory and history. He drew a dividing-line between them. He argued that history sets in when 'social memory is fading or breaking up'; that history is something unitary ('there is only one history'), while there are several collective memories; and that history is characterized by demarcations, while collective memory is more fluid and gradualist. Most striking, perhaps, is his tendency to bracket out the historian from the influence of social groups, past or present. He or she appears transcendent, or at least striving for objectivity and impartiality.[9] This notion of the historian as somehow independent of the interests and vagaries of memory or indeed any other influence other than scholarly integrity still informs present-day views, even if it has been severely undermined in recent decades, not least by postmodernism. So we arrive, then, at a dichotomous understanding of the relationship between memory and history in modernity which contrasts starkly with the altogether more harmonious relationship they enjoyed in pre-modern perceptions. History becomes the necessary corrective to memory, even its antithesis, not something embodied within it.

In providing fundamental insights into the function and operation of memory at individual and collective level respectively, Freud and Halbwachs revealed how individual and social behaviour was shaped by it. Memory was no longer an enormous thesaurus one carried in one's head and accessed when required, rather it was a volatile and malleable property which, on the collective level, had the power to influence the course of world events. Of the factors that ultimately brought down the fragile interwar peace in Europe, surely one of the most influential was memory: namely the deeply resentful memory of what were felt in some quarters to be the unfair terms of the post-World War I peace treaties (Versailles, Trianon), coupled with bitterness towards those who imposed or were perceived to have benefited from them. As Jay Winter has argued, it was World War I which 'brought the search for an appropriate language of loss to the centre of cultural and political life'.[10] But the apocalyptic thinking Winter sees as so characteristic of the Great War and its aftermath had its correlative, as Roger Griffin has argued, in 'the ideologies of modern social and political movements bent on healing society from its alleged corruption and decadence'.[11] One driver behind the 'myth of palingenesis', as Griffin calls it, was surely the evocative force of collective memory, which imagined the past not just in terms of racial purity, but also in terms of a territorial integrity, of a putative correspondence between boundaries of state and boundaries of race. It was in the name of this memory that the powerful revisionism practised by Nazism in the 1930s and by various central and eastern European states prior to and during World War II was launched.

Memory after World War I, then, for all its preoccupation with mourning and its cultivation of forms of memorialization, included an aggressive revanchist component. This changed radically after World War II. Now, collective memory – admittedly after some fits and starts – focused on ensuring that such acts of aggression never happened again. This process began, at the latest, with the adoption of the Convention on the Prevention and Punishment of the Crime of Genocide by the United Nations General Assembly on 9 December 1948. Auschwitz, in part at least the end result of a warped collective memory which imagined a history of anti-German Jewish conspiracy, now stands at the centre of a culturally constantly reinforced collective memory in which the spirit of memory is prevention, not destruction (whether commitment to prevention has proven effective, however, is open to debate). So while the *writing* of history and the operations of collective memory may be understood as contrasting processes, there can be no doubt that the impact of memory on the *course* of history would seem fundamental to developments certainly in the twentieth century – and, arguably, in preceding centuries, too.

In particular, what Anne Fuchs has called 'impact events' or what Dipesh Chakrabarty has described in terms of 'historical wounds' led to a politics of regret that was based on memory.[12] In fact, Chris Lorenz has recently argued that much of our recent history resembles a past that does not cool off any more. Instead it remains toxic, corrosive and ambiguous. It stays in a 'hot state', something reflected by the popularity of 'post-traumatic', 'catastrophic' and 'haunting' histories, which frequently involve issues of memory. If this is correct, then one of our common-sense presuppositions, namely that the hot present cools off and gives way to the past and that this amounts to a change from memory to history is no longer correct. Instead history and memory have entered a much more ambiguous and at the same time intimate relationship.[13] Added to this, there is a lot of evidence that, from the 1980s onwards, we are in fact dealing with a different time regime. If the modern time regime until then oriented attention and expectation towards the future and operated under the concept of progress, a concept that devalued the past and left it to antiquarians, the resources of the future seemed a spent force by the 1980s: fear of a nuclear Armageddon, environmental disaster, overpopulation and recurring economic crises left the future looking bleak. It rapidly ceased to be the vanishing point of our hopes and dreams. In turn the past became increasingly the anchor-point of our search for meaning and arguably the motor of that past was memory.[14] While memory has an appeal in societies short of utopian futures, memory history, as Jay Winter has argued, can also serve to be the basis of 'minor utopias'.[15] Given the popularity of concepts of memory in these diverse contexts, it seems unsurprising that historians, increasingly, have been turning their hand to analysing the nature, extent and long-term effects of memory. To the traditional branches of historiography such as social, military, economic and diplomatic history, another has been added: the writing of the history of memory.

Historians of memory

Arguably, in addition to Maurice Halbwachs, it was the so-called Annales School in the 1920s – a school which came to dominate French historiography – which first took social attitudes seriously as a focus of historical study. As Alon Confino points out, in focusing on the history of mentalities (*mentalités*), the Annales School took an interest not just in 'the history of collective representations, myths, and images', but also, as a facet of this, in the history of memory. Pierre Nora, so important for contemporary historiographies of memory, is himself a third-generation Annaliste.[16] Of fundamental importance, too, is the rise of oral history as a branch of historical study in the 1970s and 1980s. Oral historians have from the beginning been acutely aware of the need not just to integrate the perceptions and experiences of ordinary people into accounts of the past, but also to examine the relationship between the so-called objective history of events, and the 'subjective' memory of them.[17] Indirectly, at least, the emergence of discourse analysis in the 1970s was also of importance for the development of historians' interest in memory. In his pathbreaking book *Metahistory*, Hayden White set out to 'treat the historical work as what it most manifestly is: a verbal structure in the form of a narrative prose discourse'.[18] While White was not claiming that the essentially poetic and rhetorical nature of historical narrative invalidated its claim to truth, his examination of its literary qualities drew attention to the positionality of the historian, his or her 'stance' and locatedness within a particular discourse. As Patrick Hutton has suggested, White's work helped to trigger discussions about historiography in which the 'question of how history is constructed began to crowd out that of how historians gather and evaluate data' – a question which led back to memory, which, according to Hutton, had been since ancient times 'the inspiration for, as well as the source of, our inquiry into the past'.[19]

Of enormous importance for the developing interest of historians in memory, moreover, was the long-term impact of the Holocaust and of World War II in general. Legacies of guilt, complicity and suffering impacted on states domestically and internationally, an impact which took on political, judicial and cultural form, particularly in the two Germanies, but not only there. The imprint of the past on the present, it seemed, had never been so palpable. Reactions to this past, of course, were mediated through a particular understanding and approach. Norbert Frei, for instance, coined the term 'politics of the past' to designate the way in which political interests in West Germany shaped responses to the Nazi past.[20] Peter Novick's study of memory of the Holocaust in America sought to explain how, after 20 years of neglect, the subject 'boomed' in the 1970s against the background of an evolving culture of victimhood which had not been present after the war.[21] An equally groundbreaking study by Henry Rousso on memory of Vichy France sought to account for waves in patterns of reception: according to Rousso, a period of repression was followed by a phase of 'resistancialism'; between 1971 and 1974, this myth of resistance was shattered, paving the way for the 'reawakening of Jewish memory' and the increased importance of the Occupation period in French political discourse.[22]

Significant, too, was the end of the communist period and the apparent triumph of western liberalism. Famously, this was hailed by Francis Fukuyama as the 'end of history'.[23] If history had come to an end, then all that remained, as it were, was to give oneself over to the multiple subjectivities of memory. Cultural historian Andreas Huyssen, while not sharing the radicalism of Fukuyama's view, nevertheless argues that the traditional notion of history as objective and distinct from memory has been coming under increasing pressure during the twentieth century as a result of a number of factors including the critique of historiography as a tool of domination and ideology, post-Nietzschean attacks on linearity and causality, and postcolonial critiques of western history as implicated in 'an imperialist and racist Western modernity'. Huyssen argues that the crisis of history contrasts with a current 'hypertrophy of memory'.[24] Memory and history alike are thus questioned in relation to the kind of narrative hegemonies they construct, and the multiplicity of narrations over time has drawn attention to the layering of time and to palimpsestic readings of memory.[25] These views would seem to stand in opposition, however, to those of Pierre Nora, who has repeatedly, and somewhat nostalgically lamented the passing of memory, which he sees as having been swallowed up by an ever-accelerating history as constant change destroys the social fabrics required for the development of a lived memory of the past.[26] In that case, as Polish historian and philosopher Krzysztof Pomian has argued, memory has become the victim of history;[27] perhaps it has even been superseded by it. What is certain is that the end of communism and the emergence of new states from its shadow led to a recuperation, indeed effervescence of personal and national memories long repressed – especially in states which had experienced two (or more) bouts of totalitarian rule under Nazism and Stalinism. 'Decommunisation' in the former Soviet lands, but also processes of lustration and transitional justice in other parts of the world (particularly in South Africa) indicate that remembering and overcoming the past has become a central feature of the way states set about building new identities. The very vitality of memory, then, as a social and political issue over the last twenty years has alerted historians to it as an object of study.

Approaching the historical study of memory

In which ways do historians approach this topic? For many historians – not least Peter Novick and Henry Rousso cited above – Maurice Halbwachs' writings on collective memory represent the most significant starting-points for approaching memory of the past. Translated into English as *On Collective Memory*, Halbwachs' pathbreaking book *Les cadres sociaux de la mémoire* (1925) had an almost immediate effect for historical study.[28] His ideas, as Alon Confino has pointed out, were picked up by the founders of the Annales School, Lucien Febvre and Marc Bloch, to whom he developed 'a close professional friendship'.[29] The notion of collective memory has since proven fruitful for newer generations of historians who seek to understand history not just in terms of high politics, diplomacy and economics, also as one of the attitudes profoundly connected to particular images of the past. There is, in other words, no point or period in history which itself is not influenced by previous history. This observation is self-evident on one level: clearly, we live in a world which is the product of centuries of evolution. But the study of collective memory is more interested in how certain *understandings* of what came before – regardless of the accuracy of such views – inform, underpin and reinforce thinking, action and reaction in the present. To see the world through Halbwachs' eyes is to appreciate, moreover, that these understandings are essentially social phenomena, even as they are realized at the level of individuals: 'one may say that the individual remembers by placing himself in the perspective of the group, but one may also affirm that the memory of the group realizes and manifests itself in individual memories'.[30] We all belong to one or indeed several social groups, groups whose coherence and identity depend to a considerable extent on a shared view of the past. These groups are the social frameworks (*cadres sociaux*) which shape our individual memory. Halbwachs has subsequently been criticized for advocating a rather reified view of collective memory. The criticism is perhaps unfair: Halbwachs makes clear that, while ideas about the past evolve and circulate within groups, they only actually *exist* within the minds of individuals. Nevertheless, a certain semantic elasticity seems inherent to the term 'collective memory'. Usually we see it used as a metaphor for shared views, but in some accounts, too, collective memory seems to take on a life of its own, appearing almost as a kind of supernatural presence controlling the way we think. Moreover, in Halbwachs' model, the degree to which individual memory really is individual might be open to debate. At times, it seems the most he would concede is that our individuality, as remembering beings, consists in the always distinct form of intersection between group memories we, as individuals, embody.

The idea of collective memory, despite its difficulties (to which we will return), has proven enormously fruitful and inspirational for historians. This is particularly true of scholars examining the way states, state governments, political parties and other elite groups have sought to encourage views of the past which serve their own ends. This is not to say that these bodies do not believe in the views they promulgate, but it is to say that there is often a convenient symmetry between the promotion of these views and the acquisition, consolidation and extension of power. It is not to say, either, that these views are necessarily false (though they might be). But they are often one-sided or tendentious in a manner that invites comparison with the subjectivities of memory rather than with the (supposed) objectivity of historiography. They are usually formed by what has been called 'presentism', best understood as the generation of images of the past adapted to suit the interests of the present. Such views, systematically and programmatically disseminated (in school education, for example, or through state museums), can take on the form of 'master narratives', possibly displacing alternative readings to the margins and subcultures of society. In the case of the German Democratic Republic, for instance, the official doctrine of antifascism, which glorified the memory of communist resistance against Nazism, served to justify the power exercised by state leaders, who had themselves (in some case, rather tenuously) contributed to this resistance. Jeffrey Herf's classic account of the 'master narrative' of German communism in the GDR examines its operation.[31] And as Patrick Wright has shown, the emergence of the 'heritage industry' in 1980s Britain was Margaret Thatcher's way of seeking to bolster support for her controversial and divisive policies of neoliberalism by associating them with the glories of Britain's past.[32] Reimagining the past in more ideal terms was one aspect of the 'invention of tradition' which Erich Hobsbawm identified as a salient element of nationalism and the nation-state;[33] this reimagined past then played its part in establishing an 'imagined community' in the present, often to compensate for and paper over real social and economic divisions and fissures.[34]

When we speak of the 'own ends' of state governments, however, we should not conceive of this too narrowly. It is not just about securing or keeping a firm grip on power. To a significant degree in some cases at least, in seeking to mobilize the population behind a particular view of history, states seek to rally support for policies they believe to be in the national interest. Yael Zeruvabel has shown how the foundation of the state of Israel in 1948 was accompanied and followed by a Zionist 'reconstruction of symbolic continuities and discontinuities in Jewish history' designed to 'support the ideology of national revival'.[35] As the back cover of her book puts it, Zeruvabel explores how Israeli memory 'transformed events that ended in death and defeat into heroic myths'. When post-Communist central-eastern European states began remembering the oppression of communism, this was not simply to celebrate the overcoming of that oppression, but also – and more significantly, as James Mark has shown – out of a concern that communism might not be dead and buried after all: as Mark puts it, communism's continuing hold on the present needed to be confronted and weakened.[36] Heiko Pääbo's study on collective memory in the newly independent states of Estonia, the Ukraine and Georgia highlights the degree to which what he terms 'dissimilative' elements have been woven into the fabric of new foundation narratives; these narratives, in other words, stress the long-established distinctness of Estonians, Ukrainians and Georgians in an attempt to disentangle their history from that of the Soviet Union and today's Russia and furnish as it were historical evidence of the right to independence.[37] The reimagined past of the master narratives generated at state level is usually a heroic one, but it can also centre around tales of victimization (e.g. of Estonians by Soviet Russia and Nazism). As Eviatar Zeruvabel has shown, moreover, reimagining the past is not just about *what* events we choose to remember ('commemorative density'), but about how we shape this memory.[38] Thus collective memory imagines the past in terms of narratives, for instance, either of progress, or decline, or circularity, or continuity, or discontinuity; it depends what best serves current interests.

However, the notion that the state monopolizes images of the nation's past has also been challenged by historians. After all, it would be difficult to prove how far such images actually penetrate the minds of citizens, or how far they mesh with existing views within society, and it may be the case that they contradict such views. Yael Zeruvabel uses the term 'countermemory' to designate the presence of an alternative memory 'which directly opposes the master commemorative narrative'.[39] In his important book on commemoration in the United States, John Bodnar suggested the term 'vernacular culture' to describe the way citizens, organized as groups, seek to develop commemorative spaces, forms and practices which reflect how *they* want to remember historical events –[40] usually events that the members of the groups in question have themselves experienced and through which they are bonded by ties of what Jay Winter has called 'fictive kinship'.[41] Often, vernacular memory and official memory do not go hand in hand. Bodnar illustrates this through the example of Vietnam. The veterans behind the idea for a Vietnam Veterans' Memorial wanted a site where they could remember their pain, show reverence to the dead and indeed even express a sense of grievance at the way the state had treated them. While Maya Ying Lin's design certainly catered for a sense of grief, 'the powerful and dominant interests of patriots and nationalists could not let a text composed only by and about ordinary people and ordinary emotions stand alone'.[42] Hence the addition of a statue of heroic soldiers. The case of the Vietnam Veterans' Memorial is perhaps unusual in the solution it provides to competing memory: two memorials in one. More often than not, memorials and commemorative rituals have recourse to a vague inclusive rhetoric which allows a variety of readings, mediating the needs of different groups and the contrasting interests of 'top-down' and vernacular memory.

So while historians have applied the theory of collective memory to their analyses of the relationship between state power and memory, they have in general moved away from the idea that there is one, centrally driven or dominant collective memory, arguing for a more nuanced and differentiated approach which takes account of the sheer variety of memories within a society and of the different groups which have a stake in promoting these. Thus sociologist and historian Jeffrey Olick has written of the need to avoid the 'substantialism' of the notion of a unitary or consensual collective memory in favour of a 'process-relational' approach which takes account of its fluid and evolving nature.[43] As becomes clear from Neil Gregor's richly textured study of post-war Nuremberg, to speak of 'German' memory of the war in the 1950s would be to overlook the different constituencies vying for representation and their visibility in processes of commemoration.[44] The same would surely hold true of French society during the same period. Indeed so frustrated did Jay Winter become with the term 'collective memory' – insisting that 'states do not remember; individuals do, in association with other people' – that he suggested replacing it with 'collective remembrance', a term connoting the actual act of remembering, as done by specific groups at a specific place and time.[45] Dissatisfaction with the term 'collective memory' derives, then, from tendencies to use it in a reified and transcendent way, often as if it were a product of politics, or of a unitary social will, yet politics are rarely homogeneous (at least in democracies), nor do societies possess a singular soul. Too close an association of the term with the national risks eliding the memory of different social groups. Such groups may evolve due to commonalities of experience, generation, class or ethnicity, for instance.

Thinking in terms of patterns of national memory also erroneously implies that gender differences are of little importance in understanding the history of memory. Countering such assumptions, oral historians began to probe the gendered nature of memory from the late 1970s on.[46] Psychology and sociolinguistics have also drawn attention to the possibility that men and women actually remember differently.[47] In many ways, oral history and women's history developed in parallel. Indeed the two are intertwined. If oral history was seeking 'to introduce the missing voices of the underprivileged ... feminists wanted to demonstrate the vital role played by women past and present through a reconstruction of the past which for the first time gave adequate attention to the contributions of women'.[48] As far as oral history is concerned, recuperating the social, economic and cultural role of women (against the background of a male-dominated and male-focused historiography) can be done either by trying to identify traces of their influence in past oral traditions, or by the practice of oral history – interviews and the like – in the present. In either case, recent historical research has been able to reinscribe women's memory into a history from which they had often been excluded. Thus in her book on memory and gender in medieval Europe, Elisabeth van Houts shows not just that medieval sources such as Latin chronicles and the lives of saints were often crafted from oral traditions, she also stresses that these traditions were often transmitted by women, and the testimony and memories of women provided chroniclers with an important resource.[49] Such reinscription is not just necessary for the more distant past. Cheryl McEwan recently provided a critical gloss on South Africa's Truth and Reconciliation Commission. While it has done much to empower the oppressed to speak of their experiences and to create a kind of post-colonial 'people's archive', it has produced only 'a partial truth because of the absence of women's testimony, especially relating to everyday violence'.[50] Historians have recently also endeavoured to write the history and memory of the Holocaust from the perspective of women's experiences and women's memoirs and testimony.[51] Yet 'engendering the Holocaust', as Janet Liebmann reminds us, has not been without its critics. As she further points out, even a scholar such as Ruth Bondy, who has done valuable research into women's experience and memory of the Holocaust, feels bound to express reservations towards her own approach: 'Zyklon B did not differentiate between men and women'.[52]

While analysing the way we experience and the way we remember events in terms of gender, or of group affiliations and identities may do much to counteract tendencies to approach memory in terms of national imaginaries, it does not necessarily obviate the risk of reification. According to Jeffrey Olick, breaking collective memory down into different sets of collective memory according to whether it is, for instance, official or vernacular, ethnic or generational, 'does not necessarily eliminate the tendency to reify the new categories'. Olick warns against a tendency in oral history research, for instance, to simply counterpose the supposed authenticity of 'vernacular memory to the "truth" of historical memory'.[53] In suggesting the term 'collected memory' as an alternative, Olick emphasizes the need to recuperate the role, power and perspective of individuals within groups, restoring to them something of that individuality smothered by the adjective 'collective'.[54] That said, the globalization of Holocaust memory suggests there may be a need not only to look 'below' the level of the national when seeking to understand collective memory in its full variety, but also 'above' it towards transnational memory frameworks which transcend 'national containers'. The work of Daniel Levy and Natan Sznaider into the 'cosmopolitan memory' of the Holocaust, as they call it, points in this direction.[55]

If there is such a thing as a collective memory, then it certainly can no longer be imagined as something imposed, rigid or timeless. Rather it represents a constantly shifting and fragile consensus, dependent for the form it takes at any given time upon the relative power and interaction of a number of different memory contingents. Nor can it be imagined as uniform in its mode of operation. Cultural historian Jan Assmann introduced the important distinction between two parallel 'memory frames' which he terms communicative and cultural memory. Communicative memory comprises 'memories which refer to the recent past', i.e. memories which are shared by contemporaries and extend, normally, over three to four generations. Communicative memory thus evolves over time. Whereas communicative memory is linked to personal experience and social interaction, cultural memory is a 'matter of institutionalised mnemotechnics'. Usually, it focuses on fixed moments in the past, and takes a set form embodied in, for instance, texts, images and rituals through which societies and groups celebrate and commemorate defining moments.[56] Assmann's distinction is helpful: biographical memory and the memories we share with others do not extend further back than our own lifetime, yet we also come together to commemorate, say, Verdun, or to celebrate Bastille Day, or the 4th of July, even though these are clearly not events we experienced ourselves. They are, however, founding moments in the history of British, French and American identity. On the one hand, communicative and cultural memory can overlap. The first memorial to be erected at Buchenwald concentration camp after liberation was constructed by former prisoners themselves, who sought to give cultural form to communicative memory. Today's memorials at Buchenwald, however, are the expression of post-war generations with no experience of the camp. On the other hand, communicative and cultural memory can appear to conflict with one another. As recent research in Germany has shown, while the issue of German crime under Nazism, a staple of German public education, is sincerely acknowledged and regretted in public and broad cultural discourse, within individual families, post-war generations have a habit of exonerating their parents or grandparents of responsibility for Nazism.[57] What counts in public does not necessarily apply in the private sphere.

What Assmann calls cultural memory has been the subject of intense study by scholars of sociology, cultural and literary studies, art and architecture. But this does not mean that historians have not also been drawn to it. By and large, of course, historians gravitate towards archives. It may well be, as the introduction to a recent volume of essays on memorialization puts it, that such archive-based research is valuable because 'it looks beyond the neat models and paradigms that necessarily characterize broad-brush narratives of post-1945 cultural memory', drawing attention to the 'messy complexity of memorial activities as they are lived out'.[58] If sociologists might look for underlying paradigms of memory, while literary and art scholars may feel more inclined to investigate aesthetic language and matters of form, historians would, on this reading, look to explore how memorials, memorial sites, exhibitions or commemorative practices – to name but the most obvious vectors of cultural memory – came to be built or evolved. Indeed, we have many historical studies which reconstruct the web of political, social, and economic considerations, as well as the complex interplay between interest groups which feed into cultural memory production. One thinks, here, for instance, of Jonathan Huener's book on the politics of commemoration at Auschwitz between 1945 and 1979, or Harold Marcuse's study of the legacies of memory at Dachau, both of which are extensively sourced and show a precise attention to the historical contingencies upon which memorialization depends (see the chapter in this volume by Wulf Kansteiner).[59] To a degree, too, historians remain wary of grand theoretical narratives; in the introduction to his book on Nuremberg, for instance, Neil Gregor points out that, when some began to speak more openly about the Holocaust, this was not because of a 'return of the repressed', but a result of developments in the political culture of West Germany which made it possible to renegotiate the 'compromise between speaking and keeping quiet'.[60]

Yet for all that historians might favour a more archive-driven approach, and one focused on understanding the actual mechanics of cultural memory production, it would be misleading to suggest that they are not interested in matters of aesthetics. Examining the history of memory inevitably requires paying close attention not just to the various groups, factors and forces which contribute to this history, but also to the cultural forms in which meanings are conveyed, which in turn necessitates exploration of these forms themselves. Indeed, any serious approach to the history of memory is inherently interdisciplinary. The umbrella term 'memory studies' may suggest, quite wrongly, a separate discipline, or a coherent approach across disciplines. It might also imply a high level of interdisciplinary collaboration, and while there are such interdisciplinary research projects (one thinks, for instance, of the various European *lieux de mémoire* projects, examined in this volume), most researchers working on memory do so as individuals. Nevertheless, any approach to the history of memory requires of the historian a chameleon-like ability to adopt a multitude of perspectives, as she or he seeks to understand the relationship between political and social memory patterns and the cultural forms through which they are mediated, and which themselves can impact on such patterns (as the intense reception of the 1979 *Holocaust* miniseries in West Germany surely demonstrates).[61] It can also require an ability to 'read' culture not just at the 'micro' level of individual memorials, films, or works of literature, or other distinct iconic forms, but also at the 'macro' level of whole landscapes and cityscapes. Thus art historians Mark Crinson and Paul Tyrer, in a recent case study of Manchester, argue that post-industrial Britain's urban rejuvenation programmes increasingly rely upon 'a symbolic vocabulary that plays on the industrial past'. They come to the somewhat polemical conclusion that memory, far from being a positive influence in this instance, operates 'within development as a mechanism of control, exercised by business interests towards the maximisation of profit'.[62] That architectural modernism seeks to overwrite bombed cityscapes with progressive narratives is a conclusion reached by Jörg Arnold in his recent study of the long-term effects of bombing on German cities.[63] Cultural historians also need to pay attention to the *absence* as well as the *presence* of markers of memory, as Jennifer Jordan recently showed in an excellent study of recent urban change in Berlin which included an examination of planned yet unbuilt memorials.[64]

Conceptualization of this volume

The chapters which follow examine how historians have written about the history of memory. They discuss and develop many of the ideas sketched out above. While their function is to introduce students to the way various theoretical models have been applied to the historiography of memory, they do not simply represent these models or provide an overview of their implementation in the field of history writing. They also highlight problematic aspects of the theories concerned, and of the manner of their implementation in particular contexts. Theirs is a *critical* assessment of the history of memory. The reader will, however, not find every theory used in writing the history of memory in this book, nor will she or he find a discussion of every aspect of the relationship between history and memory. The chapters provide an analysis of how memory has shaped history, and our understanding of history, but they do not aim to be exhaustive. The book aims to make students acquainted with some of the main trends in writing the history in memory, as an avenue to further research.

The volume begins with a chapter by Gordon Shrimpton addressing the subject of the relationship of memory to the writing of ancient history. Ancient history could come in the form of prose or poetry. It was often oral in character, and was composed from memory. To distinguish here, then, between history and memory would be inapposite, to say the least. History was memory, and memory history in Ancient Greece and Rome.

Shrimpton examines the way in which historians in ancient times collected, assembled, remembered and recalled the past. Theories of collective memory, as his contribution proves, can be of particular analytical help in seeking to understand the way stories were formed and transmitted in a largely oral culture, before they were written down by the historian – whose dependence on precisely this transmission made it difficult given the relative paucity of alternative sources to produce a version of the past truly distinct from popular memory. In her chapter on memory and history in the Middle Ages, Kimberly Rivers demonstrates how historians have likewise applied theories of collective memory to the subject of medieval memory, particularly with regard to the commemoration of the dead. She shows how historians studying the medieval period nevertheless apply the theories of Halbwachs with critical caution, questioning his rather dismissive attitude to the idea of individual memory, or the opposition set up in his writings between collective and individual memory. Rivers also points to the influence of theories about orality and literacy on historical study of the medieval period, and to the importance of theories of mnemonics, the principles of which are also illuminated by Shrimpton in a classical context. Indeed, as Kimberley Rivers points out, medieval mnemonics originated in part in classical theory, as well as in Christian monastic meditative practice and pedagogical practice. Rivers examines how historians have evaluated the transition from orality to writing as of the eleventh century, and concludes with a discussion of studies into medieval theories of how memory actually worked.

Most of the present book focuses on the modern period. In her contribution, Mary Fulbrook takes a close and critical look at the application of Maurice Halbwachs' collective memory theory to the historiography of memory. She points to the range of approaches that have been inspired by this theory, but sets out to demonstrate that some important aspects of Halbwachs' thinking may have been overlooked or at least not have been as systematically applied as others. Fulbrook cautions against equating representations of the past (e.g. memorials, films, commemorative practices), a frequent focus of historical study, with the 'collective memory' of a society. Mapping such representations onto 'national identity' risks reifying the notion of collective memory in a manner which overlooks not just the fluid and contested nature of that memory – which many historians do indeed acknowledge – but also the complex and shifting relationship between individual and collective, past and present. The more central insight deriving from Halbwachs, Fulbrook argues, may be the one that individuals cannot articulate personal memories outside of 'collectively derived and ever changing frameworks of social discourses'. Towards the end of her survey of collective memory theory as applied to historiography, Fulbrook emphasizes the importance of examining memory from the perspective of the 'remembering agent', namely the individual, whose memory and understanding of the past develops depending on the 'communities of experience' and 'communities of identification' to which she or he belongs – communities that are not to be understood as fixed entities, but whose core values and perceptions are subject to change, changes which in turn impact upon the way the individual remembers her or his past.

Precisely this need to understand the preconditions and circumstances of individual memory lies at the heart of Lynn Abrams' chapter on the transformations of oral history. As Abrams points out, oral history narratives can serve as a historical source: how else can we learn, for instance, about the lives of those whose experiences have not been recorded in any other form? Even where interviewees might 'misremember' the past, the very discrepancies between remembered and actual experience can shed light on the way memory works. Abrams explores in her chapter the impact of collective memory theory on oral history, while also stressing the importance of autobiographical memory: for it is the connection between collective and individual memory that preoccupies the oral historian. The oral historian is acutely aware of the 'memory frames' within which personal memory, as expressed by interviewees, is formed and articulated – frames shaped by social factors, present interests and public discourse in general, and sometimes, too, in response to the 'memory frames' of the interviewer. Thus it is that Abrams reinforces Fulbrook's point about the way in which memories develop in relation to 'communities'. Her contribution also shows that, in a contemporary culture fascinated with memory, the often-heard criticism of oral history, namely that interviewees do not remember correctly, becomes redundant; for what comes to matter more is the exploration of how such memories come to take the shape they do, not whether they are true or not.

A concept that would seem to be situated somewhere between the collective and the individual is that of the generation, the subject of Wulf Kansteiner's chapter. Kansteiner begins by tracing the origin of the concept of generations back to the writings of Halbwachs, Emile Durkheim and Karl Mannheim. As Kansteiner goes on to show, the notion of generations appears to offer an innovative and neat heuristic tool to historians, challenging traditional attempts to explain social thinking in terms of family genealogies, class, gender or race. The latter categories, strongly diachronic in their focus, are replaced with a synchronic model of explanation which emphasizes common experience and consciousness. Kansteiner examines in particular the role that generational theory has played in the historiography of memory. Of fundamental significance is the question whether the root of generations is formed by common experience, or a common memory, i.e. are they constituted *through* an event, or *in response to* an event, in the interests of the generational group concerned. Then there is the question of the impact of generations. Kansteiner examines the crucial distinction often made between generations of history that make history (such as the first post-World War I generation in Germany, so important for the success of Nazism), and those that 'only' produce memory culture, such as the 1968 student movement. He concludes with a discussion of the relationship between memory, generation and trauma.

In their contribution to the present volume, the editors, Stefan Berger and Bill Niven explore the significance of collective memory theory in relation to understanding the relationship between national history and national memory. The rise of history in the nineteenth century was accompanied by a tendency to construct an image of memory as the 'other' of history in view of its assumed subjectivity, even if professional historians, committed as they often were to creating historical master narratives to undergird the nation, nevertheless implied that there was a national memory – albeit one authenticated by history. By the latter half of the twentieth century, however, it had become increasingly difficult to sustain a singular, unifying perspective on national history. Faced with this dilemma, the French historian Pierre Nora came up with the idea of rewriting national history as the history of national memory; if there was, by now, no agreement on how to narrate history, then perhaps some unity could be found in agreeing on the historical 'sites' or 'realms' – understood in the broadest sense – around which national memory might cluster. As Berger and Niven go on to argue, the constructivist turn in nation and nationalism studies as of the 1980s drew attention to the fact that national history and identity were 'invented' rather than given. This not only called into question the idea that there could be any 'authentic' historical narrative, it also helped to dissolve the perceived difference between history and memory, and pave the way towards recognizing the existence of a multiplicity of intertwined, mutually dependent and reinforcing histories and memories – which have been the subject of numerous recent historical studies.

A subject touched on in Berger and Niven's chapter, namely the concept of *lieux de mémoire* or 'realms of memory' introduced by Pierre Nora, forms the focus of the following chapter by Benoît Majerus. Majerus's chapter is the first of four concluding chapters which explore in depth, through case studies, some of the issues outlined in the opening chapters, illuminating these from a particular perspective. After outlining the genesis and principles of the French 'realms of memory' project, Majerus shows how it became 'one of the major export products of recent French historiography'. The resulting seven-volume *Les lieux de mémoire* edited by Nora found its way into most western (though few eastern) European national libraries, and parts of it were translated into English and German. More significantly, perhaps, the project gave rise to a number of parallel, if differently inflected 'realms of memory' projects – with accompanying publications – in other countries such as Italy, Germany, Austria and the Netherlands. As Majerus argues, the very methodological openness of the original French 'realms of memory' concept, which was theoretically informed solely by the work of Maurice Halbwachs, made it readily adaptable to a variety of national and indeed regional and local discourses. Part of the attractiveness of the *lieux de mémoire* concept rests in its potential for transnational cultural transfer and dialogue, yet, as Majerus shows, this potential has not yet fully been realized. The different national projects do not necessarily 'speak' to one another, and the whole *lieux de mémoire* enterprise remains marked by a French-German axis which represents the 'old' rather than the 'new' Europe.

In this connection, Majerus also points out that, in general, eastern European, post-communist countries have not yet really engaged with the opportunities for writing the history of memory which Nora's concept might afford (although a German-Polish *lieux de mémoire* project is nearing completion).[65] Having only recently emerged from the grip of communism, the initial concern of these countries was to create or recreate a national history to underpin their new-found independence; in France, which looks back on centuries of nation-building, such a national history had long existed, indeed it had begun to crack with age, and it was precisely these fractures which inspired Nora to forge a new identity around memory, rather than history. In his chapter on historiography and memory in eastern Europe, Attila Pok demonstrates that contemporary historiography in eastern Europe, in its attempts to throw off the shackles of the communist view of the past, has nevertheless been prone to as much myth-making as the intellectual regime it sought to discredit. In their critique of the internationalist communist master narrative (according to which all socialist countries develop in the same way towards socialism), post-communist European countries have sought to emphasize national distinctiveness and national historical continuity in a manner that is no less tendentious. Moreover, while these countries may not yet have begun to examine the 'history of memory' within their borders, they have quickly set about creating their own national *lieux de mémoire* to supplant the Soviet-focused memorialization of the communist era.

The common theme linking the final two case-study chapters of the volume is the Holocaust. In his contribution, Peter Carrier shows how it was above all reflection on the Holocaust that triggered histories of memory. The Holocaust was not just an event of horrendous enormity in itself; it also cast a deep and lingering shadow over the post-war world, as individuals, groups, indeed whole countries sought, in various ways and for various reasons connected respectively to questions of victimhood, perpetration and collaboration, to come to terms with its legacy. The impact of the Holocaust as memory, then, was so profound that, in time, it became as important to endeavour to understand the patterns, shifts and tensions within this memory, to understand the *history* of Holocaust memory, as it did to continue researching the Holocaust itself. There developed a new brand of historical writing, a metagenre, which Carrier terms 'Holocaust memoriography'. Given that studying the history of this memory meant seeking to comprehend not just its political and social, but also its psychological, ethical, and linguistic dimensions, and the interconnections between these, Holocaust memoriography is an essentially interdisciplinary enterprise. As Carrier goes on to demonstrate, historians of Holocaust memory have responded to the stimulus of other disciplines in their analysis, while other disciplines have been enriched by the work of historians. Exploring throughout his chapter the various perspectives and debates within Holocaust memoriography, Carrier examines the study of the politics of memory, the significance of the Historians' Dispute ('Historikerstreit') in West Germany in the 1980s for the development of a historiography informed by memory, and the 'language of memory' in Holocaust memoriography.

Carrier's chapter is followed by Richard Crownshaw's, the concluding chapter in the volume. Crownshaw's focus is on monuments. As Crownshaw points out, James E. Young has distinguished between memorials in the broader sense, a term which might refer to anything from a memorial day to a memorial book, and monuments, which Young sees as a subset of memorials and which he defines as 'the material objects, sculptures, and installations used to memorialize a person or a thing'.[66] More than any other form of memorialization, perhaps, it is monuments which have been the subject of political use and abuse over the centuries, as rulers and states sought to immortalize their achievements in stone. While the impact of the Holocaust on post-1945 memorialization was profound, ultimately ushering in a period of more sceptical, critical and reflective memorialization – especially with the advent of the so-called 'countermonuments' in the 1980s, a concept explored by Crownshaw –[67] this impact did not necessarily mean the end of politicization. The construction of a Holocaust Memorial right in the middle of Berlin, as Crownshaw points out, could be taken to demonstrate Germany's moral 'coming of age' – and its right to a prominent place on the international stage. But the main focus of Crownshaw's chapter is on the need to *historicize* monuments in a manner which goes beyond evaluating their political significance. In reference to the work, for instance, of Jennifer Jordan and Alon Confino, Crownshaw argues that a history of monuments must examine the whole process of genesis, construction and reception, if we are to understand the interplay of artistic intention, political agendas, social memory discourse, media influence and personal response – which can often differ radically from individual to individual, and from the intentions of monument makers and sponsors.

What does the future hold for the history of memory? As this book was developing, two important publications appeared which emphasize the need to think more about the relationship between memories: Michael Rothberg's *Multidirectional Memory*, and Max Silverman's *Palimpsestic Memory*.[68] Rothberg is a professor of English, Silverman a professor of French; their interest is mainly in culture (literature and film). In essence, both publications draw our attention to the way different memories of colonialism and the Holocaust interact, with one memory being 'visible' in and defining itself in relation to the other. Rather than compete, these memories – ideally – enhance each other. Future historians of memory might want to take their cue from Rothberg and Silverman. What would a history of the *intersection* of 'collaborating' memories look like? Even where memories compete, they develop their profile *in relation to* other memories. While we know there are multiple 'sites of memory', how are these mapped out in our minds?

Perhaps that really is a question for the future. For if the present is still a time of the emergence, perception and analysis of memories in their multiplicity, then the future will hold the key to their sedimentation.

Notes

1 For an online version of Plato's *Meno*, see http://classics.mit.edu/Plato/meno. html (accessed 3 June 2012).

2 As Raffaella Cribiore puts it, 'memory was the foundation of all knowledge in a world that could not rely on easily consulted books, tables of contents and indexes, library catalogues, and electronic search tools'. See Raffaella Cribiore, *Gymnastics of the Mind: Greek Education in Hellenistic and Roman Egypt* (Princeton and Oxford, 2001), here p. 166.

3 Mary Carruthers, *The Book of Memory: A Study of Memory in Medieval Culture* (Cambridge, 2008 [2nd edn]), p. 36.

4 See the excerpt from Cicero's *De Oratore* in Michael Rossington and Anne Whitehead (eds), *Theories of Memory: A Reader* (Edinburgh, 2007), pp. 39–4, here p. 40.

5 Benedict Anderson, *Imagined Communities: Reflections on the Origin and Spread of Nationalism* (London, 2006), esp. pp. 37ff.

6 Friedrich Nietzsche, *The Use and Abuse of History* (New York, 2010), p. 7.

7 Hermann Ebbinghaus, *Über das Gedächtnis* (Darmstadt 1992 [reprint of original 1882 edition]).

8 Sigmund Freud, *Zur Psychopathologie des Alltagslebens* (Frankfurt, 2006).

9 See 'Maurice Halbwachs: From the Collective Memory', in Rossington and Whitehead, *Theories of Memory*, pp. 139–43.

10 Jay Winter, *Sites of Memory, Sites of Mourning: The Great War in European Cultural History* (Cambridge, 1995), p. 5.

11 Roger Griffin, *Modernism and Fascism: The Sense of a Beginning under Mussolini and Hitler* (Basingstoke, 2007), p. 8.

12 Anne Fuchs, *After the Dresden Bombing. Pathways of Memory, 1945 to the Present* (Basingstoke, 2011); Dipesh Chakrabarty, 'History and the Politics of Recognition', in Keith Jenkins, Sue Morganand Alan Munslow (eds), *Manifestos for History* (London, 2007), pp. 77–86. Also: John Torpey, 'The Pursuit of the Past: a Polemical Perspective', in Peter Seixas (ed.), *Theorizing Historical Consciousness* (Toronto, 2004), pp. 240–55, who provides a strong argument against 'a veritable tidal wave of memory' eroding precisely a belief in the future.

13 Chris Lorenz, paper delivered to the conference 'Zwischen Gedächtnis, Geschichte und Identitätskonstruktion: was ist ein Erinnerungsort und wie entsteht er?', Institute for Social Movements, Ruhr-Universität Bochum, 13/14 December 2012. On the essential ambiguity of realms of memory, see also the contributions in Moritz Csáky and Peter Stachel (eds), *Mehrdeutigkeit. Die Ambivalenz von Gedächtnis und Erinnerung* (Vienna, 2002). One of the most thorough attempts

to come to terms with this intimate relationship between history and memory, stressing the role of history in supporting, correcting and revising memory, is Paul Ricoeur, *History, Memory and Forgetting* (Chicago, 2004).

14 François Hartog (ed.), *Les usages politiques du passé* (Paris, 2001).

15 Jay Winter, *Dreams of Peace and Freedom: Utopian Moments in the Twentieth Century* (New Haven, CT, 2008).

16 Alon Confino, 'Memory and the History of Mentalities', in Astrid Erll and Ansgar Nünning (eds), *A Companion to Cultural Memory Studies* (Berlin and New York, 2010), pp. 79–84, here p. 78.

17 For an account of the importance of memory in oral history, see Paul Thompson, *The Voice of the Past: Oral History* (Oxford, 2000), pp. 173–89.

18 Hayden White, *Metahistory: The Historical Imagination in Nineteenth-Century Europe* (Baltimore and London, 1975), p. ix.

19 Patrick H. Hutton, 'Mnemonic Schemes in the New History of Memory'. *History and Theory* 36:3 (1997), 378–91, here p. 380.

20 Norbert Frei, *Adenauer's Germany and the Nazi Past: The Politics of Amnesty and Integration* (New York, 2002).

21 Peter Novick, *The Holocaust and Collective Memory* (London, 1999). For a fascinating study of the rise of 'competitive victimhood', readers able to read French should consult Jean-Michel Chaumont, *La concurrence des victimes: génocide, identité, reconnaissance* (Paris, 2010).

22 Henry Rousso, *History and Memory in France since 1944* (Cambridge [Massachusetts] and London, 1991).

23 Francis Fukuyama, *The End of History and the Last Man* (New York, 1992).

24 Andreas Huyssen, *Present Pasts: Urban Palimpsests and the Politics of Memory* (Stanford, California, 2003), pp. 3ff.

25 Reinhart Koselleck, *Zeitschichten: Studien zur Historik* (Frankfurt/Main, 2000).

26 See, for instance, Pierre Nora, 'Between Memory and History: Les Lieux de Mémoire'. *Representations* 26 (1989), 7–24, esp. p. 7.

27 See Krzysztof Pomian, 'De l'histoire, partie de la mémoire, à la mémoire, objet d'histoire'. *Revue de métaphysique et de moral* 1 (1998), 63–110.

28 Maurice Halbwachs, *On Collective Memory*, trans. by Lewis A. Coser (Chicago and London, 1992).

29 Confino, 'Memory and the History of Mentalities', p. 79. For more on the Annales school, see Peter Burke, *The French Historical Revolution: Annales School, 1929–1989* (Cambridge, 1990). See also Mary Fulbrook, *Historical Theory* (London and New York, 2007), p. 129.

30 Halbwachs, *On Collective Memory*, p. 40.

31 Jeffrey Herf, *Divided Memory: The Nazi Past in the Two Germanys* (Cambridge [Massachusetts] and London, 1997), esp. pp. 13–39.

32 Patrick Wright, *On Living in an Old Country: The National Past in Contemporary Britain* (Oxford, 2009), p. 3.

33 See Eric Hobsbawm, 'Introduction: Inventing Traditions', in Eric Hobsbawm and Terence Ranger (eds), *The Invention of Tradition* (Cambridge and New York, 2007 [15th printing]), pp. 1–14.

34 See Anderson, *Imagined Communities*.

35 Yael Zeruvabel, *Recovered Roots: Collective Memory and the Making of Israeli National Tradition* (Chicago and London, 1995), p. 33.

36 James Mark, *The Unfinished Revolution: Making Sense of the Communist Past in Central-Eastern Europe* (New Haven and London, 2010), here p. xiv.

37 Heiko Pääbo, *The Potential of Collective Memory Based International Identity Conflicts in Post-Imperial Space* (Tartu, 2010).

38 Eviatar Zeruvabel, *Time Maps: Collective Memory and the Social Shape of the Past* (Chicago and London, 2003).

39 Zeruvabel, *Recovered Roots*, p. 10.

40 John Bodnar, *Remaking America: Public Memory, Commemoration, and Patriotism in the Twentieth Century* (Princeton, 1992).

41 See Jay Winter, 'Forms of Kinship and Remembrance in the Aftermath of the Great War', in Jay Winter and Emmanuel Sivan (eds), *War and Remembrance in the Twentieth Century* (Cambridge, 1999), pp. 40–60.

42 Bodnar, *Remaking America*, p. 6.

43 Jeffrey K. Olick, *The Politics of Regret: On Collective Memory and Historical Responsibility* (New York, 2007), p. 89ff.

44 Neil Gregor, *Haunted City: Nuremberg and the Nazi Past* (New Haven and London, 2008).

45 Jay Winter, *Remembering War: The Great War between Memory and History in the Twentieth Century* (New Haven and London, 2006), pp. 4–5.

46 See the 'Women's History Issue' of *Oral History*, 5:2 (1997).

47 See 'Gender Differences in Memories for Speech', in Selma Leydesdorff, Luisa Passerini and Paul Thompson (eds), *Gender & Memory*, 2nd edn (New Brunswick and London, 2007), pp. 17–30.

48 Selma Leydesdorff, Luisa Passerini and Paul Thompson, 'Introduction', in Leydesdorff, Passerini and Thompson (eds), *Gender & Memory*, pp. 1–16, here p. 4.

49 Elizabeth van Houts, *Memory and Gender in Medieval Europe, 900–1200* (Buffalo, 1999).

50 Cheryl McEwan, 'Building a Postcolonial Archive? Gender, Collective Memory and Citizenship in Post-Apartheid South Africa'. *Journal of Southern African Studies* 29:3 (2003), 739–57, here p. 746.

51 See Carol Rittner and John K. Roth (eds), *Different Voices: Women and the Holocaust* (New York, 1993).

52 Quoted in Janet Liebman Jacobs, 'Women, Genocide and Memory: The Ethics of Feminist Ethnography in Holocaust Research'. *Gender and Society* 18:2 (2004), 223–38, here p. 229.

53 Olick, *The Politics of Regret*, p. 24.

54 Ibid., p. 23.

55 See Daniel Levy and Natan Sznaider, 'Memory Unbound: The Holocaust and the Formation of Cosmopolitan Memory'. *European Journal of Social Theory* 5:1 (2002), 87–106; also Levy and Sznaider, *The Holocaust and Memory in the Global Age* (Philadelphia, 2005).

56 See Jan Assmann, *Das kulturelle Gedächtnis: Schrift, Erinnerung und politische Identität in frühen Hochkulturen* (Munich, 2002), here pp. 48–56. Assmann's book has recently appeared in English under the title *Cultural Memory and Early Civilization: Writing, Remembrance, and Political Imagination* (Cambridge, 2011).

57 See Harald Welzer, Sabine Moller, Karoline Tschuggnall, '*Opa war kein Nazi*': *Nationalsozialismus und Holocaust im Familiengedächtnis* (Frankfurt am Main, 2002).

58 Bill Niven and Chloe Paver, 'Introduction', in Bill Niven and Chloe Paver (eds), *Memorialization in Germany since 1945* (Basingstoke and New York, 2010), pp. 1–12, here p. 8.

59 Jonathan Huener, Auschwitz, Poland, and the Politics of Commemoration, 1945–1979 (Athens, 2003); and Harold Marcuse, Legacies of Dachau: The Uses and Abuses of a Concentration Camp, 1933–2001 (Cambridge, 2001).

60 Gregor, *Haunted City*, p. 15.

61 See http://www.zeitgeschichte-online.de/site/40208179/default.aspx (accessed 3 June 2012).

62 Paul Tyrer and Mark Crinson, 'Totemic Park: Symbolic Representation in Post-Industrial Space', in Mark Crinson (ed.), *Urban Memory: History and Amnesia in the Modern City* (London and New York, 2005), pp. 99–120, here pp. 99–101.

63 Jörg Arnold, *The Allied Air War and Urban Memory: The Legacy of Strategic Bombing in Germany* (Cambridge, 2011).

64 Jennifer A. Jordan, *Structures of Memory: Understanding Urban Change in Berlin and Beyond* (Stanford, 2006).

65 See the five-volume series edited by Robert Traba and Hans Henning Hahn, *Deutsch-Polnische Erinnerungsorte*, published by Ferdinand Schöningh. So far, only volume 3 has actually been published, but the others are due to appear in the course of 2013/2014.

66 James E. Young, *The Texture of Meaning: Holocaust Memorials and Meaning* (New Haven and London, 1993), p. 3.

67 For developments since the countermonument, see Bill Niven, 'From Countermonument to Combimemorial: Developments in German Memorialisation'. *Journal of War and Culture Studies* 6:1 (2013), 75–91.

68 Michael Rothberg, Multidirectional Memory: Remembering the Holocaust in the Age of Decolonization (Palo Alto, 2009); and Max Silverman, Palimpsestic Memory: The Holocaust and Colonialism in French and Francophone Fiction and Film (Oxford and New York, 2013).

Further reading

Astrid Erll and Ansgar Nünning (eds), *A Companion to Cultural Memory Studies* (Berlin and New York, 2010).

Andreas Huyssen, *Present Pasts: Urban Palimpsests and the Politics of Memory* (Stanford, California, 2003).

Jeffrey K. Olick, *The Politics of Regret: On Collective Memory and Historical Responsibility* (New York, 2007).

Paul Ricoeur, *History, Memory and Forgetting* (Chicago, 2004).

Michael Rossington and Anne Whitehead (eds), *Theories of Memory: A Reader* (Edinburgh, 2007).

Peter Seixas (ed.), *Theorizing Historical Consciousness* (Toronto, 2004).

CHAPTER ONE

Memory and history in the ancient world*

Gordon Shrimpton

The ancient Greeks and Romans produced a large body of literature, much of it quite brilliant, but, paradoxically, theirs was an oral culture. Plato, the prolific philosopher, decried writing as a threat to the cultivation of memory.[1] In general, they saw writing as an aid to memory, not a replacement for it. This chapter addresses the subject of the relationship of memory to the writing of ancient history. Historians needed to cultivate their own powers of memory (below), but their task also included collecting the memories of their informants. Ancient historians did not write with the reactions of other historians uppermost in mind. Their audience would be the 'general public' at times, more frequently the literati. Their information came from communities who were concerned to develop and protect an image of themselves, the more heroic the better. These communities used their monuments, temples and public places as tokens of achievement, and their local historians probably addressed themselves to celebrating this achievement.

Ancient history could take the form of poetry or prose. As poetry, we know of historical tragedies such as Aeschylus's *Persai*, and the lost *Capture of Miletus* by Phrynichus. Otherwise the ancients accepted Homer's epics the *Odyssey* and *Iliad* as history. Vergil's *Aeneid* is a setting of legendary Roman history, and Lucan's *Pharsalia* is a poetic reworking of the memory of the Roman Civil War. In prose, the main focus of this chapter, we have three main types of history: local or epichoric history, general or universal history, and a form of biography, which is really character delineation extracted from historical anecdotes.

Historians usually focused on military conflict, the rise and fall of empires. Herodotus of Halicarnassus started it in the fifth century with his leisurely description of the east-west conflict that Croesus of Lydia set in motion in the sixth-century BCE with his attacks on Asiatic Greek states and which culminated in the Persian invasion of Greece in 480 BCE. Some of his more noteworthy successors include Thucydides of Athens (c. 460–c. 399 BCE), Polybius of Megalopolis (c. 200–c. 118 BCE) from among the Greeks, and on the Latin (Roman) side Livy (59 BCE–17 CE) and Tacitus (c. 56–c. 118 CE). Their works have proved definitive to a large extent. 'Modern narratives of the Peloponnesian War or the early Roman Principate are frequently little more than respectful rehashes of Thucydides or Tacitus, supplemented where possible by archaeology or epigraphy'.[2]

The general model for historical production in a predominantly oral society would be: (1) the historian collects peoples' memories of the chosen subject (Greece), or becomes familiar with the public memory (Rome), (2) files those memories in his own memory, (3) assembles a text in his mind and (4) writes it from memory and, finally, (5) in the process of reading it back, or making it available, to the community from which he obtained the information, puts into words the community's collective memory of the event.

1 The historian collects people's memories of the chosen subject (or becomes familiar with the public memory)

What else could he have collected? Since von Ranke, we want historians to collect hard evidence. They should visit the cities of the key players, ransack their archives, study public monuments, write down the texts of any inscriptions visible in public places, collect the correspondence and written memoirs of key generals and politicians (if available), consult log books and official records, and cross-question any surviving eye-witnesses in the light of the material evidence. Most ancient historians did take note of inscriptions and monuments at times. Significantly, however, they did not use them as evidence to check the reliability of a story; if anything, the flow of evidence worked in the other direction. The story took precedence to verify, or justify the use of, the monument.[3] More significantly, the monument, statue, inscription or what have you worked as a token (Gr. *sema*, Lat. *nota*), as an aide-memoir, a prompt to bring the story to mind.

On the subject of ransacking archives, the first-century BCE historian, rhetorician and commentator, Dionysius of Halicarnassus, tells us that the local historians of Greece did just that, reproduce the contents of temple archives. In addition, we hear of a lost *Collection of Inscriptions* by the Aristotelian, Craterus. On the other hand, the great Felix Jacoby observes: '. . . in ancient contemporary historiography documents play a secondary role without exception'.[4]

So the dilemma becomes evident. A body of inscriptions, archival records, written memoirs and the like can act as the repository for information, the memory, of the events to be reported by the historian, to be sure, but to the extent that the historian chooses to be guided rather by the public recollection of the events he will need to file a considerable body of material in his own mind in preparation for writing (below), a major feat – one that requires demonstration if we are to believe that it was even possible.

2 The historian files the memory (-ies) he has collected from his informants in his own memory

The two most analytical of the ancient historians, Thucydides and Polybius, divided the stuff of history into two categories: speeches and action.[5] At first this distinction might seem puzzling because a speech is a historical action like any other occurrence, but it is meaningful from the point of view of the historian. This is because a historian like Thucydides who wrote his history as an eyewitness to the Peloponnesian War must approach a speech in a way that differs from the account of a military engagement. Regarding the action he says: 'With respect to the noteworthy deeds of the war I did not think it right to record them from just anybody, nor as they seemed right to me, but I was present at some and from my other informants I put myself out for *akribeia* as far as I was able concerning each event'.[6] And of the speeches he says: 'I have found it difficult **to remember** the [very *akribeia*][7] of the speeches which I listened to myself and my various informants have experienced the same difficulty; so my method has been, while keeping as closely as possible to the general sense of the words used, to make the speakers say what, in my opinion, was called for by each situation' (my emphasis).[8] 'There is no way to get around the incompatibility of the two parts of that statement', comments Moses Finley. 'If all speakers said what, in Thucydides' opinion, the situation called for, the remark becomes meaningless. But if they did not always say what was called for, then, insofar as Thucydides attributed such sentiments to them, he could not have been "keeping as closely as possible to the general sense of the words used"'.[9]

Like most scholars Finley assumes that Thucydides' difficulty with the speeches was one of accurate reconstruction: do you make speakers say what was really said or what suited the occasion? But Thucydides himself identifies the problem as one of memory. Did Thucydides believe that a person could commit 'a speech' (below) to memory while it was being delivered? Since Mary Carruthers' studies of memory in the Middle Ages, we know that medieval scholastics were capable of remarkable feats of memory, feats that make learning a single speech at one hearing look relatively easy as long as the mind was well trained and in practice.[10]

Plato's *Phaedrus,* written in the generation after Thucydides' death, shows how a young man would set about committing a speech to memory. In this case, Phaedrus has a written text with which to work, but the technique is worth noting. Socrates wants to hear the speech, which was written by Lysias, the famous orator. Although Phaedrus has the text on a scroll with him, reading directly from the scroll is not considered. Socrates wants to hear Phaedrus recite it. Phaedrus has not yet memorized the words, but he can go through the speech in order *by headings* starting from the beginning.[11] The key expressions are: 'by headings', 'in order' and 'starting from the beginning'. Together they comprise a method of immediate memorization, one that to date scholars have not recognized in connection with ancient historical recording.

a   **by headings.** Plato's *Timaeus* begins ostensibly the day after the completion of the *Republic.* The company, less one person, proposes to continue the discussion but first they wish to refresh their memories of the previous day's deliberations. The group urges Socrates to go over the subject again 'in brief' starting from the beginning. Socrates obliges. When he has finished, he announces that he has gone through it 'by headings', and asks if he has omitted anything. Timaeus replies that Socrates has recalled 'the very things that were said'.[12] Here is the key to the Thucydidean dilemma: the company sees no meaningful difference between a two or three page recapitulation and the dialogue itself, one that filled several books.

Now the conversation turns to a promise that Critias, one of the group, made. He says that the subject of the *Republic* reminded him of a story that he had heard as a small boy from his grandfather many years ago. He declares that he set his mind to recalling the story as soon as the previous day's discussion ended. He gives an abbreviated version first, then declares that he is ready to repeat the story not just 'by headings' but exactly as he first heard it 'detail by detail'.[13] The process of recollection is well illustrated here. The headings bring back the main argument to mind; this skeletal outline then provides a framework for the recollection of the details. We find confirmation of this idea in a work by the Athenian historian and commentator, Xenophon. He wrote a *Life* of Agesilaus, King of Sparta. He concludes the work by recapitulating his subject's excellence 'by headings to make his virtue easier to remember' (*Life of Agesilaus* XI).

The use of headings is as old as Homer (eighth-century BCE). Toward the end of the Odyssey, when Odysseus has returned home to Penelope, he tells her about his marvelous experiences among the monsters and witches of the strange worlds he visited. Readers of the *Iliad*, book nine in particular, will remember that Agamemnon agrees to make reparation to Achilles, listing off a mass of treasure and honours that he will give Achilles for returning to battle. Three messengers are sent to Achilles, namely Odysseus, Ajax and Phoenix. Odysseus speaks first and lists off the gifts Agamemnon offers almost verbatim. So how will Homer deal with this scene in which Odysseus must tell Penelope the story of his wanderings? Those adventures consumed about four entire books. Rather than repeat four books verbatim, however, Homer briefly recapitulates Odysseus' adventures: 'He related first how he overcame the Cicones, then how he reached the fruitful land of the Lotus-Eaters; the crimes of the Cyclops and afterwards his own vengeance on him for the brave comrades piteously devoured' (and so on).[14]

After Homer, summarizing a text by headings was a preliminary to full memorization. Homer's mnemotechnics are still being studied,[15] but we can say that from Plato's time on, the headings' method was in use for over a millennium. Photius of Byzantium (c. 810–c. 893 CE) put on a remarkable display of memory to show that he had read the twelfth book of Theopompus' history. Photius was Patriarch of Byzantium and a great scholar. Many works from antiquity that are now lost to us were known to him. A certain Menophanes was claiming that book twelve of Theopompus' *Philippica* was not to be found in his time. Photius refutes him by reciting the contents of the book by headings: 'the twelfth book includes: concerning Acoris King of Egypt how he made treaty with the Barcaeans and acted on behalf of Evagoras of Cyprus in resistance to the King of Persia; how Evagoras came into the rule of Cyprus unexpectedly' (and so on).[16] Photius, like many of the western scholastics of the centuries after his time, committed the books he had read to memory. They carried their libraries in their heads, though we may never know just how accurately they retained it all.

Herodotus concealed his use of mnemonics so well that scholars have not generally suspected that he availed himself of the techniques of artificial memory. By all appearances he was a professional mnemon, a prose Homer for the great Persian War. As for Thucydides we must either accept Moses Finley's dilemma and convict him of inconsistency in reconstructing speeches, or assume that he used a method of memorizing a text as he heard it. The model of Critias in Timaeus comes to mind or that of Phaedrus, or even Photius. If he filed the speech in his mind 'by headings' then rehearsed the headings afterwards using them as a skeleton onto which he could attach what he felt to be the necessary words, the product would be the exact same speech to a member of his ancient audience just as the recapitulated version of the *Republic* was to the little group at the beginning of *Timaeus*.

    b   **in order.** Aristotle (384–322 BCE) wrote a brief but very important treatise *On Memory and Recollection*. He observes correctly that memory is associative, that it follows a sequence. So, 'when one is looking for something in the memory, one needs to find a starting point, usually the beginning of the whole chain, then move along it. Order is necessary. It can be natural (some things are naturally associated) or artificial, a mathematical (or numerical) sequence is easiest'.[17]

'Memory', remarks Raffaella Cribiore, 'was the foundation of all knowledge in a world that could not rely on easily consulted books, tables of contents and indexes, library catalogues, and electronic search tools'.[18] A disorganized memory, however, is of no use. In the dialogue *Theaetetus*, Plato imagines a person who has acquired much knowledge but has kept the items of knowledge in mind like birds in an aviary. They fly around at will with the result that the owner may be said only to own them but not have control over them.[19] Earlier, Plato had likened the memory to a block of wax with images pressed into it. As long as the images stay in place, knowledge is secure. One does not confuse eleven with twelve, for example, because the impressions, staying in place, retain their sequence (i.e. we learn eleven as one higher than ten and one less than twelve).[20] The question raised in this dialogue is the nature of knowledge. Plato seems to assume that unless we have things filed securely and *tidily* in our memories, we cannot regard them as knowledge.

In the Hellenistic age, scraps of papyrus from the sands of Egypt show how students began to strengthen their memories from the earliest stages of education by playing games with the alphabet. One such game apparently involved learning it simultaneously in both directions.[21]

c **from the beginning.** Aristotle said that the place to start one's search in the memory is 'the beginning', but a little later he turns to describe the associative quality of memory: one passes 'from milk to white, from white to air, from air to damp; from which one remembers autumn . . .'. He then goes on to remark that the best place to begin is the mid-point (of a chain of associations – his example in this case is the alphabet).[22] From the middle one can move in either direction to find the item one seeks. It would take a trained memory to do what Aristotle suggests here, however. Normally, the mind does well at the beginning of a chain of items but soon reaches overload. It may retain items at the end of the chain simply because they were the most recent, but the middle is easily lost unless the individual is trained to avoid the problem. So, if people were training their memories in Aristotle's time, it would be useful to know more about their practices and for how long those practices had been in existence. Evidently mnemonic treatises were in circulation in Aristotle's lifetime. In *On the Soul*, Aristotle briefly mentions systems that advised the use of mental images to help keep track of and locate the items in the chain.[23]

Before the Greeks adapted the Semitic alphabet to their own language, anything preserved had to be retained in someone's memory. According to the Parry-Lord thesis, Homer's poems, the *Odyssey* and *Iliad*, were preserved in the memories of illiterate bards before 'Homer' wrote them down.[24] But the advent of writing did not put an end to the use of memory, for the poems were still recited from memory by rhapsodists in competition at the great festivals and at other venues.[25] Homer belongs to the eighth-century BCE when the Greek city-states were taking shape. Unlike their powerful neighbours, the Egyptians, Babylonians and Medo-Persians, the Greeks did not build large palaces peopled by powerful nobles with scribes at their beck and call to keep public records. Instead they relied on professional memory-keepers (*mnemones, hieromnemones, epistatai*) who preserved vital records orally.[26]

Rhapsodists, mnemones and their like were professional singers and record keepers. If non-professionals were to experience the advantages of powerful memories, they would need to learn artificial memory; they would need to master skills that would enable them to remember what they needed in order to navigate an increasingly complex political and legal life without paper. The Greek poet Simonides lived in the last half of the sixth-century BCE and into the first quarter of the fifth. A story was told of him in Roman times that for some reason he was called out of a drinking party by two young men. When he was clear of the building in which the party was held, it collapsed, killing all within. Their bodies were mangled beyond recognition and this made it impossible for the relatives of the victims to identify them for burial. According to the story, Simonides helped them locate the victims by reciting the names of the banqueters recalling them as they were in their places just before the building crushed them. The Romans regarded this feat as the invention of mnemonics, place-memory (below) to be specific.[27]

Sometime in the second half of the fifth century, Hippias of Elis, the sophist, visited Sparta and Athens where he put on displays of mnemotechnics. There is an account of a discussion that allegedly took place between Hippias and Socrates found in the Platonic corpus. In this dialogue, Hippias is made to boast that he could recite back 50 names after hearing them but once.[28] Socrates responds that he did not know that Hippias possessed the mnemonic skill, a comment that implies that he did not necessarily expect all sophists to teach mnemonics, to be sure, but that he knew exactly what Hippias meant. In other words, it supposes that Socrates knew what mnemonics were even before he met Hippias.

The Hippias story shows that one teacher of rhetoric in the fifth-century BCE included mnemonics in his panoply of techniques. Since the sophists put on displays for payment and with the added expectation that they would attract students who would pay even more to learn their techniques, we may be confident that mnemonics were included if only as an 'elective' in Hippias' curriculum. Indeed, a line in Aristophanes' *Clouds* could be taken to imply that it was normal to expect an understanding of mnemonics from anyone who undertook to learn rhetoric from a master. Written in the late 420s and revised some time later, the *Clouds* lampoons Socrates, falsely no doubt, as a teacher of rhetoric, of both 'better' and 'worse' argumentation. Before this Socrates begins his instruction he asks his dim-witted pupil Strepsiades if he is a 'mnemonic'.

The ignorant Strepsiades may in fact be undergoing a version of an Athenian elementary education in Socrates' Thinkatorium. If so, the play would be a precious glimpse of the early emphasis on memory training in fifth-century Greek schooling. In this connection, we have a remarkable and mysterious text that would shed a flood of light on the question at hand if we could be absolutely confident of its date.[29] Known as the *Dissoi Logoi* (alias: *Dialexeis*) and dated by most scholars to about 400 BCE, this little work is probably the earliest discourse on rhetorical training to survive. It is written in a simple, almost childish style with erratic spelling, facts that suggest it could have been written by a juvenile. After several paragraphs of repetitive drills, the treatise introduces the subject of memory:

> 9. The greatest and finest contrivance to have been found is memory. It is useful for everything—wisdom and life in general. This is what you do <first>: if you apply your mind, [that way] the idea [*gnome*] is better perceived as it goes through the following exercises. Second, you practice, whenever you hear it [a thing?]. By hearing and speaking the same things many times—what you have learned comes to mind in its entirety. Third, you store in the mind whatever you hear adjacent to things you see. Examples: it's necessary to remember Chrysippus; store him beside some gold [*chrysos*] and a horse [*hippos*]. Another: Pyrilampe, store her beside fire [*pyr*] and shining [*lampein*]. That is how you proceed with names. As for things, this is what you do. For bravery, you store that beside Ares and Achilles; for bronze, beside Hephaestus; cowardly deception, beside Epeus . . .[30]

Alas, the text breaks off at this point leaving us with a plethora of questions.

If an Athenian of the fifth century wanted to master mnemotechnics, it is likely that he or she would learn some version of place memory. What is 'place-memory'? There is a very clear description of one place-memory system in Jonathan Spence's *Memory Palace of Matteo Ricci*. 'In 1596 Matteo Ricci taught the Chinese how to build a memory palace. He told them that the size of the palace would depend on how much they wanted to remember'. The larger the better, but one could begin on a limited scale. 'One could create modest palaces or one could build less dramatic structures. . . . [I]f one wanted an intimate space one could use just the corner of a pavilion, or an altar in a temple, or even such a homely object as a wardrobe or a divan'. '[H]e explained that these palaces, pavilions, divans were mental structures to be kept in one's head, not solid objects to be literally constructed out of "real" materials'. 'The real purpose of these mental constructs was to provide storage spaces for the myriad concepts that make up the sum of our human knowledge. To everything that we wish to remember, wrote Ricci, we should give an image; and to every one of these images we should assign a position where it can repose peacefully until we are ready to reclaim it by an act of memory'.[31]

A vexed passage in Thucydides book five, viewed since the late nineteenth century as a statement of Thucydides' chronological method, should be studied in this context. Scholars have had difficulty making sense of it and have resorted to emendation – essentially re-writing the Greek text – to make it say what it 'should'.[32] The core statement in the unaltered (received) text translates as follows: 'A person should reckon by years not preferring to entrust the numbering off of names of archons or honorific titularies in any place as a system of signposts to bygone events. There is no precision that way – how a name at one place follows on after ones at the beginning or middle [of the war]. But, if one numbers by summers and winters, as I have written it, he will find, from the portions that each year has the capacity to contain, that there occurred ten summers and an equal number of winters in this first war'.[33] The mnemonic features of this passage are unmistakable.

Thucydides has finished his description of the ten-year Archidamian War. He pauses to explain the arrangement of his material. He had meticulously divided his narrative by numbered years (first year of the war, second year and so on) and by seasons within each year. The result, as he observes, is 20 seasons. As a chronological statement this information is useless, but as a mnemonic, it alerts the reader who wishes to commit the war to memory to prepare 20 places, rooms if you like in the style of Matteo Ricci, into which to file the events of the war. A person wishing to scan the stored information looking for some event may wish to start at the beginning or, as Aristotle suggested, at the middle of the war. Doing so would be problematic if Thucydides had chosen the wrong system of notation (signposts). City-states reckoned the passage of the years according to the name of an important office holder who gave his or her name to the year: archons for Athens, priestesses of Hera at Argos or ephors at Sparta, but the official years of these places began in different months of the solar year. Confusion might arise, therefore, or an Athenian might lose track of the order of the archons. Numbers are simpler and more universal.[34]

This was a bold experiment on Thucydides' part, arranging his history to invite memorization, but it cannot be called a success by ancient standards. Although his unfinished history was continued by Xenophon, Theopompus and at least one other, no one imitated his mnemonic style. Indeed no surviving history from antiquity reflects his approach. Moreover, we know of but one person who actually memorized the entire work in late antiquity, and in the judgment of Isidor of Damascus, it did nothing to improve his style.[35] Isidor's remark illustrates what happened to history after Thucydides, at least partially. Thucydides wrote 'The War' as he calls it, with the expectation that people would want to know it. This knowledge would be useful because similar things would happen in the future owing to the constancy of human nature.[36] But the generation that followed had a different agenda. Historians emerged from rhetorical schools like Isocrates' *Technai,* where they mastered style, and passed on *exempla* for the moral guidance of future generations.[37] These developments gave the historian timeless appeal. One could always read the rhetorical historians like Ephorus and Theopompus, pupils of Isocrates, for style years after their content had lost all relevance, and their charming stories and moral lessons were not lost on readers as late as Roman times.

3 and 4 The historian assembles a text in his mind and writes it from memory

The process of memorative composition is well explained by Carruthers and Small.[38] Carruthers aims to illustrate medieval monastic meditation, and one of the consequences of careful meditation can be a new literary composition. She shows how writers from Boethius back to Cicero and Romans of the republican period 'wrote' their compositions in bed. Putting stylus to papyrus (or vellum) was often the last step in the production of the piece. At this stage, dictation to a scribe was the likely process for wealthy Romans as opposed to sitting at a desk with a writing tool. Written notes are attested, however.[39]

Small shows how Roman and Greek historians who compiled their histories from written texts nearly always follow a single source for each episode despite the fact that they had read widely and so knew other versions. The problem, argues Small, is that the seamless flow of the narrative makes interruptions for variant versions disruptive. Carruthers explains the problem more completely.[40] Disruptions invite the state known to the medieval scholastics as *curiositas,* another word for fornication (=a form of going astray). If the mind is led astray, then it loses its thread and confusion reigns. A. R. Luria illustrates the difficulty even more graphically. His subject, Shereshevski, used to give displays of mnemonics several times a day. A problem he encountered was not forgetting so much as skipping from one sequence to another that he had memorized earlier in the day. In this case, the effect was the same as forgetting. In other words, even the most experienced mind gets lost when it tries to track more than one sequence at a time.[41]

The danger of losing the thread could have been controlled perhaps by keeping a written scroll in view. But if they did this, then recollecting variant versions from time to time should have posed no serious difficulty. The fact that they did not interrupt their seamless narratives for alternative versions strongly suggests that these historians worked from memory and not directly from a written text.

5 The historian puts into words the community's collective memory

Individuals remember not communities,[42] but communities can and do influence the impressions that individuals have of their past. The human memory is susceptible to suggestion.[43] Related subsequent experiences influence the individual's recollection of the event. Given time and repetition, the memory can acquire details that crowd out the original experience. There is a good example of this in Tom Harrisson's *Living through the Blitz*. A woman kept notes of her activities at the time of Britain's declaration of war in September 1939. She was by herself practising the piano and did not hear Chamberlain's speech broadcast over the BBC. About thirty years later, her notes forgotten, she 'remembered' gathering around the wireless with friends and neighbours listening to Chamberlain's speech. Her individual memory has undergone a collectivization: in fact alone at the piano, she 'remembers' huddling with friends and neighbours. Away from the wireless in fact, she 'remembers' what virtually every English person remembered from that moment, the broadcast of Chamberlain's speech.[44]

'Memory' often refers to the experiences a person stores mentally, but it is also used to mean commemoration – that which a community selects for itself from its past to identify itself for the future. The community selects what it will commemorate in public monuments and ceremonies and directs what will (or should) be obliterated from individual memories sometimes spontaneously and sometimes by decree. The historian has a role to play in this process of commemoration, selection and collectivization.

'[H]istory according to Herodotus depended on the sense of a common Greek identity that was consolidated in the Persian Wars'.[45] For Britain, the Second World War either changed the national identity or at least offered it a new dimension. Tom Harrisson complains of the public pressure to 'glossify' the courage of the British people in defiance of the Blitz, which began as part of the propaganda during the bombing.[46] With the war in progress England would never admit publically that the British spirit was cowed as a result of the bombing. Years later, letters to newspapers commenting on corruption and cowardice often on the part of the 'city fathers' in bombed cities were met by angry rebuttals insisting on the calm courage displayed by everybody during the bombing.[47] The evidence of behaviours that did not fit with the 'glossified' picture came from consulting the files of the

Mass Observation project. Mass Observation began in 1937 and continued through much of the bombing, well into 1941. It called on people from all parts of Britain to keep detailed diaries and submit them to a central data bank. The diaries were opened to the public in the early 1970s. Harrisson's book records his shock at the discrepancies between the rosy way the British people remembered their courage during the blitz and the way they had actually behaved.[48]

A collective or community recollection of an event will require some time to develop, for it will only succeed by a process of selection, suppressing memories that do not fit the pattern. Pressures toward conformity come from two, or three, directions, 'above', 'below', and within.

1   **From within:** From the studies conducted by Bartlett[49] and even Harrisson, it is evident that most people's memories tend to assimilate themselves to the community experience. People with trained memories learn how to use bizarre images as signposts to strengthen recall, but without training, Bartlett's subjects showed a strong tendency to neglect or even reject unfamiliar information at the very point of cognition. The usual result is the 'homogenisation' of the memory toward the culturally familiar. In the case of the woman practising piano, the individual experience was completely obliterated.

2   **From below:** An underlying body of experience shared by the community can help shape the way it perceives and remembers historical events. Peter Burke speaks of schemata, past perceptions that shape present memories.[50] A schema, he says, is 'associated with the tendency to represent (or indeed to remember) one event or one person in terms of another'. (p. 102) A considerable amount of Herodotus's material owes its shape to a substratum of epic and folk tales.[51] One schema is the heir to a throne raised far from the royal palace who is found miraculously and returns. A variation of this pattern is found in Livy where Romulus and Remus are raised by a she-wolf before they return to their people and help to build Rome.[52] In Herodotus it is the story of Cyrus who is sent away as a baby to die, and given to a shepherd who raises him instead of killing him.[53] Eventually he, like Oedipus in the play by Sophocles, is returned to his family to assume the throne. A second pattern is the prideful monarch or tyrant who presumes too much and meets an unfortunate end, perhaps by divine retribution. This schema is announced most emphatically in the first half of book one, the pride and downfall of Croesus of Lydia.[54] It re-emerges in book three with the ironic downfall of the tyrant Polycrates of Samos.[55] The ultimate defeat of Xerxes the invader is also built on this schema. As he enters Europe he displays hybris by having the Hellespont flogged

for breaking his pontoon bridge,[56] but a little later Herodotus shows him more humbled than presumptuous when he reviews his mighty invasionary force. Instead of flaunting his power, he weeps for the brevity of life.[57] The stories of Croesus and Polycrates belong to a generation or two before Herodotus' time, but Xerxes' invasion took place early in his lifetime. It is tempting to conclude that the schema of Xerxes the hybristic, tyrannical invader needed perhaps another generation before the Greek people could bring their 'memory' of the details into conformity with the schema.

3 **From above:** The Romans were the masters at controlling public memory, particularly during and after the Principate of Augustus. The weapon they used was *damnatio memoriae*,[58] which generally included the erasure of the person's name from all public monuments and the defacing or destruction of representations of him in public statuary. The fact that *damnatio* called attention to the targeted person, in a way that ensured that he would be remembered as the person missing from the inscription or monument, actually made it more devastating.

Damnatio is reactive to the perceived failure or treason of the subject, but the Roman approach could be emphatically proactive as well. In the first century of the Common Era the Romans faced the challenge of negotiating the culmination of a prolonged civil war that saw the demise of the Republic (freedom as some of them saw it) through to the birth of one-man rule, the Principate. The skill displayed by Augustus (and his successors) in manipulating public perceptions is remarkable. In particular, Augustus needed to convince people that he was not a destroyer, but a builder – that he had somehow restored the Republic – and that Rome could expect stability under his rule. In that peculiarly Roman assemblage of statues of republican heroes, buildings and open space called the Augustan Forum, Augustus displayed and celebrated a convenient image of history before the eyes of the people who moved about in that space. 'Focusing not merely on the new *princeps* and his family', remarks Gowing, 'Augustus' Forum was an architectural and artistic declaration of the restored Republic. Certainly no Roman monument more ably showcases the seamless blending of past and present, public and private, domestic and foreign, Republican and imperial. It brought into public view the same sort of connections with the past that were being made in literature, most notably in Vergil's *Aeneid* . . . and Livy's *History*'.[59]

As for the Athenians, while they built up their naval empire after the defeat of the Persians in 479, they built up their 'history' as well. They took to appointing leading orators to celebrate their city's achievements in public speeches, funeral orations, given in the spring over the fallen.[60] These communal images shaped history. Greek historians often assumed that their counterparts spoke for their cities or associated groups: Thucydides seems to refer to Herodotus as 'the rest of Greece';[61] Herodotus attacks the account of Egypt written by Hecataeus of Miletus, calling him 'the Ionians'.[62]

While things went well, speeches and ceremonies celebrated Athens's glorious past, but in unhappy times the response would be different. Athens lost the bitter Peloponnesian War in 404, and fell immediately into civil war. The civil struggle, which featured open conflict between the oligarchs and democrats, was settled in the winter of 403/2. To stabilize the political climate and bring peace to the city, the parties agreed to an amnesty: 'no one was to call to mind past evils' (Gr. *mnesikakein*), an obvious attempt to settle, probably by public decree, the political future by controlling the memory of the past. This amnesty has been studied in two recent books,[63] but neither study notices the extent to which the Athenians were already in the habit of naturally shedding uncomfortable memories in service to a self-image of political convenience. In fact, over the two centuries before 403/2 about half of that time had been consumed by civil conflict, often extreme. Open fighting had erupted on more than one occasion. Strange to say, the sources that mention this civil strife, Herodotus and Aristotle, include Athenian casualties extremely rarely, none in situations in which it is quite counterintuitive to suppose that Athenians could have avoided shedding Athenian blood. The evident purging of ugly memories was accomplished by the collective will of the Athenian people with no interference from a (say) controlling Augustus Caesar or even from a public decree.[64]

Composition by and through the collective memory

The picture of ancient history as a collection of memories in service to the collective memory will seem unpalatable to some, no doubt. We all know how unreliable memory is. Works cited in this chapter by Tom Harrisson, F. C. Bartlett and Daniel Schacter leave little doubt of the failings of the human memory and its ability to create – to be fictive. But as Hedrick pointed out, fictive or not, most of our modern history books are 'little more than respectful rehashes' of one ancient history or another. Documents have the ability to take us back to the very moment in question like the Mass Observation records, but such records did not exist in any abundance in antiquity and one ancient historian actually displayed scorn toward a rival who sought out what little was there.[65]

There need be no doubt that stories about the past existed in the collective memories of ancient societies. The real question concerns the relationship of these stories to ancient 'historical' literature. We can sharpen focus on the question by taking a more recent example. Gillian Tindall pointed out how the residents of Kentish Town, a borough of London, held vivid memories of a pastoral past, barns, cows grazing and the like, right in and around their neighbourhood. Their stories, generally based on misunderstandings of the remains of old buildings, were reinforced by reports and discussions in local newspapers.[66] Of course, there had been a time of greenery before modern structures, but that time was well beyond the reach of living memory.

Kentish Town supplies two models for us to test against the ancient evidence: memories in the community might simply become its 'history' without significant alteration thanks to some form of written record (like the newspaper reports). Or they might be subject to critical examination by a researcher who transforms them into, or rejects them in favour of, a well-documented account. We can take a third model from Homeric studies. Thanks to the work of John Miles Foley and other comparativists, we may regard 'Homer' not as a single person who wrote two great epics, but rather as a kind of personification of a process that may have taken centuries, one in which the epics were developed by means of a sustained interaction between performers (guslars, rhapsodists) and the community.[67] The 'text' develops in the collective memory of both performers and listeners (an oral version of the Kentish Town people and their newspapers).

People tell stories about an ostensible past, but it has seemed improbable to some scholars that 'the people' could create a great epic. Discoveries since 1949, however, have revealed the existence of long oral epics in the Soviet Union and elsewhere.[68] These epics are seen as 'texts' held in the collective memory of a people. The decision to set these texts down in writing demands a special commitment of time and resources. The *Iliad* and *Odyssey* of Homer are evidently the results of such a process.[69]

This Homeric model continues into the historical period with the production of history. Writing nearly three hundred years after the appearance of the written Homeric epics, Herodotus produced his monumental history of the Greco-Persian conflict. In his own words, he frequently identifies his source as a story in circulation (Gr. *logos legomenos*).[70] On more than one occasion he declares that his task is to report what people say, but not necessarily to believe it.[71] He tells the story of Phrynichus of Athens, who wrote and produced a play called the *Capture of Miletus* (by the Persians). This event had seriously upset the Athenians and they did not want to be reminded of it. They fined Phrynichus heavily and commanded that the play never be produced in Athens again.[72] No one was free to tell the community what it did not want to hear. On another occasion, Herodotus declines to provide information because he knows it will be met with disbelief.[73] These are but glimpses of ways in which the collective could control and intimidate the individual reporter.[74]

The inference is inevitable that the individual did not have the freedom to establish truth independent of the community. The Greeks had a handful of words for truth, but the most common one from about the time of 'Homer' right through classical times was *aletheia*. It means 'the absence of *lethe*', and lethe means 'forgetfulness', or 'obscurity'. So truth means 'clarity' or 'fullness of memory'. But if the individual was not permitted to be a reliable vessel, then 'truth' was the way the community remembered things.

Evidence from antiquity is always too sketchy to permit dogmatic conclusions, but we are fortunate to have a clear case of the spontaneous generation of a historical 'text' that found its way into historiography. The city of Thebes rose to ascendancy in Greece in the late 370s and stood as the leading power for about a decade or perhaps a little more, eclipsing both Sparta and Athens. We can trace the development of the Athenian tradition regarding Thebes by studying the way Athenian orators in public meetings describe its fortunes. From the 360s to the 330s their allusions to Thebes become increasingly circumstantial until a recent history of the city takes shape in the Athenian mind. Now enter the historians (Ephorus and Callisthenes) who set this 'text' down in writing and flesh it out somewhat.[75]

On the face of things, the above argument makes ancient historiography akin to the fictions of Kentish Town, or the distortions of British popular memory after World War II. Was there no control over their story telling? They used generally accepted 'knowledge' such as the characters of well-known persons as tests of the veracity of a story,[76] but this idea of verification is troublingly circular since the characters were usually built up from historical narratives. Nonetheless, the existence of two somewhat independent traditions, one in the biographical stream and the other in the historical one, could have acted as something of a brake on free invention.[77]

Competition was probably a more effective restraint. The Greek communities generally nursed their own local traditions, which included, as Dionysius said, the ransacking of temple archives. We should not assume, however, that this 'ransacking' was methodical or in any way scientific, or that it kept local traditions faithful to the facts. The one thing that could keep braggart cities honest was the criticism of opponents. The two most striking examples of ancient historians working critically with documents are found in assaults on local traditions. Thucydides uses inscriptions to expose an error in the way his fellow Athenians celebrate the winning of their freedom; and the Chian historian, Theopompus, attacks what he calls the 'crowing' of the Athenians by attempting to prove that some of their celebratory inscriptions were fakes.[78] Sometimes local traditions in one place overlapped with another locality. In that case, it was possible to set the two versions against each other as a test.[79]

In the case of the Romans, the use of individual characters as tests of the veracity of a historical narrative may have some limited value. For the Romans, remembering was not a passive thing, especially when the subject was from the senatorial class. Families did not ignore family tombs, which bore inscriptions describing the achievements of the dead. The Romans took caring for their dead through family rituals and public festivals very seriously, as Gowing points out. 'We need think only of Roman funeral rites, the *laudatio funebris*, or the wax portrait masks, the *imagines*, of the ancestors that adorned the atria of Rome's political elite. The explicit purpose of such masks was, again according to Cicero, to preserve the *memoria* of the deceased'.[80] While these Roman habits do nothing to establish the absolute veracity of their historical reporting, they do show that there tended to be a continuous thread stretching from the present and reaching directly to the past. By contrast, there was a gap – a clear break – of 30 years between the Mass Observation records and the attempts at recollection that Harrisson used to expose the feebleness of human memory.

Finally, we might do well to ask what really matters. The woman who never heard Chamberlain's speech knew what it contained. How useful is it for us to know who was playing the piano in Britain when war was declared in September of 1939?

Notes

* Special thanks to Dr Jan Zwicky for reading and commenting on this chapter.

1 Plato, *Phaedrus* 274C–275B. See Plato, *Euthyphro, Apology, Crito, Phaedo, Phaedrus* (The Loeb Classical Library [hererinafter=LCL], Cambridge, MA, 1914 [reprint 2005]), pp. 560–65.

2 Charles W. Hedrick Jr., *Ancient History: Monuments and Documents* (Oxford, 2006), p. 66.

3 Gordon S. Shrimpton, *History and Memory in Ancient Greece* (Montreal and Kingston, 1997), pp. 118–19 and ff.

4 Dionysius of Halicarnassus, *Critical Essays*, vol. 1 (LCL, 1974 [reprint 2000]), 479–81; Felix Jacoby, *Atthis. The Local Chronicles of Ancient Athens* (Oxford, 1949), p. 170.

5 Thucydides 1.22 (LCL, 1919 [reprint 2003]), vol. 1, pp. 38–41; Polybius 36. 1 in *The Histories* (LCL, 1927), pp. 354–7. See Mary Frances Williams, 'Polybius' Historiography and Aristotle's *Poetics*'. *Ancient History Bulletin* 21 (2007), 18, 55–7. Polybius insisted that the historian should report what was truly said on any occasion, but does not explain how one should recover that truth. Thucydides spoke to eye-witnesses (or ear-witnesses).

6 Thucydides 1.22.2, *op.cit.*, vol. 1, pp. 38–41.

7 The Greek word *akribeia* is often translated 'accuracy' but it did not mean that, particularly in Thucydides' time. It meant something like 'orderly precision' or 'integrity' and is often a characteristic of people, the upper class in fact. So when Thucydides announces that he did not get his information from just anybody but went out of his way for *akribeia*, he identifies his constituency. See Gordon S. Shrimpton, 'Accuracy in Thucydides'. *Ancient History Bulletin* 12 (1998), 71–82.

8 Thucydides 1.22.1, *op.cit.*, vol. 1, p. 48.

9 Moses I. Finley, 'Introduction', in *Thucydides: History of the Peloponnesian*

War, trans. by Rex Warner (London, 1972), p. 26.

10 Mary Carruthers, *The Book of Memory: A Study of Memory in Medieval Culture* (Cambridge, 1990), pp. 156–8, and 61–2 particularly.

11 Plato, *Phaedrus* 228D, *op.cit.*, pp. 416–17.

12 Plato, *Timaeus* 17B–19B, in *Timaeus, Critias, Cleitophon, Menexenus, Epistles* (LCL, 1929 [reprint 2005]), pp. 16–23.

13 Plato, *Timaeus* 26C, *op.cit.*, pp. 44–5.

14 Homer, *Odyssey*, Book 23. The translation is by Walter Shewring, *Homer: The Odyssey* (Oxford and New York, 1980), p. 284.

15 Two recent studies are: Elizabeth Minchin, 'Spatial Memory and the Composition of the *Iliad*', and Anna Bonifazi, 'Memory and Visualization in Homeric Discourse Markers', in E. Anne Mackay (ed.), *Orality, Literacy, Memory in the Ancient Greek and Roman World* (*Orality and Literacy in Ancient Greece, Volume 7*) (Leiden, 2008), pp. 9–34, and 35–64.

16 Translated by Gordon S. Shrimpton, *Theopompus the Historian* (Montreal and Kingston, 1991), pp. 231–2.

17 Aristotle, 'On Memory and Recollection', 451a18–452a7, in *On the Soul, Parva Naturalia, On Breath* (LCL, 1936 [reprint 2000]), pp. 298–303.

18 Raffaella Cribiore, *Gymnastics of the Mind: Greek Education in Hellenistic and Roman Egypt* (Princeton and Oxford, 2001), pp. 165–6.

19 Plato, *Theaetetus*, 197 C-E, in *Theaetetus, Sophist* (LCL, 1921 [reprint 2006]), pp. 206–9.

20 Plato 195D-E, *op. cit.*, pp. 200–1.

21 Cribiore, *Gymnastics*, p. 165.

22 Aristotle, 452a 13–26, *op.cit.*, pp. 304–5.

23 Aristotle, 427b 19, *op.cit.*, pp. 156–7.

24 Albert B. Lord, *The Singer of Tales*, 2nd edn (Cambridge, MA, 2000).

25 Walter Burkert, 'The Making of Homer in the Sixth Century B.C.: Rhapsodes versus Stesichorus', in J Paul Getty Museum (ed.), *Papers on the Amasis Painter and his World* (Malibu California, 1987), pp. 43–62; Barbara Graziosi, *Inventing Homer: The Early Reception of Epic* (Cambridge and New York, 2002), pp. 18–40.

26 See James Allan Evans, 'Oral Tradition in Herodotus', in Evans, *The Beginnings of History: Herodotus and the Persian Wars* (reprint from *Canadian Oral History Journal* 4 [1980], 8–16) p. 281; also Edwin Carawan, 'What the *Mnemones* Know', in E. Anne Mackay (ed.), *Orality, Literacy, Memory* (Leiden, 2008), pp. 163–84.

27 David A. Campbell, *Greek Lyric III* (Cambridge, MA: Loeb Classical Library, 1991), pp. 351, 374–9.

28 Plato, *Hippias Maior*, 285e in *Cratylus, Parmenides, Greater Hippias, Lesser Hippias* (LCL, 1926 [reprint 2002]), pp. 352–3. Compare: The Elder Seneca, *Controversiae*, vol. 1 (LCL, 1974), pp. 3–5.

29 Thomas M. Conley, 'Dating the So-called *Dissoi Logoi*: A Cautionary Note'. *Ancient Philosophy* 5 (1985), 59–65.

30 Hermann Diels and Walther Kranz, *Die Fragmente der Vorssokratiker* II (Dublin and Zurich, 1969), pp. 405–16.

31 Jonathan D. Spence, *The Memory Palace of Matteo Ricci* (New York, 1984), p. 1.

32 The most recent attempt was Otto Lendle, 'Zu Thukydides 5.20.2'. *Hermes* 88 (1960), 33–40.

33 Thucydides 5. 20, 2–3, in *Thucydides* vol. 3 (LCL 1921 [reprint 2006]), pp. 40–1.

34 Gordon S. Shrimpton, 'Time, Memory, and Narrative in Thucydides'. *Storia della Storiografia* 28 (1995), 47–54.

35 Clemens Zintzen (ed.), *Damasci Vitae Isidori Reliquae* (Heldesheim, 1967), fragment 138.

36 Thucydides 1.22.4, *op.cit.*, vol. 1, pp. 38–9.

37 Frances Pownall, *Lessons from the Past: The Moral Use of History in Fourth-Century Prose* (Ann Arbor, 2004).

38 Mary Carruthers, *The Craft of Thought: Meditation, Rhetoric, and the Making of Images, 400–1200* (Cambridge, 1998), pp. 173–9; Jocelyn Penny Small, *Wax Tablets of the Mind* (London and New York, 1997), pp. 185–8.

39 Small, *Tablets*, pp. 188–91; John Marincola, *Authority and Tradition in Ancient Historiography* (Cambridge, 1997), pp. 180–1.

40 Carruthers, *The Craft of Thought*, pp. 82–3.

41 Alexander R. Luria, *The Mind of a Mnemonist: A Little Book about a Vast Memory*, trans. by Lynn Solotaroff (New York and London, 1968), pp. 31–3 and especially pp. 68–9.

42 Amos Funkenstein, 'Collective Memory and Historical Consciousness'. *History and Memory* 1 (1989), 5–26; N. Gedi and Y. Elam, 'Collective Memory—What is it?'. *History and Memory* 8 (1996), 30–50.

43 D. Schacter, *The Seven Sins of Memory* (New York, 2001), pp. 112–14.

44 Tom Harrisson, *Living through the Blitz* (London, 1976), pp. 45–6, 325–6.

45 Thomas Harrisson, 'Herodotus and the Origins of History', in Peter Derow and Robert Parker (eds), *Herodotus and his World: Essays from a Conference in Memory of George Forrest* (Oxford, 2003), p. 255.

46 Harrisson, *Living through the Blitz*, pp. 324–5.

47 Ibid., pp. 327–30.

48 Ibid., p. 13.

49 F. C. Bartlett, *Remembering: A Study in Experimental and Social Psychology* (Cambridge, 1932).

50 Peter Burke, 'History as Social Memory', in Thomas Butler (ed.), *Memory: History, Culture and the Mind* (Oxford, 1989), pp. 102–4.

51 Wolf Aly, *Volksmaerchen, Sage, und Novelle bei Herodot und seine Zeitgenossen* (Göttingen, 1921).

52 Livy 1. iv-vii, in *History of Rome. Books I-II* (LCL, 1919), pp. 16–31.

53 Herodotus 1.108–29, in *The Persian Wars* (LCL, 1920 [reprint 2004]) vol. 1, pp. 138–69.

54 Herodotus 1.6–91, *op. cit.*, pp. 8–119.

55 Herodotus 3.40–44, 120–125, *op.cit.*, vol. 2, pp. 52–9, 148–55.

56 Herodotus 7.35, *op.cit.*, vol. 3, pp. 346–9.

57 Herodotus 7.46, *op.cit.*, vol. 3, pp. 358–61.

58 Alain Gowing, *Empire and Memory: The Representation of the Roman Republic in Imperial Memory* (Cambridge, 2005), p. 2.

59 Gowing, *Empire*, p. 138.

60 Nicole Loraux, *The Invention of Athens: The Funeral Oration in the Classical City*, trans by Alan Sheridan (Cambridge, 1986). Now see especially: Haijo Jan Westra, 'Memory, Myth and History in the Athenian Funeral Oration: The Collusion between Orator and Public in the Discourse of Commemoration', in Ulrich van der Heyden and Andreas Feldkeller (eds), *Border Crossings: Explorations of an Interdisciplinary Historian* (Stuttgart, 2008), pp. 411–24.

61 Thucydides 1.20.3, *op. cit.*, vol. 1, pp. 38–41.

62 Herodotus 2.15, *op. cit.*, vol. 1, pp. 290–3; Shrimpton, *History and Memory*, pp. 168–86.

63 Nicole Loraux, *The Divided City: On Memory and Forgetting in Ancient Athens*, trans by Corinne Pache and Jeff Fort (New York, 2002, first published in France, 1997); Andrew Wolpert, *Remembering Defeat: Civil War and Civic Memory in Ancient Athens* (Baltimore, 2002).

64 Gordon Shrimpton, 'Oh, those Rational Athenians! Civil War, Reconciliation, and Public Memory in Ancient Athens (Ca. 630–403)'. *Mouseion* 6 (2006), 293–311.

65 Shrimpton, *History and Memory*, pp. 66–7.

66 Gillian Tindall, *The Fields Beneath: The History of One London Village* (London, 1977), pp. 128–9.

67 John Miles Foley, *Homer's Traditional Art* (Pennsylvania, 1999), pp. 33–4.

68 Lauri Honko (ed.), *Textualization of Oral Epics* (Berlin and New York, 2000), p. 3.

69 Minna Skafte Jensen, 'The Writing of the *Iliad* and the *Odyssey*', in Honko (ed.), *Textualization*, pp. 57–70.

70 Herodotus 8.118, *op. cit.*, vol. 4, pp. 120–1.

71 Herodotus 2.123; 4.195; 7.152, *op. cit.*, vol. 1, pp. 424–5; vol. 2, pp. 396–9; vol. 3, pp. 462–3.

72 Herodotus 6.21, *op.cit.*, vol. 3, pp. 166–7.

73 Herodotus 1.193, *op.cit.*, pp. 242–5.

74 Shrimpton, *History and Memory*, pp. 168–86.

75 Gordon Shrimpton, 'The Theban Supremacy in Fourth-Century Literature'. *Phoenix* 25 (1971), 310–18.

76 Anthony J. Woodman, *Rhetoric in Classical Historiography: Four Studies* (London, 1988), pp. 78–87; Dionysius of Halicarnassus, *On Thucydides* 8, p. 5.

77 Shrimpton, *History and Memory*, pp. 115–16.

78 Ibid., pp. 146–7.

79 Herodotus 8.94, *op.cit.*, vol. 4, pp. 90–3.

80 Gowing, *Empire*, p. 14.

Further reading

Mary Carruthers, *The Book of Memory: A Study of Memory in Medieval Culture* (Cambridge, 1990).

Raffaella Cribiore, *Gymnastics of the Mind: Greek Education in Hellenistic and Roman Egypt* (Princeton and Oxford, 2001).

Alain Gowing, *Empire and Memory: The Representation of the Roman Republic in Imperial Memory* (Cambridge, 2005).

Nicole Loraux, *The Invention of Athens: The Funeral Oration in the Classical City*, trans. by Alan Sheridan (Cambridge, 1986).

Albert B. Lord, *The Singer of Tales*, Second edn (Cambridge, MA, 2000).

Alexander R. Luria, *The Mind of a Mnemonist: A Little Book about a Vast Memory*, trans. by Lynn Solotaroff (New York and London, 1968).

Frances Pownall, *Lessons from the Past: The Moral Use of History in Fourth-Century Prose* (Ann Arbor, 2004).

Daniel Schacter, *The Seven Sins of Memory* (New York, 2001).

Jocelyn Penny Small, *Wax Tablets of the Mind* (London and New York, 1997).

Gordon S. Shrimpton, *History and Memory in Ancient Greece* (Montreal and Kingston, 1997).

Rosalind Thomas, *Oral Tradition and Written Record in Classical Athens* (Cambridge, 1989).

CHAPTER TWO

Memory and history in the middle ages

Kimberly Rivers

People in the Middle Ages had a profound respect for the possibilities that a powerful memory afforded, regarding it as a treasury of hidden riches.[1] When admirers discussed the mental abilities of the philosopher Thomas Aquinas (1224/25–1274), they praised his powerful memory: 'his memory was extremely rich and retentive: whatever he had once read and grasped he never forgot; it was as if knowledge were ever increasing in his soul as page is added to page in the writing of a book'.[2] In turn, the followers of St Francis of Assisi (c. 1181/82–1226) saw his memory as grounds for sanctity. His biographer, Thomas of Celano, said that whatever St Francis read in the Sacred Books was then written 'indelibly in his heart. His memory took the place of books'.[3] Yet medieval people also inherited from antiquity a sense of memory's inherent weaknesses, following Seneca in his assessment that 'memory is, of all the parts of the soul, the one most delicate and fragile'.[4] Many a medieval charter begins with a comment about the need to write down its contents because of the potential failures of memory. This tension between the need to remember – particularly apparent in a culture still dependent on oral traditions – and a transition toward writing is reflected in the scholarship about memory and history in the Middle Ages, which has recently attracted a good deal of attention.

One can argue that four major theories about memory have influenced historians treating the medieval period (roughly 500 to 1500 AD) in the past half-century, two coming from outside the discipline of medieval history, and two arising from the works of medieval writers themselves. The first two include Maurice Halbwachs' ideas about collective memory, which have obviously been important in the whole field of historical writing, and theories about orality and literacy, which historians have borrowed from literary studies. The latter field necessarily includes treatment of memory. The second two theories, which arise from the medieval period itself, include theories of mnemonics, i.e. how to remember things, and theories about how the human brain functioned and was able to think and remember, which came to affect how people thought about the past. In each of these areas, I will first discuss the theory of memory involved and then some ways that historians of the Middle Ages have incorporated theory into their work. One of the most important theories about memory to influence scholars studying the Middle Ages has been the work of Maurice Halbwachs on collective memory.[5] Halbwachs was a French sociologist working in the 1920s and 1930s who was interested in the ways that social groups affected human experience. His basic insight was that the memories of individuals are mediated by the social groups to which they belong. For him, this influence on an individual's memory by others begins in the family: Halbwachs points out that one's own memories tend to come back when other members of one's family relate them to us and that we often remember things when other people ask us questions.[6] In a very real sense, one cannot recall one's own past without one's family and friends. What is true for an individual also holds true for society as a whole: groups within society, such as nobles, peasants, workers, as well as nations, recall their pasts through frameworks set up by these groups. These frameworks are the rituals, ceremonies, stories, even written histories that groups and nations use to connect the present to the past. According to Halbwachs, 'it is in this sense that there exists a collective memory and social frameworks for memory; it is to the degree that our individual thought places itself in these frameworks and participates in this memory that it is capable of the act of recollection'.[7]

The implications of these theories often take time to understand. One of the most important is that Halbwachs did not think that our memories are capable of preserving a crystal-clear record of the past; rather, the past is always reconstructed based on present needs.[8] Thus, a society's understanding of a particular event could change quite radically from one generation to the next, as each new generation had different reasons to recall such an event.

Medieval historians have perhaps been slower to apply Halbwachs' insights to their field than historians of modern history. One way that medievalists have followed modern historians is to look at issues of commemoration, i.e. how medieval society consciously chose to recall as a society certain events from the past. Because of the perception that people in the Middle Ages were obsessed with death, judgement and the afterlife, a number of historians have examined the ways in which the living remembered or commemorated the dead. Scholars working particularly in Germany and the Low Countries have seen *memoria* as 'a key organizing principle, not only in medieval theology but in every aspect of medieval life', and have sought to understand the myriad ways in which medieval people donated chapels, paintings, altars and alms to churches and various religious groups in return for their prayers. For the living, the portraits of past donors in chapels, the stained glass windows and the hearing of the names of the dead during the liturgy served to preserve the presence of the dead within the community. For instance, Charlotte Stanford looks at the ways that funerals allowed the living first to remember the dead and then provide a structured way to forget them, arguing that some of the elite tried to stave off anonymity through anniversary services and perpetual masses.[9] Other scholars have noticed a heightened cult of remembrance after the Black Death (1348/49) in some parts of Europe. In Italy, for instance, from 1360 to the 1370s, there was increased demand for individual portraits and figures within larger artistic compositions. In Flanders art historians have found that commissions of portraits as seen in wills hit a high point in 1400, when there was a major incidence of plague.[10]

Two examples of works by medieval historians employing Halbwachs' theories are James Fentress and Chris Wickham's *Social Memory* (1992) and Patrick Geary's *Phantoms of Remembrance* (1994).[11] Fentress and Wickham, among others, have criticized Halbwachs for putting too much emphasis on social factors and not enough on the individual. The phrase 'collective memory' seems to imply some sort of 'group mind' that makes many people uncomfortable, and appears to negate the individual's ability to recall things on his or her own. For this reason, Fentress and Wickham have preferred to use the term 'social memory' instead.[12] In their view, individual memory is made 'social' by talking about it and sharing relevant memories with others. Groups then construct their own image of the world by deciding on an 'agreed version of the past'.

Part of their book examines a variety of theories about memory, including, in addition to collective memory, orality and literacy, mnemonics and psychological studies of how human memory actually functions. An important aspect of how they see individual memories affecting history are the studies conducted by Frederick Bartlett in 1930s Cambridge, which showed that people look for meaning or patterns even in a series of meaningless data. Bartlett gave his subjects a story with no real meaning and then asked them to recall it. He found that the participants gave their own interpretations of the story in order to remember it and that they tended to forget the parts of the story that did not fit their interpretation.[13] These results apply to historical memory in that groups create their own interpretations of the past and tend to forget the details that do not support their versions. Both Fentress and Wickham and Patrick Geary stress the importance of these studies in the creation of history.[14]

Fentress and Wickham have applied these ideas to medieval history and especially to the way that historians have used medieval sources in their own work. They distinguish between two extremes in attitudes of modern historians toward medieval sources: one view comes from a positivist tradition and assumes that if the historian can detect the bias of ancient and medieval writers and root out errors, they can get at the truth of the past. The problem with this approach for Fentress and Wickham is that facts are removed from their original context and lose the memory of the past in the original text.[15] The second view is a textual approach that concentrates on the context of the writer. Historians employing this approach believe that medieval historians can be used only to understand the historians themselves, not 'facts'. In this view, it is the historians themselves who are decontextualized.[16] Their view is that modern historians need to abandon their distinction between historical and literary texts, which they see as artificial, and instead regard 'the "objective" and the "subjective" as indissoluble'. Their goal is to get at the relationship 'between the world as it empirically was, and the world as it was represented by writers'.[17]

Practically what this approach means is that historians need to examine how medieval historians used their material, especially oral sources (inasmuch as one can determine what oral sources were used by a medieval writer). They want to get at an idea of 'the usable past', i.e. what seemed worthwhile for medieval historian to take from earlier sources and incorporate into their own works. 'What aspects of the past seemed relevant to historians to play around with for their own purposes is perhaps the key question: and when it is put in this form one can see that the question can cover oral and written commemorations, just as it can cover "true" and "false" pasts'.[18] They see this approach as opening up a vast field of analysis for historians. One example of how this approach elucidates medieval history can be seen in the works of Gregory of Tours, who wrote an account of the Frankish Kingdoms in sixth-century Gaul. They see Gregory as being the first major writer to provide a medieval, rather than an ancient, history of the world. Gregory does not even seem to realize that the Roman Empire is gone and is exceedingly proud of his family connections to the Roman senatorial tradition. Fentress and Wickham then examine why Gregory wrote the kind of history he did. Rather than writing a structured, political narrative, he chose to cast God as the causal agent in history and focused on two organizing frameworks: the lives of the Frankish kings and the lives of bishops in Gaul. The authors note that the lives of the kings give pegs to a dynastic narrative, but that the lives themselves are told in the style of folk motifs. For Gregory, the kings define the 'national', political history. As counterpoint are the bishops, seen as the highest Christian authorities and the arbiters of spiritual life. Fentress and Wickham see the bishops as representative of family memories; since most early medieval bishops came from important noble families, their histories reflect the local memories. The juxtaposition of kings and bishops shows the contrast between national and local interests and how hard it was for kings to impose their will on the localities.[19] There is a tension between local and national memories, and in the Middle Ages, the local memories tend to prevail.

Patrick Geary has applied some of these same theories to the history of eleventh-century Europe in his book *Phantoms of Remembrance*. Like Fentress and Wickham, he sees too much opposition set up between individual and collective memory in the followers of Halbwachs' theories. He also sees too stark an opposition drawn by some historians between collective memory, which is seen as relying on oral transmission, and history, which is seen as relying on written sources. He sees no reason why collective memory has to end when written history begins, and indeed gives examples of medieval writers drawing upon collected oral memories to write their histories.[20] He also posits that the way memories of the past are stored affects what we can know about history and that one must thus consider why documents from the past are preserved and the motives of the institutions that preserved them.[21]

As part of that consideration, Geary draws upon a list of what could be considered useful processes for remembrance, including visual associations, analogy, logical patterns, and labels and names.[22] He then tries to employ these processes actively in creating a history of medieval memory. Asking the question, 'what things are good to remember with?' he goes back to the four things named above and concludes that texts, people's names, and land and physical objects that by analogy or physical association might connect past and present were all perceived as good for remembering with at the turn of the millennium.

He sees the eleventh century as a major turning point in medieval history and that what we know, or think we know, of the eleventh century and the early Middle Ages, depends more than we have realized on what historians and writers of the time consciously chose to preserve of their own past.[23] The eleventh century was a time of competition for power, and the past could be used to acquire power.

> The right to speak about the past also implied control over that which gave access to the past – the "relics" by which the past continued to live into the present. How these tangible or unwritten relics of the past were preserved, who preserved them, and who could therefore make them to disappear were thus fundamental aspects of power and authority.[24]

This was a time when medieval authors reassessed the degree to which ideas from the past could be useful to the present, and to a larger degree than we might expect, decided that many records of the past were not useful. One example of this is the way that Western churchmen desirous of reforming the church created collections of canon law that supported their ideas. In this sense they were creating a bridge to a new past.[25] In the process of selecting and emending records from the past, the editors jettisoned what they felt they no longer needed. One of Geary's main points in the book is that written documents were kept for specific reasons in the Middle Ages and that those reasons need to be kept in mind when interpreting documents.[26] Overall, Geary thinks that if his study contributes anything to the scholarly debate over the 'mutation' of the year 1000, 'it is that the most profound transformation of this period was in the nature of the written record'.[27] People had a new sense that 'the received past no longer coincided with the present'.

For Geary, this sense that there was a momentous change around 1000 in attitudes towards the documentary record affects his view of the second of the main theories about memory in the field of medieval history, and that is the place of memory in the transition from orality to literacy in medieval Europe. Anthropologists and literary scholars have long been interested in the effects of orality and literacy upon a given culture. By orality, scholars mean a culture in which knowledge is transmitted orally without the benefits of writing. By literacy, scholars mean a culture in which knowledge is transmitted primarily through writing. Medieval scholars have tended to see medieval Europe as a time of transition between orality and literacy, because of the period's seemingly sharp divide between a literate elite of monks and clerics and an illiterate laity. Memory is involved because of the presumption that oral culture requires more reliance on memory than a literate culture. However, scholars have argued over when the transition to literacy occurred and over the degree to which the laity were illiterate.

Brian Stock's *The Implications of Literacy* brought the topic of literacy into the mainstream of medieval scholarship. He saw a kind of rebirth of literacy in the eleventh and twelfth centuries and tried to tease out the effects of literacy on related modes of thought at the time, which he saw as the 'implications of literacy'.[28] Stock did not think that literacy overtook orality in this period, but rather that the two became interdependent: 'oral discourse effectively began to function within a universe of communications governed by texts'. He also coined the phrase 'textual communities', the idea that groups could form around texts and their interpretation, whether or not they were written down.

One of the implications of literacy that Stock explores is the degree to which the way one transmits knowledge affects the way that one thinks and perceives the world. He argues that in an oral culture, memory becomes the 'storehouse of meaning' and that the 'mnemonic devices through which epic, legal and religious information is recalled help to structure the way in which the individual thinks about the facts transmitted'.[29] These kinds of changes led to a debate over the proper end of knowledge itself. One of the big changes in twelfth-century Europe was the rise of schools and schoolmasters. First in the cathedral schools and later in the new universities, such as Paris, Oxford and Bologna, masters began to teach the liberal arts, law, medicine and theology to students who travelled across Europe to take classes with them.[30] These new teachers saw the world differently than had the monks who had formerly dominated religious education, and they debated the role of knowledge and experience in medieval intellectual life. This debate about the ends of knowledge was perhaps most clearly drawn in the lives of Peter Abelard, who taught in the schools of Paris, and Bernard of Clairvaux, the famous abbot of the Cistercian abbey of Clairvaux.[31] 'Was its proper function, as St Bernard asserted, a meditative dialogue between one's inner self and God, or was it, as Abelard seemed to imply, the production of logically defensible statements about the knowable?'[32] Stock saw in the rise of the masters a concurrent rise in independent texts and a kind of separation between the knower and knowledge that was not present in early medieval intellectual thought. This change in view was at the heart of the fight between Abelard and St Bernard, where Abelard took a view of knowledge as separate and Bernard saw knowledge and texts as a way to gain personal experience through meditation (*meditatio*).[33] Both views would continue to have a following, through scholastic masters following in Abelard's footsteps, and members of religious orders following in Bernard's.[34] For each side, memory would also continue to play a vital role, as will be seen below.

Michael Clanchy has in some ways illustrated Stock's point that oral discourse in the twelfth century could function in a world dominated by texts. In his biography of Abelard, he stresses that twelfth-century masters in the schools did not initially write much down. Their fame depended on oral reports of their teaching. In fact, for the inhabitants of the early schools, parchment, writing and books were hard to come by and were more bound up with monastic experience than the scholastic one.[35]

One of the most ingenious ways in which these ideas have been applied to medieval history can be found in Michael Clanchy's book *From Memory to Written Record*, about the transition from reliance on memory to written documents in the day-to-day workings of government in medieval England from the mid-eleventh to the early fourteenth century. Clanchy argues that the Norman Invasion of Anglo-Saxon England in 1066 under William the Conqueror constituted a decisive moment in the workings of government and thinks that the 'growth in the uses of literacy is indicated by, and was perhaps a consequence of, the production and retention of records on an unprecedented scale (unprecedented, that is, in England)'.[36]

Clanchy outlines the ways that the Normans introduced and standardized written documents into government between 1066 and 1307, and considers the surviving numbers of documents from this period in English history as evidence of his thesis. He notes that some 2000 charters and writs survive from Anglo-Saxon England, while from the thirteenth century, well after the Normans were established in power, tens of thousands survive. Clanchy also thinks the increasing use of documents in government helped to spread a 'literate mode' in English society to the extent that by Edward I's time (1272–1307), writing was familiar to everyone. For instance, at the time of Edward the Confessor in 1066, only the king possessed a seal to sign his name; by Edward I's reign even serfs were required by statute to have one.[37]

Clanchy is careful not to privilege literacy over oral culture and sees writing as a 'technology' that was separate from the ability to read.[38] He credits the new styles of writing developed in monastic *scriptoria* (writing work-rooms) with paving the way for future acceptance and extension of literacy among the general populace.[39] The entire argument of the book hinges on the idea that English culture shifted from a dependence on memory in the eleventh century to one that was much more heavily dependent on the use of written records by the thirteenth century. He certainly does not think that the entire population was literate by this point, but rather that the government relied more on written documents as proof and that the people as a whole understood the use of written texts. He also argues that as people became more literate, they depended less on memory for their personal recording needs and had to use written notes as much as a modern literate person would.[40] He examines the kinds of mnemonic systems that will be discussed below, but concludes that these were moving towards the page, seeing new indexing systems used in manuscripts as a move from memory to written record.[41] Several scholars have come to similar conclusions on this last point.[42]

The ideas of Stock and Clanchy have not gone unchallenged, however. Geary thinks that both scholars have a better understanding of the complexities of eleventh- and twelfth-century Europe than they do of the earlier period and thus tend to overestimate the degree to which pre-eleventh-century Europe was dominated by oral discourse.[43] The lack of written documentation does not reflect a lack of literacy, but rather a different understanding of the purposes of writing and a loss of written records. On the whole his stance is that early medieval people created and preserved written records if they had a specific reason to do so and not otherwise. One might conclude that while the increase in surviving written documentation in Europe from the twelfth-century on is indisputable, the reasons for the smaller numbers of documentation in the earlier period are in dispute. Is it because pre-twelfth-century culture was based more in oral traditions or is it because the keepers of documents then had reasons to jettison written records that had once existed?

As part of their considerations of memory in medieval culture, all of these historians give some consideration to the issue of how people who did not always have constant recourse to books, parchment and notes recalled things through mnemonic schemes. The theory of mnemonics involves the techniques that medieval people consciously used to remember things they had read or heard and might wish to use again in a speech, literary composition or educational setting. Anyone who has ever made up a little verse or acronym to study for a test has employed a mnemonic device. There were a number of different mnemonic schemes available in the Middle Ages, some originating in Christian monastic meditative practice, some in pedagogical practice and some in classical rhetorical theory. One of the best-known variations was the mnemonic scheme described in the Roman rhetorical handbook, the *Rhetorica ad Herennium* (first-century BC). According to its anonymous author, anything could be remembered through the use of images and places. One had first to memorize an ordered set of mental places, i.e. mnemonic spots, such as various parts of a church or sections of a well-known street or house. Once one had a visual memory of a series of such locations, then one could set in these places mental images of the things one wished to remember. These images were meant to be as striking and active as possible in order that they might stick in one's memory. To retrieve the images, one simply revisited the memorized places in order, and the images would remind one of what one had memorized.[44]

This mnemonic technique was known in the classical and medieval period as 'the art of memory' or artificial memory, that is, a set of techniques designed to aid natural memory, which was seen as being naturally weak and subject to mistakes. The groundwork of the scholarship on the topic was laid by Ludwig Volkmann's 1929 article on the 'Ars memorativa', Helga Hadjú's *Das Mnemotechnische Schrifttum des Mittelalters* (1936), Frances Yates' *The Art of Memory* (1966) and Paolo Rossi's *Clavis Universalis* (1960).[45] Volkmann and Hadjú provided initial forays into the mnemonic arts of the medieval and Renaissance periods but hardly exhausted the material or its implications for European culture. Yates traced the history of the ancient art of memory up through the Renaissance, when it inspired hermetic philosophers like Giordano Bruno to search for the key to universal knowledge. Rossi documented the function of mnemonics in the development of the scientific method.

Because both Rossi and Yates were most interested in the Renaissance material, little work was done on the medieval period until recently. Mary Carruthers' *The Book of Memory* (1990) concentrated on the role of mnemonics in the audience and presentation of medieval literary works, while her second book, *The Craft of Thought* (1998), considered how early medieval monks created their own monastic rhetoric with a concomitant monastic *memoria* as part of their life of prayer.[46] Her work has revealed that medieval people had many different schemes of remembering things. The system laid out by the *Rhetorica ad Herennium* described above, which for a time scholars took to be the main mnemonic technique, was actually out of favour with intellectuals from about the fourth-century AD until the early thirteenth century, when it appears to have been revived by the Franciscan and Dominican orders.[47] Medieval monks and scholars came up with other techniques as well, including using complicated mental pictures with mnemonic 'places' built into them as organizing structures for what they wanted to remember. Examples include Noah's Ark, as described by High of St Victor in the twelfth century, and cherubs and seraphs, used throughout the Middle Ages.[48]

One area where one would expect mnemonics to be useful in the Middle Ages is preaching. Medieval Europe experienced a preaching revival in the twelfth and thirteenth centuries, and since these preachers did not often use notes to recall their material, mnemonic techniques should have been very useful to them. Nevertheless, medieval preachers did not leave many explicit directions about how to remember their sermons, so the little that has remained has been examined carefully. Lina Bolzoni has analysed how the Franciscan friar St Bernardino manipulated the rules of the *ars praedicandi* to produce sermons memorable because of their careful divisions and riveting imagery.[49] I have explored how the Catalan Franciscan author, Francesc Eiximenis (d. 1394), advocated mnemonic practices in his manual of advice for preachers, *Ars praedicandi* (*The Art of Preaching*).[50] The mnemonic advice of both friars reveals how monastic and classical memory schemes were conflated by medieval thinkers.

In *The Art of Preaching*, Francesc included a section on how to remember sermons. He saw the key to remembering as order and advised one always to 'order the things to be remembered in some order corresponding to the things to be remembered'. He provided several examples of how common 'orders' could be used. For example, he advised using roads and routes to recall things. He suggested that one could devise a route between Rome and Santiago de Compostela (a major pilgrimage site in the Middle Ages). One then thought of a number of important cities between them, found important attributes of each city distinct from the others, and then imagined them all as equidistant from each other: Francesc's example list includes Rome, Florence, Genoa, Avignon, Barcelona, Saragossa, Toledo and Santiago de Compostela.[51] Then, assuming that one had eight things to remember – money, merchants, a great bridge, burgesses, oil, knights and the apostles – one placed in each city the thing that best corresponded to it, putting clerics in Rome, money in Florence, and the apostles in Santiago de Compostela.

Francesc's mnemonic advice is often very similar to the advice in the *Ad Herennium* described above, but it is not exactly the same. Rather than creating mental places that could be used over and over again, Francesc told his readers to match the thing to be remembered with a particular place that suited it; the places could not be reused so easily in such a schema. In fact, Francesc states that his plans reflect what 'the moderns' do and even says that they find Tully's rules (the medieval name for Cicero, the supposed author of the *Ad Herennium*) too cumbersome.[52] He is clearly familiar with the ancient rules but content to adapt them to late medieval practice, likely as practised by the Franciscans and in the medieval universities.[53]

Another example of medieval mnemonic practice used in preaching comes from the famous Franciscan preacher, St Bernardino da Siena. During the Lenten preparations for Easter of 1424, St Bernardino addressed the importance of penance. Instead of merely haranguing his listeners with the dire penalties awaiting those who did not confess their sins to their priest, he began his six-week programme of instruction by describing a detailed image of a seraph, one of the higher orders of angels in Christian thought. Both the listeners and the preacher were to imagine a splendid creature with six shining wings, each divided into seven parts. Onto each of the divisions of the wing, San Bernardino instructed his listeners to inscribe the theme of one of his sermons. Each wing corresponded to a week of Lenten preaching, and each day received an 'illumination' onto which the major points of the sermon could be placed. The projected divisions allowed both the preacher and the audience to remember the main points of six weeks of daily sermons by drawing them together into a visual whole.

To construct his seraph, Bernardino probably drew on both monastic habits of meditation and the new genre of the *ars memorativa* in the fifteenth century. The creation of an intricate mental image reflects monastic meditative practice; the image of the seraph with writing on its wings was already circulating in Europe in the twelfth century and became particularly popular among the Franciscan order because of St Francis's vision of the seraph.[54] Bernardino's seraph is clearly a variant of monastic practice, in which the wings and their partitions provide the places, and the written inscriptions provide the 'images' to remind one of the entire sermon. It would certainly have served his memory but also likely that of his audience, who were reminded to picture the seraph for six weeks. Moreover, the friar was well aware of the usefulness of mnemonic strategies in his preaching. In a sermon delivered on 10 April 1424, he gives an example of an illiterate priest who is taught the *Pater Noster* (the 'Our Father') by his priest through a simple mnemonic strategy. The priest tells the peasant to put the images of 20 debtors in the place of the 20 phrases that make up the prayer. Bernardino even calls the advice 'the art of memory'.[55]

St Bernardino's reference to the art of memory reflects his awareness of a new genre of treatise circulating in fifteenth-century Europe, the *ars memorativa*. Though these treatises were examined by Yates, Rossi, Hadjú and Volkmann, much work on them remains to be done. Recently, Sabine Heimann-Seelbach inventoried manuscripts of the *ars memorativa* extant in Western Europe and published her account of the relationships among the manuscripts as well as an important study in her book, *Ars und Scientia*.[56] Lucie Doleželová, Farkas Gabor Kiss and Rafał Wójcik have begun to work out the history of the *ars memorativa* in Central Europe in studies that promise to reveal much more about the history of mnemonics in the universities and among the religious orders.[57]

The last major theory about memory and history arises from medieval theories of cognitive psychology, that is, theories of how humans processed sensory information and employed it to think. The scholar most responsible for elucidating the connections between history and cognitive psychology is Janet Coleman in her book *Ancient and Medieval Memories*.[58] Her goal was 'to give an account of some of the most prominent medieval theories and practice of remembering and reconstructing the past by examining the various ways in which texts (which were written in antiquity and which spoke to the future about the authors' present), were interpreted and understood during the middle ages'.[59]

What Coleman discovers is that how medieval writers regarded the past had a great deal to do with how they regarded memory and the value that they gave to what it recorded. For instance, Coleman notes a manifold shift in attitudes toward memory and the past with the Christianization and barbarian invasions of the Roman Empire from the fourth to the seventh centuries. For one, the tenets of classical rhetorical theory, along with the rules for the art of memory that it had taught, went out of fashion and were in fact held in great suspicion by the new groups of men in power. The *Ad Herennium*'s memory system went out of fashion until the thirteenth century.

Even more significantly, a new monastic ideal took root in this period, exemplified in the works of Pope Gregory the Great (590–604). By Gregory's time, the dominant literary model was no longer based on deeds of the past but rather emphasized miracles of living men. What was wanted were 'models of current heroic sanctity', which implied a new view of memory.[60] As the Roman world collapsed around Gregory and his contemporary, St Benedict of Nursia, the details of the secular past became progressively less important, and Scripture and the writings of the Fathers of the Church took their place. *The Rule of St Benedict* required its followers to practice monastic forgetfulness (*oblivio*) and to always remember God (*semper memor*).[61] What often seems to modern readers like a quixotic insistence on miracles in early medieval writing is actually a contemporary response to crisis and a realization of what seemed important at that time. One should remember God and living saints, not one's own or the secular past.

In her chapters on the high and late Middle Ages, from the twelfth through the fifteenth centuries, Coleman focuses more on medieval scholars' interpretations of formal theories about how physical memory works. In the second half of the twelfth and the beginning of the thirteenth century, philosophers became interested in the topic with the rediscovery and assessment of the Greek philosopher Aristotle's works on the soul and on what were called the 'interior senses', as well as Arab commentaries on Aristotle's works.[62] Medieval scholars strived to understand what Aristotle's theories meant for epistemology (the science of thinking) and for how people experienced sensation, i.e. touching, seeing, hearing, and so on. A special difficulty, and one which affected medieval thinkers' views of the past, was the contrast between particulars and universals. Aristotle had declared that knowledge and science could only be derived from universals, that is, from things that affect a whole class or genus, as opposed to particulars, which affected only some of a class. Given that sensation involved particulars, how did the cognitive process come to make use of them to create universals? A great many theories arose to explain the process. The variation in the theories stemmed from Aristotle's vagueness in explaining the mediators between sensation and intellection, known as the internal senses.[63] Aristotle referred to the notion of a 'common sense', to *phantasia* (imagination), and to memory, which he said belongs to the part of the soul to which *phantasia* belongs.[64] However, he was not particularly clear in distinguishing their functions. Arabic and Medieval Latin commentators were obliged to construct a more elaborate schema to explain the function of memory and the internal senses (often grouped together as the imagination) and their connections to intelligence.

Coleman's book delineates the variation in theories among scholars from the twelfth through the fourteenth century, examining, among others, the views of Thomas Aquinas, Duns Scotus and William of Ockham in addition to Averroes. Most medieval philosophers in the thirteenth century thought that the soul had three parts: the vegetative, sensitive and intellectual or rational. Only the latter two divisions were considered to play a role in cognition. The sensitive soul directed movement and apprehension through the external senses (sight, hearing, touch, etc.), while the rational soul governed cognition and drew upon the powers of the sensitive soul through the internal senses, which acted as mediators between the external senses and the intellect. Both the external senses and the internal senses were considered part of the sensitive, rather than the rational soul. The external senses began the process of sensation by sensing their respective objects. The sensory experience was transmitted to the interior senses through what were called 'species' or 'phantasms'. The interior senses occupied three cells in the brain, the first two of which were divided into two parts: in the first cell were located the common sense and imagination, in the second cell were the phantasy and estimation and in the third memory. Each power either apprehended the species sent to it or stored some part of them away. Memory, the aspect that most concerns us here, was the final stop in the process. It stored the species received from all the other powers for future reference and could also reminisce, i.e. recollect things about the past, with the aid of the intellect.[65] The images stored in imagination and memory were then available for use by the intellect in rational thought. The entire process of sensation to intellection was one of abstraction, of removing accidents, matter and, eventually particularity, to derive an abstract concept or 'universal'. It is important to note that no part of the above description would have gone unchallenged by some medieval philosopher, as different schools of thought emphasized one power over the others.

These theories affected how individual philosophers perceived the past. Aquinas, for example, saw history as being part of the particular, which was removed through the process of abstraction as described above. For this reason, the particular details of past experience were not really understandable according to these norms. What mattered was the past as it could be seen as universal or exemplary, from the useable truths that one could draw from it. It would then fit with a virtue like Prudence, which uses past experiences to know about the future.[66] In this sense, the past is present and universal.

That view of the past was opposed most famously by the Franciscan philosopher William of Ockham (d. 1349). Ockham's theory of cognition rejected most of the process of abstraction that Aquinas and other thirteenth-century philosophers had accepted. He also rejected the realist idea of the universe that assumed that all individual things have some extra-mental existence as well as the idea of species as intermediaries between the particular individual and mind's need to think with universals.[67] He came to the conclusion that all that can be known are individuals, and that scientific knowledge, the kind that Aristotle and those following after him had sought, is derived from concepts, which in turn are based on individuals.[68]

How does this thinking affect Ockham's view of history? Because his theory of cognition allowed the intellect, like the senses, to experience individual particulars, it also allowed for the past to be known as past. 'For Ockham, true memory and recollection must always have as their subject a person who remembers his own personal experiences'.[69] One's own, individual experiences could be proved true for oneself, but not those of other people. Coleman sees Ockham's formulations about the past as being the beginning of a 'putatively Renaissance confidence in the uniqueness of the past as past, and it is based on an analysis of the intellect's capacity to know the individual past just as do the senses'.[70] According to Coleman, his formulation, known in the medieval schools as the *via moderna*, came to be one of the two main ways of viewing the past, along with the *via antiqua*, into the eighteenth century.

All four of these theories – collective memory, orality and literacy, mnemonics and cognitive psychology – have given historians of the Middle Ages new lenses through which to view the sources of the period and have hardly been exhausted. They have the power to change the way we view important contemporary political movements, most notably demonstrated in Patrick Geary's *Myth of Nations*, in which Geary employs theories of collective memory to analyse and reject the views of the past of European nationalists.[71] In the end, history is about memory, and historians are best served when they have an understanding of the many ways in which it can be viewed.

Notes

1 See, for instance, Guibert de Tournai's comments in E. Bonifacio (ed.), *De modo addiscendi* (Turin, 1953), pp. 208–13.

2 From the *Life of St. Thomas* by Bernardo Gui. Cited in Mary J. Carruthers, *The Book of Memory: Study of Memory in Medieval Culture* (Cambridge, 1990), p. 3.

3 Cited in Kimberly A. Rivers, *Preaching the Memory of Virtue and Vice: Memory, Images, and Preaching in the Later Middle Ages*, Sermo, 4 (Turnhout, 2010), p. 106.

4 Roger A. Pack, 'An *Ars memorativa* from the Late Middle Ages'. *Archives d'histoire doctrinale et littéraire du moyen âge* 46 (1979), 221–75, here p. 231.

5 Halbwachs' theories may be most conveniently accessed by an English-speaking audience in Maurice Halbwachs, *On Collective Memory*, ed. Donald N. Levine, trans. by Lewis A. Coser (Chicago and London, 1992).

6 Halbwachs, *On Collective Memory*, p. 37.

7 Ibid., p. 38.

8 Halbwachs claimed that '[c]ollective frameworks are . . . precisely the instruments by the collective memory to recollect an image of the past which is in accord, in each group, with the predominant thoughts of the society' (Halbwachs, *On Collective Memory*, p. 39).

9 Charlotte A. Stanford, 'Held in "Perpetual" Memory: Funerals and Commemoration of the Elite Dead in the Late Middle Ages'. *Interculture (IPH)* 2 (2005), http://interculture.fsu.edu/pdfs/stanford%20medieval_funerals.pdf (accessed 27 September 2011).

10 John Aberth, *From the Brink of the Apocalypse: Confronting Famine, War, Plague, and Death in the Later Middle Ages*, 2nd edn (New York, 2009), pp. 209–10.

11 James Fentress and Chris Wickham, *Social Memory* (Oxford, 1992); Patrick J. Geary, *Phantoms of Remembrance: Memory and Oblivion at the End of the*

First Millennium (Princeton, 1994).

12 Fentress and Wickham, *Social Memory*, p. ix.

13 Ibid., pp. 34–5.

14 Geary, *Phantoms of Remembrance*, p. 19.

15 Fentress and Wickham, *Social Memory*, p. 144.

16 Ibid., p. 145.

17 Ibid.

18 Ibid., p. 146.

19 Ibid., pp. 146–52.

20 Geary, *Phantoms of Remembrance*, pp. 10–11.

21 Ibid., pp. 14–15.

22 Ibid., p. 20.

23 Ibid., p. 7.

24 Ibid.

25 Ibid., pp. 114, 180.

26 Ibid., pp. 14–15.

27 Ibid., p. 178.

28 Brian Stock, *The Implications of Literacy: Written Language and Models of Interpretation in the Eleventh and Twelfth Centuries* (Princeton, 1983), p. 3.

29 Stock, *Implications of Literacy*, pp. 15–16.

30 See, for instance, John W. Baldwin, *Masters, Princes and Merchants: The Social Views of Peter the Chanter and His Circle*, 2 vols (Princeton, 1970); Alan B. Cobban, *The Medieval Universities: Their Development and Organization* (London and New York, 1975); Hastings Rashdall, *The Universities in the Middle Ages*, eds. F. Maurice Powicke and Alfred B. Emden, 3 vols (Oxford, 1936).

31 For an overview of the tensions between scholastic and monastic life, see Stephen C. Ferruolo, *The Origins of the University: The Schools of Paris and Their Critics, 1100–1215* (Stanford, 1985).

32 Stock, *Implications of Literacy*, pp. 327–8.

33 Ibid., pp. 408–9.

34 Though one should not overemphasize the differences between their approaches to education. See, for instance, Thomas Head, 'Monastic and Scholastic Theology: A Change of Paradigm?', in Nancy Van Deusen and Alvin E. Ford (eds), *Paradigms in Medieval Thought Applications in Medieval Disciplines: A Symposium* (Lewiston, NY, 1990), pp. 127–42.

35 Michael T. Clanchy, *Abelard: A Medieval Life* (Oxford and Cambridge, MA, 1997), pp. 77–9.

36 Michael T. Clanchy, *From Memory to Written Record*, 2nd edn (Oxford, 1993), p. 1.

37 Clanchy, *From Memory to Written Record*, p. 2.

38 Ibid., pp. 7, 88.

39 Ibid., p. 114.

40 Ibid., p. 120.

41 Ibid., p. 179.

42 Mary Carruthers, *The Book of Memory: A Study of Memory in Medieval Culture*, 2nd edn (New York, 2008); Richard H. and Mary A. Rouse, '*Statim invenire*: Schools, Preachers, and New Attitudes to the Page', in Robert L. Benson and Giles Constable (eds), *Renaissance and Renewal in the Twelfth Century* (Cambridge, MA, 1982), pp. 201–25; Kimberly Rivers, 'Memory, Division, and the Organization of Knowledge in the Middle Ages', in Peter Binkley (ed.), *Premodern Encyclopedic Texts. Proceedings of the Second COMERS Congress, Groningen, 1–4 July 1996* (Leiden, 1997), pp. 147–58.

43 Geary, *Phantoms of Remembrance*, p. 14.

44 *Ad C. Herennium. De ratione dicendi (Rhetorica ad Herennium.)*, trans. by Harry Caplan, Loeb Classical Library (Cambridge, MA, 1954), Book III, ch. xvi, pp. 207–19.

45 Ludwig Volkmann, 'Ars memorativa', *Jahrbuch der Kunsthistorischen Sammlungen in Wien*. Neue Folge 30 (1929), 111–200; Helga Hadjú, *Das Mnemotechnische Schrifttum des Mittelalters* (Vienna, 1936); Frances A. Yates, *The Art of Memory* (Chicago, 1966); Paolo Rossi, *Clavis Universalis: Arti Mnemoniche e logica combinatoria da Lullo a Leibniz* (Milan and Naples, 1960). Rossi's book has been translated into English as *Logic and the Art of Memory*, trans. by Stephen Clucas (Chicago, 2000).

46 Mary Carruthers, *The Craft of Thought: Meditation, Rhetoric, and the Making of Images, 400–1200* (Cambridge, 1998); Carruthers, *The Book of Memory: A Study of Memory in Medieval Culture* (Cambridge, 1990).

47 Rivers, *Preaching the Memory of Virtue and Vice*, Chapters 1–2.

48 Carruthers, *The Craft of Thought*; Lina Bolzoni, 'St Bernardino da Siena', *The Web of Images: Vernacular Preaching from its Origins to St Bernardino da Siena* (Aldershot, England; Brookfield, Vt., 2004), pp. 117–95.

49 Bolzoni has also examined the influence of memory practices on sixteenth and seventeenth-century culture: Lina Bolzoni, *The Gallery of Memory: Literary and Iconographic Models in the Age of the Printing Press*, trans by Jeremy Parzen (Toronto, 2001). Lina Bolzoni, *The Web of Images: Vernacular Preaching from its Origins to St Bernardino da Siena* (Aldershot, England; Brookfield, Vt., 2004).

50 Kimberly Rivers, 'Memory and Medieval Preaching: Mnemonic Advice in the *Ars praedicandi* of Francesc Eiximenis (c. 1327–1409)'. *Viator* 30 (1999), 253–84.

51 Kimberly A. Rivers, trans., 'Francesc Eiximenis, On the Two Kinds of Order that Aid Understanding and Memory', in Mary Carruthers and Jan M. Ziolkowski (eds), *The Medieval Craft of Memory: An Anthology of Texts and Pictures* (Philadelphia, 2002), pp. 199–200. Francesc's choice of cities reflects his upbringing in the Crown of Aragon, part of what is now Spain.

52 For examples of Francesc speaking of modern practice, see 'Francesc Eiximenis, On the Two Kinds of Order', pp. 198, 202. For interpretations of what Francesc means by his comments, see Rivers, *Preaching the Memory of*

Virtue and Vice, p. 178.

53 Francesc attended several universities in Europe, including Paris, Oxford, Rome, and Toulouse, making his familiar with scholastic practice across Europe.

54 For an example of the Seraph used as a mnemonic scheme, see Bridget Balint, trans., '[Alan of Lille], On the Six Wings of the Seraph', in Carruthers and Ziolkowski (eds), *The Medieval Craft of Memory: An Anthology of Texts and Pictures*, pp. 83–102.

55 Rivers, *Preaching the Memory of Virtue and Vice*, p. 331.

56 Sabine Heimann-Seelbach, *Ars und Scientia: Genese, Überlieferung und Funktionen der mnemotechnischen Traktatliteratur im 15. Jahrhundert; mit Edition und Untersuchung dreier deutscher Traktate und ihrer lateinischen Vorlagen, Frühe Neuzeit, Bd. 58* (Tübingen, 2000).

57 Lucie Doležalová (ed.), *Strategies of Remembrance: From Pindar to Hölderlin* (Newcastle upon Tyne, 2009); Lucie Doležalová (ed.), *The Making of Memory in the Middle Ages* (Leiden and Boston, 2010); Rafał Wójcik, *Opusculum de arte memorativa Jana Szklarka. Bernardyński traktat mnemotechniczny a 1504 roku* (Posznań, 2006); Rafał Wójcik (ed.), *Culture of Memory in East Central Europe in the Late Middle Ages and the Early Modern Period, Prace Biblioteki Uniwersyteckiej, 30* (Posnań, 2008); Farkas Gabor Kiss, 'Valentinus de Monteviridi (Grünberg) and the Art of Memory of Conrad Celtis', in Rafal Wójcik (ed.), *Culture of Memory in East Central Europe in the Late Middle Ages and the Early Modern Period* (Posnań, 2008), pp. 105–18.

58 Janet Coleman, *Ancient and Medieval Memories. Studies in the Reconstruction of the Past* (Cambridge, 1992).

59 Coleman, *Ancient and Medieval Memories*, p. xiv.

60 Ibid., pp. 120–1.

61 Ibid., pp. 127–8.

62 See Rivers, *Preaching the Memory of Virtue and Vice*, pp. 79–86, for an overview of the relationship of cognitive psychology to mnemonics. For more thorough discussions, see Nicholas H. Steneck, *The Problem of the Internal Senses in the Fourteenth Century*, Ph.D. diss., University of Wisconsin, 1970; Richard Sorabji, *Aristotle on Memory* (Providence, 1972); Murray Wright Bundy, *The Theory of Imagination in Classical and Medieval Thought* (Urbana, Illinois, 1927); Henry A. Wolfson, 'The Internal Senses'. *Harvard Theological Review* 28 (1935), 69–133; Deborah L. Black, 'Estimation (*Wahm*) in Avicenna: The Logical and Psychological Dimensions'. *Dialogue* 32 (1993), 219–58. Also useful as a condensed explanation is Alastair Minnis, 'Medieval imagination and memory', in Alastair Minnis and Ian Johnson (eds), *The Cambridge History of Literary Criticism. Volume 2: The Middle Ages* (Cambridge, 2005), pp. 239–74.

63 Black, 'Estimation (*Wahm*) in Avicenna', p. 219.

64 Aristotle, *De memoria et reminiscentia* 450ᵃ.

65 The above depiction is based on Steneck, *The Problem of the Internal Senses*, pp. 10–15.

66 Coleman, *Ancient and Medieval Memories*, p. 455.

67 Ibid., p. 503.

68 Ibid., pp. 500–9.

69 Ibid., pp. 523–4.

70 Ibid., p. 526.

71 Patrick Geary, *The Myth of Nations: The Medieval Origins of Europe* (Princeton, NJ, 2002).

Further reading

Lina Bolzoni, *The Web of Images: Vernacular Preaching from Its Origins to St Bernardino Da Siena* (Aldershot, England, 2004).

Truus van Bueren and Andrea van Leerdamed (ed.), *Care for the Here and the Hereafter: Memoria, Art and Ritual in the Middle Ages* (Turnhout, 2005).

Mary Carruthers, *The Craft of Thought: Meditation, Rhetoric, and the Making of Images, 400–1200* (Cambridge, 1998).

—, *The Book of Memory: A Study of Memory in Medieval Culture*, 2nd edn (New York, 2008).

Michael T. Clanchy, *From Memory to Written Record*, 2nd edn (Oxford, 1993).

Janet Coleman, *Ancient and Medieval Memories. Studies in the Reconstruction of the Past* (Cambridge, 1992).

Lucie Doležalová (ed.), *The Making of Memory in the Middle Ages* (Leiden and Boston, 2010).

James Fentress and Chris Wickham, *Social Memory* (Oxford, 1992).

Patrick J. Geary, *The Myth of Nations: The Medieval Origins of Europe* (Princeton, NJ, 2002).

—, *Phantoms of Remembrance: Memory and Oblivion at the End of the First Millenium* (Princeton, NJ, 1994).

Maurice Halbwachs, *On Collective Memory.* trans. by Lewis A. Coser. ed. by Donald N. Levine, *The Heritage of Sociology* (Chicago and London, 1992).

Sabine Heimann-Seelbach, *Ars und Scientia: Genese, Überlieferung und Funktionen der mnemotechnischen Traktatliteratur im 15. Jahrhundert. Mit Edition und Untersuchung dreier deutscher Traktate und ihrer lateinischen Vorlagen. Frühe Neuzeit, Bd. 58* (Tübingen, 2000).

Kimberly A. Rivers, *Preaching the Memory of Virtue and Vice: Memory, Images, and Preaching in the Later Middle Ages, Sermo, 4* (Turnhout, 2010).

Paolo Rossi, *Logic and the Art of Memory.* trans by Stephen Clucas (Chicago, 2000).

Brian Stock, *The Implications of Literacy: Written Language and Models of Interpretation in the Eleventh and Twelfth Centuries* (Princeton, 1983).

Frances A. Yates, *The Art of Memory* (Chicago, 1966).

CHAPTER THREE

History-writing and 'collective memory'

Mary Fulbrook

'Collective memory' studies by now constitute a variegated and complex field. There is a wide range of theoretical approaches and associated conceptual vocabularies, as well as an array of rich and detailed studies of particular topics, themes and areas. The interest in social or collective memory dates back a long way – on some views, at least a couple of thousand years – but what concerns me here is the recent and current situation.[1] Although the remarks below have more general relevance, I shall take examples primarily from the area of twentieth-century European history and particularly the Holocaust, where some of the differences in theoretical approach can be delineated most clearly.

The 'memory boom'

There has, over the last few decades, been a memory boom in at least two senses. Among historians and social scientists there has been a heightened interest in the area of what may roughly be designated as 'collective memory'; and in the wider public sphere there has been an apparently heightened historical consciousness, evident in north America and in eastern as well as western Europe. An increasingly commercialized and professional concern with public history, particularly in western societies, has fostered not only growing interest in the past among wider non-professional circles, but also stimulated the interest of historians in the topic of historical consciousness, the relations between history and memory, and the significance of remembrance activities for historical developments. With the overthrowing of communist regimes in eastern Europe, perceptions of the past that were at odds with official representations of history have been able to compete for space and voice in new and more diverse, often emotionally laden and strongly contested landscapes of remembrance and memorialization. Not all of this activity relates to 'memory' in the more restricted sense of that which is recalled by those who have personally experienced an event or period, but much has been subsumed under an arguably ever more inflated concept of 'collective memory'.

The 'memory boom' in the public sphere went alongside and partially prompted the increased interest in the history of 'collective memory' among scholars. Memorialization itself is far from new: statues, memorials, and rituals of remembrance in public spaces have always been used for political, religious and social purposes throughout the centuries. But there were significant shifts in character and scale in the decades after World War II. The uses of historical representation for political purposes were striking among eastern European states, constraining although not entirely precluding diversification until after 1990. In western states, there was a combination of professionalization, decentralization, democratization and commercialization during the last three or four decades of the twentieth century: an exponential growth in what might be called the 'historical tourism industry', inviting public identification with selected aspects of the past, alongside new kinds of identity history. Voices from the past – whether the eyewitness testimonies of those who had lived through the wars of the twentieth century, or the imputed subjectivities of seventeenth-century settlers in New England – were harnessed to the task of 'bringing the past alive'. Reconstructed seventeenth- and eighteenth-century settlements, as in Plimoth Plantation or Old Sturbridge Village in the USA, with a commitment to historical authenticity and educational goals, must be counted alongside commercial sites for popular 'experience' (the London Dungeons), or the more sober development of museums and archives with an associated memorial mission, from the early post-war Museum of the Shoah (*Centre de Documentation Juive Contemporaine*, CDJC) in Paris to the United States Holocaust Memorial Museum (USHMM) in Washington. Forms of historical representation and commemoration were shaped and inflected by contrasting national and international contexts. The 750th anniversary of Berlin in 1987, for example, gave rise to competing official self-representations on both sides of the Berlin Wall. States were however not the only actors. There were also regional, local and special interest group projects of identity building – experiencing different constraints on either side of the Iron Curtain – reflecting social changes and tensions across and within geopolitical and temporal borders. The 200th anniversary of the French Revolution in 1989, for example, was marked both by 'official' celebrations and regional revivals or constructions of local heritage.

Across Europe, with marked variations in timing, details, patterns of contestation and opposition, and eventual outcomes, aspects of the Nazi past and the legacies of occupation were excavated, displayed and commemorated. The Holocaust sites in Poland were variously appropriated by Communist narratives of political heroism and later retrieval of narratives of Jewish resistance and victimhood. The collapse of the Cold War stimulated widespread debates over how to represent and remember the overlapping and succeeding experiences of dictatorship and repression through the 'age of extremes', complicated in many eastern European states by the complex heritage of multiple occupations by dominant powers.[2] In all these attempts, however overlain by educational missions (more so in some cases than others), notions of 'heritage', legacy and identity in the present were clearly as much at stake as any attempt at reconstructing or representing 'the past as it really was'. Given their significance in the present, these aspects of the past were seen to be something more than mere 'history'; thus, they could be conflated into notions of collective memory.

This supposed 'memory boom' in the public sphere was accompanied by a boom in historical memory studies. In what respects and why did the forms and shapes of public memory appear to change so much in the closing decades of the twentieth century – or did they? What were longer continuities and subtle changes in the 'sites of memory', metaphorical as well as literal? Could one write a history of collective memory, and how it varied from place to place? One need only think, for example, of Pierre Nora's acclaimed multi-volume project tracing French 'sites of memory' (see the chapter by Benoît Majerus in this volume), or the comparable projects carried out by Étienne François and Hagen Schulze in Germany, or the works by James Young on Holocaust memorials, or those by Jay Winter and others on the Great War, to register the boom not only in public memory but also in studies of these phenomena.[3] Indeed, the memory boom and the boom in memory studies went hand in hand. As Pierre Nora memorably put it:

> [M]emory today exercises such a powerful hold on our minds that commemorative bulimia has all but consumed all efforts to control it. No sooner was the expression *lieu de mémoire* coined than what was forged as a tool for maintaining critical distance became the instrument of commemoration par excellence.[4]

Among some scholars, even the very notion of memory, now so fashionable, became something of a red rag. As Norman Finkelstein comments, using Peter Novick's work on the Holocaust as his immediate target:

> Currently all the rage in the ivory tower, "memory" is surely the most impoverished concept to come down the academic pike in a long time. With the obligatory nod to Maurice Halbwachs, Novick aims to demonstrate how "current concerns" shape "Holocaust memory."[5]

Even without buying into the kind of polemics developed by Finkelstein or sharing his critique of Novick, it began to seem that the notion of 'collective memory' on occasion ran the risk of claiming a great deal more than it could actually deliver.

Yet despite this double boom, historians barely agree on what they mean by 'collective memory'. Despite the exponential growth of the field, there is as yet no consensus on theoretical approaches. It is of course perfectly legitimate to explore the appropriation and instrumentalization of particular images of the past, the construction of historical myths, or the ways in which people are enjoined to remember, to identify with particular values, or to adopt certain attitudes towards a constructed 'heritage'. But in some respects, the study of historical representations at this level has displaced any concern with the inevitably collective aspects of individual memory in the strict sense of the term. A highly fruitful area of study has thus been relatively ignored, swamped as it has been by excessive focus on merely one aspect of the problematic. This becomes clear if we consider in more detail the potential inherent in the theories of one of the founding fathers of current memory studies, Maurice Halbwachs.

Halbwachs' double legacy: The 'remembering agent' and the location of memory

Theoretical approaches may roughly be divided into two very general camps, with further subdivisions within and across these camps. These differ with respect to what might be called the 'remembering agent' and the closely related issue of whether or not there is a 'real experience' on which 'memory' is based.

The broadest division has to do with whether or not analysts of 'collective memory' assume that their subjects – the individuals, groups or other collectives who are engaged in 'memory work' – have themselves actually experienced the events or phenomena in question; in other words, whether the word 'memory' is used in a literal or a metaphorical sense. Some scholars are quite happy to deploy the term 'memory' irrespective of whether or not this relates to a personally experienced past. Other scholars, however, argue that we should actually talk about 'remembrance', 'commemoration' (and similar terms), rather than 'memory', when the agents have not themselves actually lived through and personally experienced the events that are being 'remembered'. On this view, 'memory' should be reserved for representations made by those who did indeed live through the events and periods remembered.

This distinction is not trivial. For both approaches are in principle present in the work of the scholar most suited to the accolade of 'founding father' in this area, Maurice Halbwachs. Yet it is really only the former insight, perhaps influenced by Halbwachs' teacher, Émile Durkheim, that seems to have had most impact on historians of collective memory. This relates to the ways in which public practices, such as rituals of remembrance or commemorative ceremonies, connect with the attempted construction or would-be reinforcement of a particular kind of collective identity. As Paul Connerton puts it:

> With exemplary lucidity, [Halbwachs] demonstrated that the idea of an individual memory, absolutely separate from social memory, is an abstraction almost devoid of meaning. . . . Yet Halbwachs, even though he makes the idea of collective memory central to his inquiry, does not see that images of the past and recollected knowledge of the past are conveyed and sustained by (more or less) ritual performances . . .[6]

And it is precisely this aspect of Halbwachs's work which Connerton himself seeks to develop, drawing attention to 'commemorative ceremonies' that 'prove to be commemorative only in so far as they are performative'.[7] The same selective strand of development is prevalent in numerous historical works and related theoretical literature. A casual glance at what comes under collective memory studies reveals a significant concentration on public representation, practices of remembrance, films and works of creative literature, that have little or nothing to do with actual memories or personal experiences of individuals.

But the more central insight deriving from Halbwachs, that no individual can articulate personal memories outside of collectively derived and ever-changing frameworks of social discourse, has been less well developed. Halbwachs' own focus was very much on living individuals, ·who as members of particular social groups participate in fluctuating, changing memory communities:

> While the collective memory endures and draws strength from its base in a coherent body of people, it is individuals as group members who remember. While these remembrances are mutually supportive of each other and common to all, individual members still vary in the intensity with which they experience them.[8]

In one of his most programmatic statements on the nature of collective memory, Halbwachs asserts that:

> the continuous development of the collective memory is marked not, as is history, by clearly etched demarcations but only by irregular and uncertain boundaries. . . . The memory of a society extends as far as the memory of the groups composing it.[9]

There is no particular reason why, for all his insights, Halbwachs' classic work should be taken as a founding testament in historical studies of collective memory; there is inevitably (as with all classics that have endured) much that is dated in his discussions of both memory and the nature of history as a scholarly discipline. But this particular strand of his thought has received far less by way of development than that of public representations. And there has to date been remarkably little by way of analytic attempts to bring these levels together in a coherent overall theoretical framework.

Collective memory as public representation: The community as remembering agent

In the first camp, then, are those approaches where the primary focus is on some collective body or community as primary 'remembering agent'. Collective memory in these approaches is generally seen as, in principle, separable from actual memories of past experiences; it may or may not relate to these. The focus in these kinds of study of 'collective memory', however inflected and conceptualized, is on a collective unit of analysis – whether the state, the region, the locality, the family, the 'memory community' or at any other level. The key point is the passing on of a particular form of historical consciousness, irrespective of whether or not this relates to a personally experienced past.

Many historical studies of 'collective memory' focus predominantly, if not entirely, on the level of public representations – through the study of memorials, museums, historical sites, films and novels, parliamentary debates, media reports, war crimes trials and other activities in which selected aspects of the past are 'made present' again. Henry Rousso, for example, defines this 'new field of study' as 'the study of the evolution of various social practices and, more specifically, of the form and content of social practices whose purpose or effect is the representation of the past and the perpetuation of its memory within a particular group or the society as a whole'.[10] Such studies often posit 'the nation' or other collective units as essential subjects, as in Rousso's intriguing and suggestive but somewhat anthropomorphic representation of the development of the 'Vichy syndrome' in terms borrowed from individual psychology, including 'Neurosis', 'Repressions' and 'Obsession'.[11] Public representations of history, in whatever media (including films and novels) are very often 'mapped onto' analyses of changing patterns of, for example, 'national identity', as in the case of German 'coming to terms with the past' (*Vergangenheitsbewältigung*).

While some of the earlier approaches to national memory traditions tended to iron out the degrees of contestation and emphasize the functions of commemorative practices for social cohesion, recent approaches are more sensitive to the ways in which dominant voices marginalize or silence the voices of those with differing views, and highlight the essentially contested character of the public outcomes of memory contests in any given case.[12] Collective memory may in this version be seen as rooted in specific groups with a distinctive set of past experiences, such as local groups or 'political communities' that contest 'national' or 'hegemonic' narratives. Robert Gildea, for example, defines 'collective memory' as 'the collective construction of the past by a given community'. He writes:

> [T]here is no single . . . collective memory but parallel and competing collective memories elaborated by communities which have experienced and handle the past in different ways. . . . [T]he past is constructed not objectively but as myth, in the sense not of fiction, but of a past constructed collectively by a community in such a way as to serve the political claims of that community.[13]

His own work seeks to explore the ways in which 'political communities have struggled to win acceptance for their own presentation of French history as universal and objective'.[14] Many other such examples could readily be adduced. In appropriating the legacies of Halbwachs, Émile Durkheim has by now, as it were, been supplemented by an implicit dose of Max Weber (more rarely Karl Marx). Such approaches, with their focus on the political instrumentalization of particular views of the past – whether at the level of the state or of distinctive groups or 'memory communities' within or across the borders of any given context – also tend to reduce 'collective memory' to an aspect of political ideology.[15]

Some scholars, following the work of Jan and Aleida Assmann, have focused primarily on the medium of transmission of historical consciousness: their typology seeks to prioritize the distinction between forms of 'cultural memory' embodied in artefacts, exhibitions and published media, and 'communicative memory' passed down in face-to-face encounters, through word of mouth, among people in personal contact with one another. But even in the latter sphere, where the experience is perhaps historically closer, the mode of communication is what is distinctive: the events depicted need not have been personally experienced. Informal memories and personal perceptions of an actually experienced past frequently remain beyond the scope of such studies. Even when such an aspect is included, it is often treated in terms of 'reception studies', implicitly predicated on notions of a rather one-way street in lines of influence and response.

This kind of approach generally posits a direct link between the past in question and the later community appropriating this past. There is an associated tendency, even when discussing 'transnational' collective memories or asking about 'Europeanisation' of memories, to think in terms primarily of discrete national contexts. Often these too presuppose a clear line of continuity between a particular national past and a later 'memory culture'. Aleida Assmann, for example, in discussing the possible 'Europeanisation' of a collective memory of the Holocaust, distinguishes particular 'nations' or 'states' that have what she calls an 'experiential link between the memory and the event'. She identifies as the 'four groups that have a claim to such

a memory' the following: Israel, Germany, the European nations that were
sites of genocide and 'the nations of rescuers' among the Allies. In Assmann's
analysis, some 'reflections . . . argue for historical diversity and a national
framing of Holocaust memory' but 'international measures have been taken
to transcend the national level by reshaping and standardizing this memory
in terms of a common historical reference'.[16] On this line of reasoning, if
European nations can agree on 27 January as a Holocaust remembrance day,
then a collective memory of the Holocaust functions as a basis for a common
European identity (even though the date was designated by the United
Nations General Assembly in 2005 to apply to all UN member states). This
approach tends to prioritize the significance of public representations over
individual subjective perceptions, generally within national or other clearly
bounded political frameworks, whether local and regional or supranational.
Such a focus is clearly complicated by population mobility and the passage
of generations; yet the latter aspects are often only considered when talking
about media of transmission – 'communicative memory' versus 'cultural
memory' – where the distinction tends to remain formal and typological.

One of the commonest critical reactions to otherwise significant works
in this line of approach is a sense that, for all the subtlety and richness of
the analysis of historical representations, and for all the awareness of the
essentially contested nature of any such phenomena, the subjective aspect
is often largely missing. Only rarely are attempts made to look at mutual
interactions and influences between 'private' or familial representations
and those in the public sphere. This could in principle be done with respect
to any period of history, as research on ego-documents can reveal. With
respect to recent and contemporary history, the significance of personal
involvement in the creation of 'public history' may on occasion become only
too clear. This was the case, for example, in a series of German debates in
the mid and later 1980s: the 1985 Bitburg controversy when US President
Reagan and German Chancellor Helmut Kohl clumsily marked the 40th
anniversary of the end of World War II with an attempt at reconciliation
over the graves of former members of the SS; the so-called historians'
controversy (*Historikerstreit*) of 1986–87, in which right-wing philosophers
and historians appeared close to celebrating the efforts of German soldiers
on the eastern front to combat the supposedly 'prior evil' of Bolshevism,
while downplaying the suffering of Jews and relativizing the Holocaust;
and the controversial speech in 1988 by German parliamentary floor-leader
Philipp Jenninger on the fiftieth anniversary of the November Pogrom
(commonly known as 'Kristallnacht', night of broken glass), a speech in
which the rupture of unspoken conventions about the sayable and the
unsayable, public scripts and private emotions, caused a major political
furore.[17] One of the key themes, indeed, of German experiences through the
turbulent twentieth century has been that of dissonance between the kinds
of account of oneself and one's role in and/or views on the past demanded
in public and those experienced in private.[18]

Approaches to collective memory in the sense of public representations of the past have little to do with any notion of 'memory' in the narrower or strict sense of the term. Other concepts, such as historical consciousness, commemorative practices, rituals of remembrance, even myth, might actually be more appropriate terms for the material under analysis. This sort of approach to collective representations is really only related to the sense of 'memory' as the injunction to ponder and recall: 'Remember, remember, the fifth of November: gunpowder, treason and plot'; or 'lest we forget' and other similar praxes, including religious anniversaries (Pesach/Easter, for example); in the sense of seeking to bring back to mind, to put the pieces together again as a whole and to bring alive in some way for a present in which such a past no longer exists in any kind of personal experience. Moreover, commercial interests may play as much of a role in such historical representations as any other kind of political or moral impulse. The fireworks, bonfires and parties that traditionally celebrate 5th November in Britain certainly now have more to do with supermarket sales than any early seventeenth-century Catholic plot to blow up parliament; Easter eggs and Christmas presents arguably also have for many secular westerners very little to do with remembering the biblical stories of Christ's life.

To restrict the notion of 'collective memory' to historical representations and instrumental appropriations of the past for collective purposes risks inflating the meaning of the term, reifying the collective which serves as the remembering agent, and potentially obscuring or ignoring the significance of the social for the construction and framing of subjectively experienced individual memory.

Collective memory as the social articulation of individual experience: The remembering self in historical context

Halbwachs' other major insight has to date been less well taken up by historians of collective memory. This insight is in itself twofold: first, no individual can communicate any personal memories to others outside of collective frameworks of conceptualization and narrativization; and secondly, members of social groups construct and adapt these collective frameworks in ever-changing ways, ways that are coterminous with the lives of members of these groups but extend no further than their lifetimes. The 'engrams' that are the visual traces within the brain ('the mind's eye') of a personally experienced past can only be communicated to a wider world through the use of a shared language, a discourse of mutual significance.[19] And the ways in which this language operates will change with changing frameworks of interpretation, changing patterns of employment of the past, changing concepts for describing and analysing what it is the individual wishes to communicate, in changing contexts of communication. Halbwachs' approach here to discourse is in a formal sense somewhat similar to the 'structure/agency' problematic that has also been much discussed; people participate in rule-guided communities of perception as well as action and are able both to play by and alter these rules over time.

Thus the other major approach to collective memory starts by positing the existence of 'remembering agents' who have personally lived through and experienced, in some way, the past in question. They cannot recount this past to others without the use of shared terms, common frameworks of reference, within any given communicative context. Their representations of this past will neither rely solely on, nor comprehensively represent, their own perceptions and emotional responses to events and experiences at the time; rather, their later accounts represent attempts to give meaning and significance to selected aspects of this past, as informed and framed by the priorities and discourses of the later present, and with the likely impact of their communication on the potential or actual audiences in mind. The particular form and content of the narrative of an individual's own life story will be affected not only by neurological memory traces in the brain, as well as changing physiological capacity to remember, but also by multiple social and historical contexts of narration.

Insofar as approaches in this camp deal with the significance of collective memory – as distinct from individual psychology, such as the impact of trauma on a particular person – they explore the ways in which autobiographical narratives of a personally experienced past are inherently informed and shaped by social contexts. Irrespective of the particular details of the individual life story, there are wider patterns concerning issues such as: the desire to present a certain kind of 'self' in different contexts, associated with political and social considerations and cultural conceptions of what is deemed acceptable; the purposes and likely implications of different sorts of self-presentation (as in family stories, letters, diaries and memoirs, compared with witness testimony, defence statements in legal proceedings or the scholarly investigations of oral history interviews); the presence or absence of significant others in different settings of self-presentation; the character of the narrator and the mutual expectations of interlocutor/interviewer and narrator/interviewee.[20]

It is notable that it was primarily among social psychologists and literary scholars, rather than historians, that this line of approach was most prominently developed at a relatively early date in the 'memory boom'; and here, it has perhaps had most impact in the area of Holocaust studies.[21] There is by now a wealth of research in this area, ranging from the psychotherapeutic studies of trauma and survivor memories – where finding ways of articulating a highly distressing experience in words has been found to alleviate symptoms among sufferers from Post-Traumatic Stress Disorder – to social-psychological studies of the ways in which individual life stories are produced in part as a function of small group communicative contexts.[22] Over time, too, people's life stories develop in relation to the changing situations in which different aspects of their past are variously relevant, as well as varying with their own age and changing propensity to recall; and psychologists are gaining increasing sophistication in understanding variations in autobiographical memory at the level of the individual.[23]

More generally, the implications of post-structuralist theories of the self have been taken more seriously in literary scholarship than among historians. Similarly, the debates on structure, agency and habitus deriving from the work of Bourdieu have as yet arguably had less influence on historians than on social scientists. Increasingly, however, whether or not they explicitly theorize their approach, historians are coming to explore the interrelations between individual memories, contemporaneous social relations and changing historical contexts.[24]

Theoretical frameworks among historians have been perhaps most explicitly developed in the analytic strategies of those using oral history methods, who have moved well beyond the early, empirically driven impetus to try to discover aspects of the past that had left no or few traces in the archival records, or the often politically driven emancipatory impulse to 'give voice' to marginalized and excluded groups (see the chapter by Lynn Abram in this volume). Often their focus now is on exploring and identifying the particular mentalities and strategies discernable in the life stories of individuals drawn from different cohorts, living through and reflecting on different historical periods.[25] Yet historians have barely started to integrate studies of individual self-representations or constructions of a personally experienced past into wider historical analyses of collectivities.

Frequently, historians use personal memories as near contemporary eyewitness accounts, verbal illustrations or snapshots in words: attempting to bring a sense of immediacy to analytic depictions of historical developments. This may serve to 'give voice' to historical protagonists, helping readers to understand the experiences and mentalities both of those in power and those subject to discrimination or repression, and giving colour to descriptions of everyday life; this may make for more accessible history, akin to literature rather than an analytic branch of the social sciences. But such uses of eyewitness accounts rarely address directly the character or significance of 'memory' itself and the social construction of the remembering self in such sources. The focus is still on describing events and on vivid renditions of the experiences of the time.[26]

Many historians use the memories of those who lived through particular experiences as distinctive primary sources that can be mined for information about that past that is unavailable in official archival sources. The focus then is not on 'collective memory' so much as 'collected memories', in Christopher Browning's phrase. Browning is somewhat critical of approaches that focus primarily on the narrative structure and strategies of memory with little regard for any capacity to represent the past with a degree of accuracy. Such approaches, Browning suggests, emphasise the effects of the Holocaust upon the survivors and how they have remembered and narrated, struggled and coped with these effects rather than the events of the Holocaust itself. The "authenticity" of the survivor accounts is more important than their "factual accuracy". Indeed, to intrude upon the survivors' testimonies with such a banal or mundane concern seems irrelevant and even insensitive and disrespectful.[27]

Browning also wants to distinguish his use of testimonies from the kinds of uses discussed above with respect to collective remembering agents: 'Here the key question is: How is a society's identity and self-understanding both created by and reflected in the selection from and manipulation of survivor accounts to create society's present "collective memory" of the past?'[28] In contrast to such approaches, Browning – along with many other historians – wants to use testimony as 'collected memories' to reconstruct past events, 'to construct a history that otherwise, for lack of evidence, would not exist'.[29]

Obviously a great deal depends on the purposes for which memory scripts are being used, and the principal focus of many historians is on reconstructing a particular past, rather than analysing strategies of remembering this past, or exploring the lingering legacies of a succession of ever-receding pasts for a changing later present. Even where memory is seen to be significant in historical reconstruction, it is not itself the primary focus of the account but rather a means to other ends. Sometimes the selective memories of an earlier past play a major role in a later period that is the topic of historical reconstruction – as, for example, when the alleged 'lessons of 1918' are seen to be significant in understanding support for Hitler's revisionist strategies in the 1930s. Here the emphasis is not so much on 'memory' as on political mobilization and the historical significance of a particular myth, which is explicitly treated as such.

Once historians do attempt to bring together the levels of personal and subjective constructions of the past, or the narration of directly experienced memories within different contexts and frameworks, with the wider analyses of official, hegemonic or dominant scripts about the past, the complexities of analysis of changing constructions over time begin to become all too apparent. Alon Confino and Peter Fritzsche, for example, are now asking 'how memory *forms* social relations – as opposed to the traditional way of asking how memory represents social relations'.[30] The interactions between literary, cultural, political and other representations of a contested past are also increasingly coming under historical scrutiny.[31] Some scholars have begun to explore the ways in which later narratives vary across what might loosely be called the 'literary' traditions of different groups. As Luisa Passerini points out, for example, 'gypsies' (often referred to as Roma and Sinti, although there are debates too about these terms) tended to have a culture of forgetting as 'buoyant defiance', in contrast to Jewish traditions of remembering; Passerini talks of the 'contrast between defiant silence and monumental remembrance' in their respective traditions.[32]

Some historians have begun to focus intensely on the dissonance between individual memories and the historical evidence of the time, as in Mark Roseman's exploration of one Holocaust survivor.[33] Even so, there are significant methodological reasons why it is often hard to go beyond the public sphere of representations of personal experiences. Robert Moeller, for example, explores 'how Germans transformed their pasts into public memory in the early history of the Federal Republic'.[34] But as he points out:

> [I]f Jews, expellees, and German POWs were equal at the level of rhetoric, the victims of National Socialism remained ghosts lacking faces, families, names, identities or a powerful political presence. Represented by others, they spoke for themselves only seldom. German victims, in contrast, lived, breathed, organized, demanded recognition, and delivered speeches from the floor of parliament. What Germans had inflicted on others remained abstract and remote; what Germans had suffered was described in vivid detail and granted a place of prominence in the public sphere.[35]

Analysing the ways in which West Germans cast themselves as victims through vociferous public debates, Moeller is sensitive to the difficulties of carrying out comparable research in the German Democratic Republic: 'Although many private accounts doubtless diverged from these official public pronouncements, the East German state radically restricted the room in which competing memories of the war and its consequences could emerge'.[36] The politics of 'public memory' in this sort of approach thus, for methodological reasons, continues to take precedence over the ways in which private memories are framed by social discourses.

Historians are becoming increasingly aware that collectively inflected individual memories based on 'real experiences' are both informed by and contribute to the further development of informal or local memory communities. These may, in turn, conflict with or contribute to the shaping of public representations; interest groups form and exert pressure for particular kinds of memorialization, shaping awareness and influencing patterns of remembrance and hence the perceptions of others in turn. With the shift from the essentially Durkheimian legacies of Halbwachs – focusing primarily on the supposed functions of commemorative work for 'society as a whole', or 'a nation' or another collective entity – to a more conflict-oriented approach looking at the politics of contested remembrance, there has been growing realization of the significance of interaction of different levels. These diverse approaches to historical memory studies have over preceding decades developed rich but often rather separate bodies of theoretical literature, spawning a range of theories and concepts. We have however little by way of an adequate conceptual framework that will help to provide analytic tools for exploring the interrelations among different levels.

If we are to understand the diverse legacies of aspects of the past for later generations, then a number of approaches need to be brought closer together, with care and precision, in order to analyse what has frequently been conveniently been lumped together under one vague and all-purpose carrier bag concept of 'collective memory'.

The legacies of the past: Communities of experience, connection and identification

No longer can historians remain purely at the level of public debates and media presentations, leaving individual subjectivities to the disciplinarily distinct arenas of 'reception studies', literary criticism or social psychology.

Key questions arise concerning the interrelationships among these different aspects and levels. How are the 'frames' for individual memories constructed and developed, and by whom? Who contributes more decisively in effecting shifts in the narrative strategies and discourses prevalent among particular communities, and for what reasons? How do the value systems and norms embedded in prevalent narratives develop and change? Who or which groups determine what are the dominant frameworks of interpretation and which are marginalized? What are the implications of dramatic historical ruptures and changes of regime, of population mobility or of an increasingly global and certainly transnational cultural sphere, for individuals 'making sense' of a personal past across widely different historical periods or places? What are the hidden, inchoate, 'embodied' legacies of the past in unconscious patterns of behaviour, attitudes, ways of seeing and being in the world, and with what consequences for the nature and development of community life and social relations across generations? What forms of interplay are there between political, public and media representations and private, informal, non-institutionalized memories of a contested past in different contexts? Can one discern any patterns among succeeding generations with respect to gaining distance or identifying with values quite at odds with those of parents or grandparents, and how do these vary under different political, social and cultural conditions?

What follows is not an attempt to answer these questions – which are absolutely pressing if we are to understand the legacies of the past for a later present, beyond the narrow confines of any single approach to collective memory studies – but merely a first attempt at analytic disaggregation.[37]

It may be important to widen, shift or break up the traditional units of analysis. When analysing representations of the past, a frequent approach is to adopt a well-defined, readily bounded focus: the nation state, distinct physical sites of memory (places where something actually happened, memorials constructed for purposes of remembrance), specific texts (literary, cinematic, political and so on). Historians, anthropologists and sociologists using the notion of collective memory have focused on substantive topics defined at a political, social or cultural level: social practices and rituals of remembrance, cultural modes of narration, forms of expression – or suppression or marginalization – of particular tropes of memory, set within distinctive historical and political contexts. But it may be more useful to start with a focus on 'remembering agents', analysing the movements and orientations of people themselves, as they pass through what I would like to call different communities of experience, connection and identification.

A shift of focus to communities of experience, connection and identification may serve to break the assumption of direct links between those who lived through certain experiences and later collectivities in the 'same' geographical or social space who engage in activities serving to 'remember' these experiences; but at the same time it will help to heighten our perception and understanding of both the ways in which collective discourses frame the narration of personal experiences, and the ways in which the past may have inescapable legacies for a later present in a wide range of 'places'. If we make distinctions between 'collective memory' as a set of ever-changing socially and culturally given frameworks of perception and representation through which individuals are able to make sense of and communicate their experiences to others, and 'historical consciousness' as a set of phenomena rooted in a variety of perceptions and influences not necessarily related to direct personal experience of a particular past, we may be able to develop a more complex, and more adequate, understanding of the reverberations of the past for those living in later periods and places. What then is meant by each of these concepts?

A 'community of experience' does, as the phrase intrinsically suggests, have some major set of historical experiences, events or challenges in common. Members of a 'community of experience' – whether or not they know each other, and whether or not they are aware of having had comparable experiences – have lived through a historical epoch in ways that are in some significant sense similar to each other, and different from the ways in which others lived through this period, as well as being different from the experiences of those who lived earlier, later, or elsewhere, or whose location in relation to the significant events was very different. 'Holocaust survivors', for example, form in a very general sense a community of experience, in contrast to different groups of 'perpetrators', or those who lived well before, or were born well after the period marked by Hitler's policies of genocide. But the notion of a 'community of experience' is nevertheless both fluid and complex, and qualifications need to be added right at the outset. We cannot and should not reify a 'German' or a 'Jewish' or a 'Polish' (or whatever) 'experience' of the war or the Holocaust. Of course we need to explore common aspects or features of the general situation of differently defined collectivities, by virtue of identities ascribed to them at the time, and how they were singled out (or not) for particular policies and sorts of treatment. But we also need to explore people's own self-ascriptions and individual responses to new challenges; we need to be aware of the wide variations in perceptions, choices about behaviour, routes through new situations.[38] Even at the time of Nazi persecution, for example, among groups readily termed 'victims', there were major variations. The 'experience' of life in a ghetto or forced labour or extermination camp differed according to social class, economic and cultural resources, age, gender, political and religious views, family connections, the fate of friends and relatives, the character and location of the pre-war community of origin and so on. It also differed according to personal choices about degrees of collaboration, strategies for survival and attempts at resistance. Among 'perpetrators', there were also major differences: between those at the front line of physical brutality – the Einsatzgruppen, the Gestapo, the SS, soldiers and ordinary police forces – and those who can best be seen as 'Hitler's facilitators', the civilian administrators of racist rule; between those who designed the plans, and those who carried out orders; between those who were willing, and those who succumbed to pressure. Even among perpetrators, there were individually based differences in degrees of enthusiasm or otherwise for the Nazi cause which they were empowered to drive forward, and hence their 'memories' of these events at a later date; differences rooted in politics, morality and individual views, as well as generation, milieu, class, education and so on.[39] 'Communities of experience' are thus not as simple as they might seem.

There are methodological challenges and opportunities here, as the character of 'experience' is refracted and reflected in sources produced at widely different times. Sometimes differences in experience can be reconstructed from sources produced at the time, as in contemporary letters and diaries. Often the experiences can often only be extrapolated from later reflections, and then the archaeological layers and interrelationships of changing communities of experience and identification across historical ruptures further inflect the accounts. In a sense, then, even to reconstruct presumed communities of experience we often already have to talk about the later situations in which people narrated their lives. The point for the historian of memory is then to examine precisely how such constructions varied and changed.

Different post-war political and social contexts, interpersonal relations and specific interests affect later patterns of memory and self-presentation. What people felt they could articulate, among whom, when and to what ends, and what they did not speak about, depended massively on where they made their later lives and to whom they spoke. How the past was seen and dealt with in practice – who was praised, who was pardoned and who was condemned; who rose in which social hierarchy and who was marginalized or never fitted in; what was remembered, what was repressed and what was simply forgotten – made a huge difference to people's perceptions of their own lives, as they picked up the pieces and tried to construct what has been termed, in a slightly different context of inquiry, 'life after death'.[40] The similarities between, for example, the defensive narratives among former civilian facilitators of the Holocaust when facing investigation in post-war West Germany – generally emphasizing that they had seen, heard and done absolutely nothing, and 'knew nothing about it' – is quite striking.[41] So too are typical stories in general circulation in post-war West Germany: 'train stories' suggesting they had heard only at second hand about the gas chambers; 'attempts to save a Jew' stories; stories demonstrating that one had 'always been against it' (*immer dagegen*). In the GDR, by contrast, stories of conversion when in a Soviet Prisoner of War camp might help to compensate for previous commitment to Nazism; meanwhile, claiming to have been a 'victim of fascism' might be displaced, as regime emphases shifted, by attempts to show one had more actively 'fought against' fascism. In other contexts, those who had lived through the Second World War found very different points of significance or reception for their narratives of suffering and survival. Who was deemed to have been a 'victim', a 'collaborator', a 'perpetrator', a 'resistance fighter', differed not only with actual past behaviour but also the wide variety of post-war settings in which war-time actions became salient, and self-narratives were adapted and adjusted accordingly.[42] Continuing negotiations also affected interpersonal relations, with often deep and lasting implications for intergenerational legacies.

Moreover, there is another aspect in which the past is always present, quite irrespective of strategies for highlighting or repressing of aspects of a personally experienced past. These are the ways in which people are themselves – physically, behaviourally, psychologically – actually constituted by the past in multiple ways of which they may be entirely or partially unaware. There are inchoate legacies of the past for individuals going way beyond what they may be prepared or even able to articulate. Individual experiences of the past, as coloured by later developments in changing historical contexts, shape behaviour patterns, attitudes, emotional codes and values; these have implications for interpersonal relations and the intergenerational transmission of the legacies of the past in a wide variety of ways, many of which go well beyond any narrativization or representation as 'memory' or stories. As Anne Karpf, for example, recalls:

> Somehow my parents seemed to derive from the fact of their survival not a sense of powerlessness, victimhood, or even luck, but of the possibility of control. All of life seemed purposive, actuated by choice or behaviour; nothing was down to chance. Despite the counter evidence presented by his own life, my father would quote to us in Latin that "omni homo sui fati auctor est" (every man is the author of his own fate).[43]

Such behavioural and attitudinal legacies and also narrative strategies of silencing or selectively recalling the past have been well analysed for survivors who emphasize that their children could never really know what hunger or suffering meant, or who place unbearable pressures on them for success, alongside heightened criticism of shortcomings or failings. Literary scholars as well as psychologists have been particularly active in this area, although focusing primarily on individual narratives rather than variations according to historical context and the character of the wider community in any given location.[44]

This then leads us to those who might be called 'communities of connection'. These include individuals who are inescapably connected to a salient past, without ever having personally experienced it, including (by no means all, and not limited to) second- and third-generation relatives of Holocaust survivors and perpetrators.[45] Communities of connection do not necessarily need to develop across generations, particularly in political or cultural contexts where the given past is not rendered significant; and there do not need to be individual familial links with the past to feel that a weight of connection is unavoidable, as the public culture of shame that developed in the Federal Republic of Germany, in contrast to the GDR, readily attests. Interestingly, some social psychologists argue that the particular experiences of the parents or grandparents have most impact on legacies for subsequent generations; there has again as yet been little research on the impact of different historical settings for the actually highly variable significance of the 'burdens of the past'. Marianne Hirsch's notion of 'postmemory' may be helpful here, highlighting the significance of a particularly salient past for those who did not actually live through it; but this approach has largely remained the preserve of literary and cultural scholars focusing on specific texts, with little historical research on broader patterns, variations and indeed absences of connection.[46]

Finally, all of these unconscious as well as articulated legacies develop within an ever-changing wider world. 'Communities of identification' may develop who have neither direct personal experience of a given period or event in the past, nor direct personal links, of whatever sort, with that set of experiences; and yet they may feel its lessons vividly, and may draw from it normative, emotional and cognitive, 'lessons for the future'; rather than merely 'learning about' this period as simply 'history', they may, in short, *identify* with a particular set of experiences. While not actually participating in any real 'memory' of the events in question, these communities of identification have something in common with what Alison Landsberg has termed 'prosthetic memory'. As she puts it, 'the person does not simply apprehend a historical narrative but takes on a more personal, deeply felt memory of a past event through which he or she did not live'; in contrast to dry historical knowledge, the 'resulting prosthetic memory has the ability to shape that person's subjectivity and politics'.[47] Again, there is as yet too little historical research to explore patterns and variations in the development and character of communities of identification who may act as carriers of mobilizing visions of past and future (whether or not we want to deploy the concepts of 'prosthetic memory' or 'postmemory'). Developments in the media and the technology of communications, the globalization of culture, greater mobility of individuals, all affect not only the degrees of choice people have in identifying with one or another community, but also their very perceptions of what such choices might consist in, and indeed whether or not they even feel they have a choice. Later generations may choose to identify with quite different sets of values or experiences than those of members of older generations in their 'own' group, however defined. The agents of memorialization need have no geographical or personal connections whatsoever with the previous pasts they seek to commemorate; nothing more than the knowledge of a given historical phenomenon, and a personally driven commitment to raising awareness of that phenomenon, may be the necessary link between a later community of identification and a previous community of experience, as the many projects of reconciliation and commemoration across post-war Europe serve to demonstrate. Absence of particular themes and topics, or social and political sanctions and taboos, may affect negatively the availability of certain possible patterns of later identification.

These terms clearly have to be used with some flexibility. They are in part mutually overlapping and fluid; they are intended to allow exploration of the ways in which people may participate in and be affected by the legacies of the past well beyond the realm of 'memory' proper, but also not easily viewed as history or myth. These ideas cannot be explored further here: but it should be apparent that the complexities of the ways in which the 'past is made present' cannot readily be subsumed under one simple concept of or approach to 'collective memory', let alone one that remains within discretely bounded national pots, or tied to specific sites (real or metaphorical) or that implicitly assumes that within any given unit of analysis there are direct links between a remembered past and a later present. But to explore these complexities adequately would break the bounds of this brief overview.

Conclusions

Pierre Nora concludes his massive multi-volume survey of French sites of memory with the comment:

> The present selection makes sense only for the present moment. By the time the French have settled on another way of living together, by the time they have settled on the contours of what will no longer even be called identity, the need to exhume these landmarks and explore these *lieux* will have disappeared. The era of commemoration will be over for good. The tyranny of memory will have endured for only a moment – but it was our moment.[48]

Whether or not Nora was right in this prognostication, one thing is certain: it is evident, even from the most cursory glance at this topic, that the past is ever present, with different kinds of historical understanding and interpretation shaping the ways in which the present is understood and the future made. Human beings are intrinsically both historically constituted and historically aware; and historical knowledge is an essential corrective to the inadequacy of myths that are all too easily subverted or instrumentalized to particular political ends, with radical consequences for those affected. We need then urgently to develop new ways of conceptualizing the ways in which the past constantly and continually informs a later present.

Any approach can only be evaluated in relation to the questions it is designed to address, and the kinds of answer it makes possible. I would argue that notions of collective memory need to be defined very much more precisely, and not deployed, as at present, to refer to virtually any referencing of the past in a later context where functions for identity construction, political mobilization or social cohesion (or other consequences) can be inferred for some notional collectivity, whether a 'nation' or 'society' or a political interest group or a self-defining community constructing and claiming a 'usable past'. Semantic quibbles are however probably a waste of time, given the current prevalence of the term 'collective memory' in such a wide diversity of ways, including some probably quite inappropriate places. More important than definitional debates is to look at precisely what is being analysed, and to explore links across levels and cases that currently remain under-theorized. The fundamental assumption underlying many current approaches to collective memory is that there are direct lines of some sort – however twisted and ambivalent – between an experienced past and a later 'collective memory'. This is however not always the case; human beings appropriate aspects of the world around them, including knowledge of a wide and diverse past, for all manner of purposes. The significance of a past has to do with the ways in which it has reverberations for both those who lived through it and later generations, who may or may not have specific links – personal, familial, political, ethnic, religious or any other sort – with the communities who participated in and lived through that particular past. Thus we need to explore the multiple ways in which the legacies of the past are reinterpreted and selectively reappropriated, and the manifold hidden as well as articulate reverberations of any historical era in a variety of later periods and contexts. This is however an agenda that requires quite precise differentiation and formulation of conceptual distinctions – perhaps in the process consigning the now inflated notion of 'collective memory' to an appropriate historical graveyard.

Notes

1   For a wide-ranging overview, see Jeffrey Olick, Vered Vinitzky-Seroussi and Daniel Levy, 'Introduction', in Jeffrey Olick, Vered Vinitzky-Seroussi and Daniel Levy (eds), *The Collective Memory Reader* (Oxford, 2011), pp. 3–49.

2   See, for example, James Mark, *The Unfinished Revolution. Making Sense of the Communist Past in Central-Eastern Europe* (New Haven and London, 2010).

3 See, for example: Pierrre Nora's three volume masterpiece, *Lieux de Mémoire* (see detailed references to volumes in English translation in footnotes below); Etienne François and Hagen Schulze, *Deutsche Erinnerungsorte*, 3 vols (Munich, 2001); James Young, *At Memory's Edge: After-images of the Holocaust in Contemporary Art and Architecture* (Yale, 2000), *The Texture of Memory* (Yale, 1993), and *Writing and Rewriting the Holocaust* (Bloomington, IN, 1988); Jay Winter, *Remembering War: The Great War between History and Memory in the Twentieth Century* (Yale, 2006); Jay Winter and Emmanuel Sivan (eds), *War and Remembrance in the Twentieth Century* (Cambridge, 1999).

4 Pierre Nora, *Realms of Memory, Vol III: Symbols,* trans. by Arthur Goldhammer (New York, 1998 edn), Ch. 18, Pierre Nora, 'The Era of Commemoration' (pp. 609–37), p. 609.

5 Norman Finkelstein, *The Holocaust Industry. Reflections on the Exploitation of Jewish Suffering* (New York and London, 2000; 2nd edn. 2003), p. 5. For Novick's own work, see Peter Novick, *The Holocaust and Collective Memory. The American Experience* (London, 1999).

6 Paul Connerton, *How Societies Remember* (Cambridge, 1989), pp. 37–8.

7 Connerton, *How Societies Remember*, pp. 4–5.

8 Maurice Halbwachs, *The Collective Memory*, quotation taken from the extract translated by and reprinted in Olick, Vinitzky-Seroussi and Levy (eds), *Collective Memory Reader,* p. 142.

9 Halbwachs in Olick, Vinitzky-Seroussi and Levy (eds), *Collective Memory Reader,* p. 144.

10 Henry Rousso, *The Vichy Syndrome: History and Memory in France since 1944* (Cambridge, MA, 1991), p. 3.

11 Rousso, *Vichy Syndrome,* passim.

12 See, for example: Norbert Frei, *Adenauer's Germany and the Nazi Past. The Politics of Amnesty and Integration,* trans. by Joel Golb (New York, 2002); Jeffrey Olick, 'What does it mean to normalize the past? Official memory in German politics since 1989', in Jeffrey Olick (ed.), *States of Memory. Continuities, Conflicts and Transformations in National Retrospection* (Durham and London, 2003), pp. 259–88.

13 Robert Gildea, *The Past in French History* (New Haven and London, 1994), p. 10.

14 Gildea, *The Past in French History,* p. 12.

15 See, for example, Alon Confino, 'Collective Memory and Cultural History: Problems of Method'. *American Historical Review* 102:5 (December 1997), 1386–403.

16 Aleida Assmann, 'The Holocaust – a global memory? Extensions and limits of a new memory community', in Aleida Assmann and Sebastian Conrad (eds), *Memory in a Global Age: Discourses, Practices and Trajectories* (Basingstoke, 2010), Ch. 5 (pp. 97–117), here pp. 100, 101.

17 See for example: Ilya Levkov (ed.), *Bitburg and Beyond: Encounters in American, German and Jewish History* (New York, 1987); Astrid Linn, '*Noch heute ein Faszinosum . . .' Philipp Jenninger zum 9. November 1938 und die*

Folgen (Münster, 1990); Piper (ed.), *Historikerstreit*. Further references and discussion in Charles Maier, *The Unmasterable Past: History, Holocaust, and German National Identity* (Cambridge, MA, 2003); Richard J. Evans, *In Hitler's Shadow* (London, 1989); Mary Fulbrook, *German National Identity after the Holocaust* (Cambridge, 1999).

18   On the wider issues, see Mary Fulbrook, *Dissonant Lives: Generations and Violence through the German Dictatorships* (Oxford, 2011).

19   On the origins of the term 'engrams' in the work of Richard Semon, see Olick et al., *Collective Memory Reader*, pp. 11–12.

20   See, for example, Annette Wieviorka, *The Era of the Witness*, trans by Jared Stark (Ithaca, 2006); Harald Welzer, Sabine Moller, Karoline Tschuggnall, '*Opa war kein Nazi*'. *Nationalsozialismus und Holocaust im Familiengedächtnis* (Frankfurt/Main, 2002).

21   See for by now classic examples in the field of Holocaust studies: Lawrence Langer, *Holocaust Testimonies: The Ruins of Memory* (New Haven and London, 1993); Daniel Bar-On, *Legacy of Silence: Encounters with Children of the Third Reich* (Cambridge, MA, 1989); Gabriel Rosenthal (ed.), *The Holocaust in Three Generations. Families of Victims and Perpetrators of the Nazi Regime* (London, 1998).

22   See, for example, Dori Laub, 'From Speechlessness to Narrative: The Cases of Holocaust Historians and of Psychiatrically Hospitalised Survivors'. *Literature and Medicine* 24:2 (Fall 2005), 253–65; Welzer, Moller, and Tschuggnall, '*Opa war kein Nazi*'.

23   See, for an overview of psychological approaches to individual life stories and memories, Martin A. Conway, *Autobiographical Memory: An Introduction* (Milton Keynes, 1990).

24   See, for example, Jürgen Matthäus (ed.), *Approaching an Auschwitz Survivor* (Oxford, 2009); Mark Roseman, *The Past in Hiding* (London, 2000); Alon Confino and Peter Fritzsche (eds), *The Work of Memory. New Directions in the Study of German Society and Culture* (Urbana and Chicago, 2002); Frank Biess, *Homecomings: Returning POWs and the Legacies of Defeat in Postwar Germany* (Princeton and Oxford, 2006); Robert Moeller, *War Stories: The Search for a Usable Past in the Federal Republic of Germany* (Berkeley and Los Angeles, 2001).

25   See, for example, the pioneering work by Lutz Niethammer, Alexander von Plato and Dorothee Wierling, *Die volkseigene Erfahrung* (Berlin, 1991); Dorothee Wierling, *Geboren im Jahr Eins* (Berlin, 2002).

26   See, for example, Saul Friedländer, *The Years of Extermination. Nazi Germany and the Jews, 1939–1945* (London, 2007).

27   Christopher Browning, *Collected Memories. Holocaust History and Postwar Testimony* (Madison, Wisconsin, 2003), p. 38.

28   Browning, *Collected Memories*, pp. 38–9.

29   Ibid., p. 39.

30   Alon Confino and Peter Fritzsche, 'Introduction: Noises of the Past', in Confino and Fritzsche (eds), *The Work of Memory* (pp. 1–21), p. 5.

31 See, for example, the work of one of the editors of this volume, Bill Niven, *The Buchenwald Child: Truth, Fiction and Propaganda* (Woodbridge, 2007); see also Niven (ed.), *Germans as Victims: Remembering the Past in Contemporary Germany* (London, 2006); and Niven, *Facing the Nazi Past: United Germany and the Legacy of the Third Reich* (London, 2002).

32 Luisa Passerini, 'Memories between silence and oblivion', in Katharine Hodgkin and Susannah Radstone (eds), *Memory, History, Nation. Contested Pasts* (New Brunswick and London, 2006; orig 2003), pp. 238–54.

33 See Roseman, *The Past in Hiding*. I have also attempted this with respect to a former facilitator of Nazi racial policies in Fulbrook, *A Small Town near Auschwitz: Ordinary Nazis and the Holocaust* (Oxford, 2012).

34 Moeller, *War Stories*, p. 20.

35 Ibid., p. 34.

36 Ibid., p. 19.

37 The following brief remarks relate to an AHRC-sponsored collaborative research project, based at UCL, on 'Reverberations of War in Germany and Europe since 1945'. I am very grateful to the AHRC for its generous support of this project.

38 The two senses of 'experience' are easier to render in German than in English: there is a key difference between the German words 'Erfahrung' and 'Erlebnis', both of which may be translated into English as 'experience'.

39 I have explored the role, behaviour, perceptions and later self-representations and memories of one such civilian administrator in some detail in Fulbrook, *A Small Town near Auschwitz*.

40 Richard Bessel and Dirk Schumann (eds), *Life after Death: Approaches to a Cultural and Social History of Europe during the 1940s and 1950s* (Cambridge, 2003).

41 See further Fulbrook, *A Small Town near Auschwitz*.

42 See further, for example, Mary Fulbrook and Andrew Port (eds), *Becoming East German: Socialist Structures and Sensibilities after Hitler* (New York and Oxford, 2013).

43 E.g. Anne Karpf, *The War After. Living with the Holocaust* (London, 1996), p. 14.

44 See, for example, Langer, *Holocaust Testimonies*.

45 See, for example, Bar-On, *Legacy of Silence*, and Rosenthal (ed.), *Holocaust in Three Generations*.

46 Marianne Hirsch, *Family Frames. Photography, Narrative and Postmemory* (Cambridge, MA, 1997); Marianne Hirsch, 'The Generation of Postmemory'. *Poetics Today* 29:1 (Spring 2008), 103–28.

47 Alison Landsberg, *Prosthetic Memory. The Transformation of American Remembrance in the Age of Mass Culture* (New York, 2004), p. 2.

48 Nora, 'The Era of Commemoration', in Nora (ed.), *Realms of Memory*, Vol. III, p. 637.

Further reading

Aleida Assmann and Sebastian Conrad (eds), *Memory in a Global Age: Discourses, Practices and Trajectories* (Basingstoke, 2010).

Daniel Bar-On, *Legacy of Silence: Encounters with Children of the Third Reich* (Cambridge, MA, 1989).

Christopher Browning, *Collected Memories. Holocaust History and Postwar Testimony* (Madison, Wisconsin, 2003).

Martin A. Conway, *Autobiographical Memory: An Introduction* (Milton Keynes, 1990).

Mary Fulbrook, *A Small Town near Auschwitz: Ordinary Nazis and the Holocaust* (Oxford, 2012).

Katharine Hodgkin and Susannah Radstone (eds), *Memory, History, Nation. Contested Pasts* (New Brunswick and London, 2006; orig 2003).

Lawrence Langer, *Holocaust Testimonies: The Ruins of Memory* (New Haven and London, 1993).

Peter Novick, *The Holocaust and Collective Memory. The American Experience* (London, 1999).

Jeffrey Olick, Vered Vinitzky-Seroussi and Daniel Levy (eds), *The Collective Memory Reader* (Oxford, 2011).

Mark Roseman, *The Past in Hiding* (London, 2000).

Gabriel Rosenthal (ed.), *The Holocaust in Three Generations. Families of Victims and Perpetrators of the Nazi Regime* (London, 1998).

Henry Rousso, *The Vichy Syndrome: History and Memory in France since 1944*, trans by Arthur Goldhammer (Cambridge, MA, 1991).

Jay Winter, *Remembering War: The Great War between History and Memory in the Twentieth Century* (New Haven and London, 2006).

Jay Winter and Emmanuel Sivan (eds), *War and Remembrance in the Twentieth Century* (Cambridge, 1999).

CHAPTER FOUR

Memory as both source and subject of study: The transformations of oral history

Lynn Abrams

Introduction

In Sebastian Barry's novel *The Secret Scripture* his narrator – Roseanne – tells her painful story in a secret journal. Roseanne is aware that memories can only be entry points to a past that no longer exists as a coherent time or place. She describes certain memories as 'stepping stones' which are just sufficient to permit her to conjure up a narrative of a life shaped by trauma and turmoil whilst allowing her to avoid drowning in the magnitude of what might be recalled if memory could be relied upon.[1] Memory is the bread and butter of the oral historian. Accessing the past, or versions of the past, via an oral history interview, is a process that relies upon the workings of memory, both in a neurological sense and in a social sense. Because remembering – conjuring up stories, experiences and emotions from our past lives – is an active process. One does not remember by searching around in a store room called memory. Rather, memory is a complex, fluid and contingent thing. Memories are formed by means of a neurological process in the brain but thereafter, as memories are accessed and narrated, they are subject to social influences.[2] It is decoding this process of remembering that makes oral history such a challenging endeavour and arguably oral historians have been at the forefront of theoretical and methodological advances in the field. The time has long since passed when oral historians were regularly challenged to defend their method of enquiry against charges regarding the fundamental 'unreliability of memory'. Indeed oral history today thrives on the analysis of memory construction; oral historians are interested not just in *what* is said but *how* and *why* it is said. In the words of leading oral historian Allessandro Portelli: 'what is really important is that memory is not a passive depository of facts, but an active process of the creation of meanings'.[3] Memory is both the source and the subject of study.

The historian's use of the oral history interview presupposes that this particular methodology will reveal something in addition to what one might obtain from other kinds of source. We assume that the memory source will offer up new, richer, more nuanced and more personal material. In some subject areas there may be little alternative to speaking to those who experienced an event or to endeavouring to collect the testimonies of a group traditionally silenced in conventional accounts. But even then it soon becomes clear that accessing someone's memory stories constitutes more than just a means of collecting information. Rather, facilitating a memory narrative is a way of accessing how that person constructs the self and how she or he places himself or herself within the social world. For we are nothing without our memories. Without our memory, we have no social existence as the amnesiac's experience shows; we are unable to construct a coherent story about ourselves that positions the self in time and space. In short, our memory is our roadmap. It tells us where we have been, where we are now and helps us to plan where we are going next. For the oral historian then, an interview is a means of bridging the gap between the self and society, between the individual story and the collective experience, between the past and the present.

In this chapter we consider memory firstly as a source or data and then as the subject of study, meaning we are interested in the ways in which people remember, the reasons behind the production of memory stories. Of course in practice, these two elements are intertwined. Every oral history narrative contains source material but that material has been called up by the interviewee through a series of prisms or layers of time and experience. As an historical source, memory has been criticized for its unreliability, its alleged slippery nature. The analysis of the process of remembering, on the other hand, allows the historian to contextualize the way in which memory works in the interview, to understand how memories can be conflicting, partial, meaningful and purposeful. For most oral historians the reliability of memory is important, but it is the formation and narration of memory stories that offers the key to meaning; we can begin to understand the significance of an event or experience to the interviewee from the way in which he or she positions memories within a web of meaning.

Memory is a special source. The memories people retain and remember are likely to be those that hold significance for them. Memory is personal.

It is a volatile mix containing the intensely personal as well as the public event, the detailed picture alongside the general perspective. There will be holes in memory (things forgotten) as well as things that are remembered but not expressed. In contrast to the written document – a text fixed in time and space – memory is a far more intriguing source for the historian interested in how the past is remembered as well as what is remembered. Probing someone's memory in an oral history interview is often like embarking on a journey with a stranger and a poor map. There are mutual points of recognition (common knowledge of public events for instance) but the exploration will go off on diversions and tangents, memories will be prompted by chance encounters and emotions may be brought forth by smells, images or stories. It is a heady mix.

Memory as a source

There are some areas of history impervious to the documentary record and thus largely unrepresented in historical accounts: many aspects of everyday life, the experiences of many women, workers, ethnic minorities, personal and emotional experiences as opposed to accounts of public events, the banal in contrast with the spectacular. Oral history is a necessary, and sometimes the only, methodology that offers access to information and experiences otherwise unrecorded. How else to explore the experiences of Holocaust survivors, or first-generation immigrants, members of the gay and lesbian community or people with disabilities?[4] Oral history still has an important empirical role to record and document the memories of groups and individuals who have traditionally been silenced and to document disappearing working practices, for instance, and the nitty-gritty of everyday life. Indeed this is one of its strengths: by shedding light on long forgotten skills and on unrecognized or marginalized lives, oral history not only reveals new data but may also offer the narrator some degree of legitimacy or empowerment. In the field of work for instance, many interviewees are able to expound in great detail on habitual practices and routines undertaken decades earlier. What might be regarded today as mundane tasks are described with pride, not just in the job done but in the ability to recall so accurately. This lady, born in 1924 and interviewed in 1987, recalled in considerable detail the work she undertook in a carpet mill at the age of 15. This is a short extract from her testimony:

> I was employed as a boxer. Now that's not a fighting boxer! A boxer worked for two printers and had to attend to the dyes that the printers used in the wool which was used for weaving the carpets. Well, this department was called the Print Shop, and each dye had a number, and the dye was kept in large jugs. The printer followed a pattern printed on a large board,

which was fixed to the side of her drum. The wool was wound round the drum, and the printer called the number of the dye she wanted, to the boxer. Well, the boxer, then took, she took a wooden box with the dye colour and she filled it to a certain level from the numbered jug. Every colour had its own box. The box was then put in a small carriage. Thus the name 'Boxer'. As soon as the boxer told the printer the box was ready, the printer started the undercarriage running. It was quite like a little truck running on a miniature railway. There was a wheel placed on the fixture right across the box, which dipped into the dye. And when the carriage carrying the box moved, the wheel moved across the drum, printing the colour on the wool. It was important to keep the dye at a proper level on the box because of this wheel, the wheel, y'know, that was across the box. And sometimes if there was a lot of one colour on the pattern, the printer had to stop this little carriage running, so that the boxer could top up the colour. When the printer had completed the pattern on the drum, she then rubbed the colour into the wool with a flat object. I think this was made of bone. And while she was doing this the boxer had to see that she had plenty of wool bobbins to rewind the next drum, and see that her dye jugs were filled up. And also clear around her place of work.[5]

The job this woman was describing no longer exists and her testimony is probably the only evidence we have of the boxer's work. Oral history will continue to fulfil this important role as recorder of disappearing jobs and activities, as well as recording the voices of the disenfranchised and marginalized whose experiences are not regarded as significant by the mainstream.

The difficulty of verifying personal memories recounted in an oral history interview was, for a long time, a thorn in the side of practitioners. Oral history it was said, often simply did not produce sufficient data to be checked in comparison with the favoured written sources such as chronicles, minutes of meetings, proceedings of parliament and official statistics. Alongside diaries and autobiographies, oral history was seen as subjective, retrospective and therefore somehow tainted or at least unreliable. In the early days of oral history practice, much emphasis was placed on trying to assuage the doubters, cross-checking a story told in an interview with newspaper reports for instance. Yet, there is no evidence to demonstrate either that people tell deliberate untruths in oral history interviews or that memory is especially liable to distortion. In fact memory is remarkably stable and enduring and despite anecdotal evidence, it seems that memory does not necessarily deteriorate with age.[6] We do know that some memories – known as flashbulb memories – do retain vivid and detailed images of an especially traumatic or emotional event, whereas others, memories of more prosaic experiences, are likely to be less sharp and perhaps more liable to be shaped by subsequent events and social experiences. We also know that there are gender differences in the ways in which memories are formed and subsequently narrated.[7] But even taking all these aspects into consideration, an oral history interview should still be treated on a par with other sources traditionally relied upon by historians such as minutes of meetings or newspaper reports. There is no distinction to be made between so-called reliable and unreliable evidence, as British oral history pioneer Paul Thompson effectively pointed out. All evidence is socially constructed, and many written documents were deliberately shaped to present a particular picture or interpretation of an event or phenomenon.[8]

When we do find inconsistencies or even blatant misrepresentation of what we know to be a fact, we know that there will usually be an explanation for the 'error'. Portelli's much-cited discussion of the ways in which the 1949 death of an Italian steel worker was remembered among the working-class community in Umbria is a masterclass on how to analyse and then understand the meaning of a collective misremembering of the year in which the event occurred. The written historical record shows that Luigi Trastulli was killed in that year in a confrontation with police during a factory stoppage to protest the signing of the NATO treaty by the Italian government. Yet numerous oral testimonies gathered 30 years later from rank and file workers date Trastulli's death to the occasion when more than 2000 workers were fired from the factory in 1953 which was followed by a walkout and street fights. As Portelli explains, this misremembering of the date cannot be ascribed to numerous individual and disconnected memory lapses; rather, it can be explained by the narrators shifting the death from a time and place which symbolized defeat and humiliation to a context where it could be explained as part of an event from which the workers could salvage some self-respect. 'The discrepancy between fact and memory', writes Portelli, 'ultimately enhances the value of the oral sources as historical documents. It is not caused by faulty recollections . . . but actively and creatively generated by memory and imagination in order to make sense of crucial events and of history in general'.[9]

Misremembering – or the inaccurate recollection of events – does not invalidate the oral history source. Discovering discrepancies in a person's account should alert the researcher to look for the underlying reasons for the inaccuracies which in turn might offer a deeper understanding of that person's account. Mark Roseman's sensitive analysis of the account of a Holocaust survivor, Marianne Ellenbogen, illustrates the impact of trauma on the ability to recall past experiences which in themselves were deeply traumatic. Analysing Marianne's account of her escape from Germany while her family and fiancé were deported to Poland, Roseman discovered a number of discrepancies between her version of events and the contemporaneous records. While noting that the documentary sources should not always be accepted as a true account of events, Roseman nevertheless is interested in what he calls the 'flawed' oral testimony. He concludes that her misremembering – notably she recalls that she spent the night with her fiancé before he was deported the next day – was attributable to trauma and specifically her guilt at allowing her loved ones to be taken and having herself survived. The misremembering was a way of 'trying to impose some control on a memory which could not otherwise be borne'.[10] Roseman concludes that the details of her account were ultimately not important. 'What was important was not to be exposed quite so powerlessly and passively to an unbearable past.'[11]

This is perhaps an exceptional example but the lessons may be more widely applied. In order to own one's past and to feel comfortable with that past, the memories one relates must in some way affirm or bolster that version of the past with which we feel most at ease. When memories do not fit snugly, the narrator is likely to experience discomposure, manifested in a disjointed narrative or an outward display of discomfort. Our memories serve to help us compose a usable past for ourselves.

Memory as subject

Given the fact that memory is unlike other sources, oral historians have had to turn to theorists from other disciplines in order to interpret what they have been told. The fact that memory is contingent, mutable and creative, that the ways by which people narrate their memories are influenced by the discourses circulating within culture, as well as by the intersubjective relations within the interview, and are shaped by narrative structures and forms and are expressed in performances – all of this has forced oral historians to apply theoretical models originally developed in other disciplinary contexts and, ultimately, to develop analytical frameworks distinctive to oral history practice. When it comes down to it, remembering, the articulation of memories in narrative form, requires that we pay attention to the relationship between content and form in memory stories.

It is useful at this stage to define some commonly used terms. *Autobiographical memory*, sometimes called individual or episodic memory, refers to the reconstruction of personal events or episodes of one's life containing persons, actions, objects, etc., and the belief that they have been personally experienced. *Collective memory* refers to a shared memory of an event or experience which is circulated among a group and which may shape individual memory.[12] *Popular memory* refers to the production of memory in which everyone is involved and which everyone has the opportunity to shape.[13]

Oral historians also utilize concepts of official and public memory to understand how autobiographical memory is shaped and narrated. And as memory studies develop, a number of terms have been coined to describe particular forms of memory telling. Graham Smith has coined the term *transactive memory* to refer to the ways in which memory stories can be facilitated, shaped and shared among a group of people using a shared language to recall the past.[14] Graham Dawson, in his oral history study of the Northern Ireland 'Troubles' writes about a complex interweaving of individual accounts with popular and media representation of the events which might be described as commemorative memory, a form of memory telling which has a political commemorative purpose, aiming to sustain remembrance of traumatic events as a means of maintaining a collective identity and ownership of what happened.[15] In my own research I encountered what I will call historical memory, a fusing of autobiographical memory (that is the recollection of events experienced by the narrator) with family or community memory and material from historical research. One of my respondents, a woman identified to me as a local resident and an amateur historian who knew a great deal about the lives of women in Shetland – the subject of my research – skilfully combined in her testimony all three of these elements. This is demonstrated here in the context of a discussion about the plight of unmarried women in which she references her own historical knowledge (drawn from archival sources) in the midst of an autobiographical story learned from family members:

> There was just one female that survived alone in the nineteenth century that I know of and that was Janet Russell. And she came to a cousin who was my something's grandfather and he gave her a plot of land just outside the house dykes for her to cultivate. And Janny's house is still to be seen and Janny's byre and her park and she actually survived like that with help from neighbours. But she couldna have lived without help, impossible. But that woman was one of the few felons that I've found. They were taken up for thieving potatoes at Sellivoe . . . it's in the sheriff records. And therefore her description which is something you need to hone in on is the police description of prisoners
>
> LA: yes I've seen that
>
> Have you seen it? Janny Russell as we call her, I mean it was the middle of the last century, the century before that, she was tiny with brown eyes and her sister was five feet five with blonde hair . . .[16]

Much oral history research in the past two decades has been preoccupied with the relationship between autobiographical, collective and popular memory because most oral historians are interested in what the personal experience can tell us about the general.[17] That is, they are interested in the relationship between individual or personal accounts of the past and the shared accounts upon which we all draw to shape our own versions of the past. Remembering is typically conducted using a memory frame, which we might describe as a locus or field which makes remembering possible. This may often be constructed by the interviewee in response to the interviewer's research frame or agenda but will also be informed by public discourse which serves to 'both define and limit imaginative possibilities'.[18] This does not mean that personal memory can *only* be recalled through the prism of public discourse but that there is a two-way relationship, a feedback loop or 'cultural circuit' between the personal or autobiographical account and culture.[19] A concrete example will illustrate how this works in practice. I recently conducted a series of interviews with women focusing on their life experiences in the 1950s and 60s in Britain. In the information supplied to my respondents in advance, I laid out my research frame, which was to examine the proposition that the post-war years were characterized by a shift from moral conservatism to emancipation. Clearly then, the majority of my interviews thought about my research agenda and in some cases it markedly shaped their narratives. However, they were also aware of my position as a university lecturer in women's and gender history and may have identified me as a feminist. In several cases, the resulting interviews demonstrated that my respondents' had prepared their memory frames in response to my research frame – their narratives contained stories of self-development and independence framed by their journey away from the code of respectability embodied by their mothers' generation towards a new mode of living characterized by independent decision-making and the pursual of autonomous selfhood. Deborah, for instance, recounted how she was facilitated in this journey or transformation by her schooling. Referring to the 'amazing' headmistress at her girls' school who was responsible for Deborah attending university, Deborah recalled: 'She said "I don't want you staying around here, I want you to take yourself off and experience a different sort of life" and I think she could probably see something in me I didn't see – she had amazing confidence – I was head girl – she had amazing confidence in me, you know.'[20]

Of course this narrative fits neatly with the emancipatory discourse of modern feminism, and those who narrated their lives in this way were to some extent conscious that they were keying their memories into a bigger story, that of the rise of women's independence since World War II. However, not all my respondents were able to align their memory frames with my research frame quite so snugly. Lorraine, who left the comforts and certainties of a middle-class rural home for the excitement of Glasgow School of Art in the sixties – all black polo-necks and posturing – was initially able to align her memory frame with both the public representation of that era and my research agenda. She described in much detail and with much enthusiasm the excitement of arriving at the art school, quickly discarding her twinset and pleated skirt and conjuring up a new name for herself in a bid to 'look cool at all costs'. 'It was all very long haired and I desperately wanted to look like Juliet Greco.' But when the interview moved on to her life as a wife and mother – firstly overseas and then back in Scotland – Lorraine's narrative faltered. When asked what she did on her return to Scotland, her husband ensconced in a new job, she replied: 'yes, I knew you were going to ask, em, so well then I had another baby, and then, em, oh dear, not very much em, well did the garden, did a bit of painting . . .'.[21] Her tone was much more hesitant and in some ways almost apologetic for not conforming to the implicit agenda I had set – that of the independent modern woman. Staying at home as a wife and mother jarred with Lorraine's perception of my research frame, perhaps also with what she perceived I represented as a female professor of gender history and with her own recognition that she did not fit ideally into the bigger celebratory 'feminist' narrative.

In what follows, I will explore a number of case studies drawn from my own and others' oral history research, each of which highlights a particular theoretical or methodological approach to memory. These examples illustrate how an analysis of the production of memory stories (in conjunction with a content analysis of the experiences and events remembered) can aid the historian's understanding of meaning, that is, the significance of the memory story to the narrator and in some cases, to cultural understandings and representations of the past.

Memory and intersubjectivity

Memory stories are constructed and narrated in the context of the oral history interview. That is, the selection of memories told to an interviewer and the ways in which they are narrated are influenced by the intersubjective relations between the interviewer and the interviewee. Intersubjectivity refers at the most basic level to the interpersonal dynamics between the two parties and the process by which they cooperate to create a shared narrative. The interviewer, not only by asking questions but also through appearance, gesture, accent and a host of other characteristics and actions, solicits memory stories from the interviewee which may differ markedly in the presence of a different interviewer. The interviewee constructs a subjective position for himself/herself for the purposes of the interview which draws upon available cultural constructions in public discourse but which also responds to the interviewee's perception of the interviewer. There is then a three-way conversation taking place in the interview: the interviewee with himself/herself, with the interviewer and with culture.

Intersubjective relations may either liberate or suppress memory narratives. At the most basic level, if the researcher and interviewee hit it off, if they establish a good, positive working relationship, the stories elicited are likely to be subject to less self-censorship by the narrator; in short, confidences may be shared. For feminist researchers, the oral history interview offered the opportunity to liberate women's voices from patriarchal discourses and communication strategies which in the past, it was argued, had silenced or muted women's ability to express themselves honestly. This meant moving away from the 'masculine paradigm' of the objective and impersonal research strategy and embracing subjectivity, treating the interview as shared experience in an attempt to nullify the inherent unequal power relationship and thus creating an interview environment in which women could 'speak for themselves'.[22] In her work with Chinese-American women, Judy Yung put the theory to the test. Her position as a member of the community she was researching enabled her to establish positive and trusting relationships with her interviewees which facilitated them in telling their stories from a woman-centred perspective, freed from the dominant stereotypical models and discourses traditionally employed by others to talk about their lives, such as the 'diabolical Dragon Lady' or the 'exotic Suzy Wong'.[23] But the approach is not without its problems, as Miriam Zukas discovered when she embarked on a project on the topic of friendship. Some of her female respondents treated the interview as a conversation between friends and 'confided things they would normally only say to a very close friend'.[24] But unlike a friendship which ideally incorporates the reciprocal sharing of information or confidences, the interview relationship seemed to be trading on the understanding that interviews involving women often are characterized by 'natural communication encouragement work'.

It is generally accepted that gender is a significant variable in the conduct and outcome of interviews. In her interviews with Glaswegian men for a project investigating modern Scottish masculinities, Hilary Young is clear that her subjective identity as a young, educated woman influenced the responses she elicited from her older male interviewees. The opening remarks of one respondent – 'So you've come to hear how Glasgow's men are big sissies nowadays' – were followed by a narrative that emphasized the role of women in the decline of the Scottish male's macho image, implying that women's education and freedoms had undermined the traditional role of the working-class male. There was little doubt in Young's mind that her interviewees' perception of her – as a modern, liberated woman – shaped how they chose to tell their stories.[25] A male interviewer may well have elicited very different narratives.

Self-reflexivity on the part of the interviewer can illuminate some of the ways in which intersubjectivities in the interview can shape the memory stories related. Penny Summerfield describes how her very visible pregnancy influenced the content of the narrative of one of her respondents in a project on women's experiences in World War II in that she repeatedly referred to her own pregnancy in the context of her joining and leaving the ATS. Summerfield speculates that the interpersonal dynamics of the interview, what she described as 'the unspoken and unwitting messages of one female body to another', encouraged her interviewee to actively review the meaning of her own pregnancy in the 1940s.[26]

Recognizing the role played by intersubjectivity on the memory stories produced in an oral history interview has forced historians to acknowledge the multiple voices that go towards producing memory stories. Summerfield has memorably written that not only should our analysis encompass 'the voice that speaks for itself, but also the voices that speak to it'.[27] Likewise, Graham Dawson urges us to be conscious of the multilayered process through which memory stories are produced. In the context of trying to hear stories of the conflict in Northern Ireland, Dawson perceptively remarks: 'the possibility of any individual articulating his or her own account of this multi-faceted, subjective relationship to the past depends on a relationship with others, who listen, bring to bear memories of their own, and interpret and reinterpret the meanings that are made: it is necessarily "a collective, intersubjective affair"'.[28] Dawson's observation might apply just as well to the narration of family memories as to something as public and contested as the Northern Ireland Troubles.

Memory and composure

Memory is both a psychological as well as a social process. In remembering, particularly in a public context such as an oral history interview, we attempt to position our autobiographical memories within a recognizable social context while at the same time drawing on popular cultural meanings and collective memories to legitimize our memory stories. This process has been termed 'composure' and it comprises two connected elements: the process of composing a story, and the ability of the individual to produce a coherent story or memory narrative with which he or she feels comfortable. In the words of Graham Dawson, who is credited with first coining the term: 'The social recognition offered within any specific public will be intimately related to the cultural values that it holds in common, and exercises a determining influence upon the way a narrative may be told and therefore, upon the kind of composure that it makes possible.'[29] Discomposure arises when we are unable to align personal memories with publicly acceptable versions of the past.

We all seek to achieve composure. 'We compose our memories', writes oral historian Alistair Thomson, 'so that they will fit with what is publicly acceptable, or, if we have been excluded from general public acceptance, we seek out particular publics which affirm our identities and the way we want to remember our lives'.[30] Moreover, oral history interviewers will often seek to facilitate composure in their interviewees, not least because a composed memory story often takes the form of a fluent and coherent narrative – but it is not always possible, particularly when memories do not seem to fit snugly with commonplace understandings of past events.

Alistair Thomson's analysis of the memory stories of World War I Australian soldiers (Anzacs) is the best-known application of the theory of composure by an oral historian which demonstrates the interaction between national memory or myth and personal accounts. In his interviews with Gallipoli veterans, he encountered individuals for whom private memories were entangled in the public myth of the Gallipoli campaign and the subsequent valorization of the Anzacs as archetypes of the Australian national character – so much so that some incorporated scenes from the film *Gallipoli* into their own narratives. But in Fred Farrall, Thomson discovered a man who had been unable to align his personal memories and feelings about the war with public representations of Gallipoli and of the heroic 'diggers'. Fred's memories of the war – of being scared, of losing his mates – his sense of personal inadequacy, and the fact that he did not conform to the popular image of the digger as a womanizing, drinking jack-the-lad, meant that he was unable to compose a coherent narrative. However, through the labour movement Fred found an alternative and more comfortable identity, a renewed self-confidence and a supportive peer group who encouraged him to articulate his views about the war. And by the 1980s, when public perceptions of war had changed in the light of the Vietnam War and under the influence of the peace movement, Fred found he was able to speak more freely about his memories. Finally, Fred achieved composure; there was public affirmation for his experiences and he was able to participate in the national celebration of Anzac Day. He had reconciled his personal experience with the public myth.

As I write this chapter, the 70th anniversary of the World War II Blitz is being commemorated by the British media, occasioning much memory telling by those who experienced the German air bombardment of UK cities in 1940. It is notable that the memories of many people fit comfortably within what became known as the Blitz spirit, the 'all in it together' narrative which stresses the indomitable will of the British to stand up to the relentless bombings despite the destruction of homes and the loss of many lives. Stories of bravery nestle against those of just getting on with everyday life. Those memories that counter the dominant myth appear much less frequently, and the narrators are less comfortable in the telling. But 70 years on, as the notion of the Blitz spirit has been subject to some critical comment, alternative memories can be more easily expressed and accommodated. For instance, the fact that many houses were looted in the immediate aftermath of being bombed is a story that perhaps only now may be recounted without fear of being accused of bursting the dominant image of everyone pulling together.[31]

In a series of interviews I conducted with adults who had spent their childhood in the Scottish welfare system, I encountered different ways in which individuals composed memory stories with which they could feel comfortable, which made sense to them and which allowed them to position often difficult memory stories with wider discourses on childhood and family.[32] The case of Betty is interesting because of the way in which she narrates the story of being removed from her birth city of Glasgow to a small island off the west coast of Scotland and her subsequent fostering by an elderly couple. Like most of her generation who were placed with foster families by the local authority, Betty was not an orphan. Up until the age of 60, she knew little or nothing about her birth family. When I interviewed her, she had recently met her brother and had discovered something of the circumstances of her being taken into care. Betty composed a story about her childhood that emphasized her good fortune at being boarded out with a caring family on an idyllic island, stressing the fact that she was treated as a full member of the family. In this lengthy extract, Betty describes her foster parents and the treatment she received:

> They had no children of their own, and they were seemingly desperate to have children, but she would be, but they would be, see it must have been quite a lot for them because they would be in their 50s when they got me, it must have been quite a lot for them, running the post office and running me as well, yes. But it was quite funny all the people coming in, saying hello and it was quite; another thing I can remember I loved the animals another thing I was pestering them about this, said I would get my own room, a lovely wee room, nice wee room, nice wee bed, beautiful wee room it was upstairs, next to theirs opposite the landing but when I went they thought I think we'll put her in with ourselves just now, so they moved a bed in there for me, because seemingly I was taking nightmares, terrible fright, so I was taken into their room at first but as I got stronger I kept wanting, I thought I was to get my own room so eventually I did get my own room, oh it was . . . because I'd all these memories of being in rooms with other children, you know, and I got this room to myself and we didn't have electricity or anything, I was left with a wee lamp. . . . I was never left in the dark . . . he was a quiet man . . . he wasn't a man that you would have thought should have ever have had children, he just he was so far away from children, but it was just because he didn't have any and when he did get one he didn't know what to do with it, you know, but she was very very kind, so was he but she was, I mean she was just over the moon about getting me, that must have been just what she wanted, she got this wee girl, and she was a tailoress to trade so I was always beautifully dressed and after I was there a short time you see these people used to come and inspect the house, the, inspectors would come from Glasgow and they would come in and inspect the house and that and after a while all the children were dressed the same you see, when you all went to school all the wee boys would be in grey suits on, they all had these terrible black shoes, black stockings. . . . All the boarded out children were dressed the same it was dreadful.[33]

It is notable that here Betty distances herself from 'the boarded out children' even though she was one herself and had experienced many of the same indignities they had, most memorably being driven from village to village in a black taxi, waiting for a family to choose her. Later on in the interview, Betty was at pains to contrast her experience of being treated well and as one of the family with that of her brother who had been born after she had been placed in care:

> Where I went I was very very lucky and I was accepted by that family, I mean I've got cousins all over the place, I'm not their cousin . . . and it's nice to have that. They are my family. That's what I was trying to explain to my brother. That is my family, and I've got my own family but they're

there as well but to my dying day I'll not forget them and all the kindness they showed me. I was very lucky, I was one of the lucky ones . . . . well I think compared to what my brother had I had a far happier childhood . . . well he stayed with my mother, he's older than me, and my mother went out, she had to work, she worked for Barr's Irn Bru, she scrubbed the floors and she went out to the big houses and cleaned and Andrew had to sit on the steps until she was finished you know, because she couldn't leave him, she had to take him with her, so look at the freedom that I had . . . compared to him, you know when you look at it that way, alright he lived with his mother which I didn't which you'd suppose was better for him but on the other hand I had a happier childhood.

Betty's narrative was composed in both senses of the term. On my arrival, she presented me with a booklet she had written containing a personal account of her experiences, saying 'all you want to know is there', indicating that she had already composed a story with which she was comfortable. In the course of the interview, she referred to a television programme which had recently screened about the experiences of children boarded out from Glasgow to the Hebridean islands which in some respects legitimated her own story of good fortune. But most significantly, Betty achieved composure in the sense of being able to relate a coherent narrative that met her need to belong to a family and at the same time conformed to a more general public discourse on normal family life and the appropriate upbringing for a child. She acknowledged the system of boarding out could have very negative consequences for children but was at pains to stress that she had been treated as one of the family. The interview ends with Betty reaffirming the importance of family ties:

My children . . . they just looked on aunt Kate, she was like a Granny to them, I mean it broke their heart when she died. . . . Both aunt Kate and uncle Hugh made a lot of them. . . . I certainly became one of the family, there's no doubt about it . . . . I've never actually met anyone that's had a bad word for anybody out there you know.[34]

Memory, emotion and trauma

Memory has a hard time dealing with emotion, especially if it involves anger, grief or extreme distress. Experiences that engender heightened emotion are often recalled in vivid detail with great accuracy, sometimes containing flashbulb memories, but the emotion felt at the time of the event itself is more difficult to recall; great joy or conversely serious distress may only be reported. The 'revivability in memory of the emotions' is limited, writes James. 'We can remember that we underwent grief or rapture but not just how the grief or rapture felt.'[35] However, the recollection of upsetting emotions in particular may be expressed in other ways: through disjointed narratives, incoherence, gaps or silences or alternatively by telling stories that indirectly intimate the strength of the emotions felt at the time.

In my own interviews with individuals who had experienced their childhood apart from their birth family, either in a children's home or with foster parents, issues around memory and emotion loomed large. My respondents were then in old age, but most still only had a hazy picture of the circumstances that led them to be taken into care, while some had very recently discovered these details along with, in some cases, information about surviving relatives. My intention in conducting the interviews was, firstly, to gain some empirical information about the Scottish child care system from those who experienced it, given that existing documentary sources never contained the views of the children affected by the systems in place to care for them. But I also hoped that my respondents would share with me some of their subjective feelings about their childhood in care in order that I might gain a deeper understanding of the impact of the care system on vulnerable young girls and boys. Given that a proportion of those in institutional care had experienced harsh conditions, limited contact with surviving family members and little engagement with the world beyond the children's home it was perhaps unsurprising that they were able to recall routine activities in great detail. Their memories of monotonous food, uniforms and the routine of everyday life in an institution had not faded with time, providing me with valuable data on the material conditions of institutional care. Arthur, for instance, who was taken to an orphanage in the north east of Scotland at the age of around 11, produced the following memories at the age of 86:

> It was dormitory rooms with eight at each side; Saturday was the day you were kept in which was the day I were landed in Aberlour to do all the cleaning . . . we got all the boys and girls in the one common room, dining room and you were told what was happening six months forward, it was just porridge and [indistinct] you got a little scone and a cup of tea and for your lunch there was soup either semolina on Wednesday you got a change you got plum duff . . . and at tea time at five you got tea, you got nothing else until a Sunday when you came back from church you got a piece of cheese and half slice of bread. That was a treat.[36]

Respondents also retained strong memories of flashpoints, extraordinary events which cut through the monotony of everyday routine. To take an example from Arthur again, he recounted one of the few humorous episodes – this one occurring in church – during the time he was in care:

> There was one Sunday I'll never forget. This McK. he couldn't get an "R" out, so he was reading a passage in the Bible, it was Barabas was a robber and a well known thief and he said "Bawabas was a wobber and a well known thief" and someone laughed and that happened to be the day that

the man that gave the money was there [*the orphanage's patron*] and we all got put into bed when we come home from church, didnae get a bit of cheese . . . when we come out of school through the week we got put into our bed after. Aye, I'll never forget that, you couldna help laughing could you?[37]

But these respondents had much more difficulty remembering how they had *felt* about their experiences. Few had ever talked in detail about this part of their lives – Arthur commented that having been in care meant that 'there's a stain on you, a stain, and I don't ken anything in this world that would have a stain so much. . . . I'm glad there's somebody to listen to me . . . that has always been in mind, it was always . . . to release it, I couldna get anybody to, it would be boring to speak of it'.[38] Hence, having never spoken of his experiences, he now struggled to articulate them to me. In others, memories of difficult or distressing events often brought forth fragmented, partial or incoherent responses. I asked Christine if she could recall her emotions upon arriving at the orphanage at the age of 8 following the death, in quick succession, of both her parents:

At eight you really don't, I stayed with my grandmother when my Dad died and my cousin. . . . I remember him coming up the stairs to me in the bedroom in the morning and saying "you havn't got a mother or a father", I says "I have got a mother, I havn't just got a father", "oh but there was a policeman at the door just now and told me that your mother's died as well" and that's how I was told my mother was dead, isn't it awful, however then I got back to Burghead because, I don't know how I got there but I remember seeing my Mum in her coffin, two pennies on her eyes so she must have, I just remember that, and I remember the funeral because it was the old type horse and cart you know with the black plumes, it was really old. . . . As I say I suppose you're unhappy but you just don't, you just don't remember very much about it.[39]

In the case of Annie, she used a vivid description of the clothes she was wearing upon being taken to an orphanage at the age of 6 to convey the emotions she felt at being removed from her widowed father:

It was blue costume, pleated skirts, I think I see it yet, pleated skirts, a double breasted jacket with brass buttons, and a black velour hat, black stockings and shoes, and we went into the home in that and I never saw it again. It was taken from us, and we just got a dress and a pinafore on.

LA: Were you upset by that?

You thought it was your life, you see. You just thought that's what's happening you see, we were all the same you see, there were some very nice girls in there.[40]

Unable, not surprisingly, to respond to my question about her emotions, Annie effectively conveyed these inner feelings in a flashbulb memory which arguably acted as a metaphor for strong feelings about being taken to a place in which one's individuality was quashed.

The survivors of trauma are likely to produce memory narratives that differ significantly from conventional stories about the past, in part because the interviewee has not been able to formulate a coherent memory narrative that makes sense of the events. Extensive oral history research with trauma survivors – from those who lived through the Nazi Holocaust to the victims of more recent events such as the 11 September attacks and Hurricane Katrina – have demonstrated that trauma narratives are often devoid of emotion, disjointed and incoherent. Their unease is signalled by changes in voice and observable body language. Silence is often easier than recollection. This is not because people cannot remember traumatic experiences, but because often they find it impossible to find the words and the frameworks of meaning and understanding to express themselves in ways that others would comprehend. Speechlessness is not the same as forgetting or not being able to remember. Survivors of trauma can find it difficult or impossible to tell of their experience because they are unable to find the language or the narrative structures to convey that experience. In the words of one concentration camp survivor, 'there is no language of extermination'.[41] Moreover, there are no common reference points for mutual understanding between narrator and listener. Even if a survivor is able to articulate the memory of traumatic experiences, there is no guarantee of comprehension on the part of the interviewer. This point has been repeatedly demonstrated from Primo Levi's moving explanation of why it was impossible to speak about Auschwitz, to more recent work with refugees from the Rwandan massacres of 1994.[42] And Antje Krog's account of reporting on the Truth and Reconciliation Commission hearings in post-apartheid South Africa amplifies the point. She writes that, like the witnesses who struggle to put their experiences into words and sentences, she too found it difficult to translate what she had heard into coherent reports for the media. The Commission itself understood the struggle everyone was experiencing to convert memories of trauma into understandable narratives, telling the journalists, 'You will experience the same symptoms as the victims. You will find yourselves powerless – without help, without words.'[43]

It is useful for the oral historian to recognize some of the memory strategies adopted by those who have witnessed or experienced traumatic events. Dori Laub, who has worked extensively with Holocaust survivors, has observed that traumatized individuals may only achieve what is popularly termed 'closure' when they have narrativized the experience or been able to put their experiences into a coherent story. Laub describes this as the survivor re-externalizing the event.[44] The Lockerbie disaster in 1988, when a terrorist bomb brought down an airliner on the small

Scottish town killing all on board the plane and destroying a street of houses in the town and their inhabitants, serves as an interesting example of how residents have articulated what were often searing and shocking memories. In interviews some used humour to talk about the events of that night and the weeks after, relating funny stories (a missing cat, an elderly lady offering her rescuers a glass of sherry) or a kind of gallows humour to enable the respondent to construct a manageable narrative of the events, such as one man recalling that those who were working with the recovered bodies in the local ice rink 'sit doon and have their tea in amongst them'.[45] Another strategy for speaking about horror in this instance was to focus on the everydayness of people's actions: one woman emphasized trying to maintain 'normality' for her family while her husband – a fireman – was participating in the search for bodies; another told of how she washed the clothes and prepared the belongings of the dead for return to their relatives – everyday actions which belied the terrible context in which they were carried out.[46]

Conclusions

Remembering is conducted within a complex and busy space. The oral history interview presents the narrator with a special place in which to narrate memory stories, but these stories are told in response to questions arising from a research agenda, and are recalled and crafted in a context informed by external influences. It is this process of remembering that most interests oral historians rather than the data or information that might be gleaned from a person's memory. We are curious about how people make sense of the past, how individual memory coincides with or rebuts shared or collective memory, how people use memory stories to position themselves in the present and how present-day experiences shape interpretations of the past. Memory is at the heart of all historical practice, but the oral historian is in a unique position because he or she facilitates the remembering process in a direct and active relationship with the narrator. The oral historian has the privilege of unleashing memories which invariably offer up revealing insights into personal interpretations of experience as well as contributing to a broader social understanding of the past. But with this privilege comes responsibility for acknowledging our own part in the memory process and for treating personal memory stories with respect. The words of Roseanne Clear in Sebastian Barry's novel *The Secret Scripture*, encapsulates the task of both narrator and researcher. Memory does serve as a stepping stone, allowing us to traverse the past carefully, sometimes dipping our toe in the water, at other times passing on quickly to avoid dangerous rapids but hopefully always facilitating the making sense of disparate experience.

Notes

1 S.Barry, *The Secret Scripture* (London, 2008), p.209.

2 For a lucid and accessible discussion of how memory works, see Daniel Schacter, *Searching for Memory* (New York, 1996).

3 Alessandro Portelli, *The Death of Luigi Trastulli and Other Stories: Form and Meaning in Oral History* (New York, 1991), p. 52.

4 Some examples include: Eric Marcus, *Making History: the Struggle for Gay and Lesbian Equal Rights 1945–1990* (New York, 1992); Alistair Thomson, 'Moving Stories: Oral History and Migration Studies'. *Oral History* 27:1 (1999), 24–37; Jan Walmsley, 'Life History Interviews with People with Learning Disabilities', in Robert Perks and Alistair Thomson (eds), *The Oral History Reader*, 2nd edn (London, 1998), pp. 184–97, and see all of the articles in this edition which offers comprehensive coverage of the possibilities and uses of oral history research.

5 Mrs G1., Stirling Women's Oral History Collection, Smith Art Gallery and Museum, Stirling, CD-ROM.

6 For a practical demonstration of this, see Alice M. Hoffman and Howard S. Hoffman, 'Reliability and Validity in Oral History: The Case for Memory', in Jaclyn Jeffrey and Glenace E. Edwall (eds), *Memory and History: Essays on Recalling and Interpreting Experience* (London, 1994), pp. 107–29.

7 See the collected articles in Selma Leydesdorff, Luisa Passerini and Paul Thompson (eds), *Gender and Memory* (Oxford, 1996).

8 Paul Thompson, *The Voice of the Past*, 3rd edn (Oxford, 2005), pp. 118–28.

9 Portelli, 'The Death of Luigi Trastulli', in Portelli (ed.), *The Death of Luigi Trastulli*, p. 26.

10 Mark Roseman, 'Surviving Memory: Truth and Inaccuracy in Holocaust Testimony', in Perks and Thomson (eds), *The Oral History Reader*, pp. 230–43, here p. 238.

11 Roseman, 'Truth and Inaccuracy', p. 241.

12 On the theory of collective memory, see Maurice Halbwachs, *On Collective Memory* (London, 1992).

13 For a discussion of the theory of popular memory, see Popular Memory Group, 'Popular Memory: Theory, Politics, Method', in Perks and Thomson (eds), *The Oral History Reader*, pp. 43–53.

14 Graham Smith, 'Beyond Individual/Collective Memory: Women's Transactive Memories of Food, Family and Conflict'. *Oral History* 25:2 (2007), 77–90.

15 Graham Dawson, *Making Peace with the Past: Memory, Trauma and the Irish Troubles* (Manchester, 2007); and Dawson, 'Trauma, Place and the Politics of Memory'. *History Workshop Journal* 59 (2005), 151–78.

16 Shetland Archive 3/1/396: Interview with Mary Helen Odie by Lynn Abrams. For a discussion of this interview in context, see Lynn Abrams, *Myth and Materiality in a Woman's World: Shetland 1800–2000* (Manchester, 2005), pp. 24–52.

17 For an extended discussion of the relationship between individual and collective memory, see Lynn Abrams, *Oral History Theory* (London, 2010), pp. 95–103.

18 Graham Dawson, *Soldier Heroes: British Adventure, Empire and the Imagining of Masculinities* (London, 1994), p. 25.

19 The term 'cultural circuit' was coined by Dawson. For a full discussion as it applies to oral history, see Penny Summerfield, 'Dis/composing the Subject: Intersubjectivities in Oral History', in Tess Cosslett, Celia Lury and Penny Summerfield (eds), *Feminism and Autobiography: Texts, Theories, Methods* (London, 2000), pp. 91–106.

20 Interview with Deborah by Lynn Abrams, 2009.

21 Interview with Lorraine (pseud) by Lynn Abrams, 2010.

22 On feminist approaches to oral history interviewing, see the articles in Sherna B. Gluck and Daphne Patai (eds), *Women's Words: the Feminist Practice of Oral History* (London, 1991) and Personal Narratives Group (ed.), *Interpreting Women's Lives: Feminist Theory and Personal Narratives* (Bloomington, Ind., 1989).

23 Judy Yung, 'Giving Voice to Chinese American Women', in Susan H. Armitage et al. (eds), *Women's Oral History* (Lincoln, Nebraska, 2001), pp. 87–111, here p. 87.

24 Miriam Zukas, 'Friendship as Oral History: a Feminist Psychologist's View'. *Oral History* 21:2 (1993), 73–9, here p. 78.

25 Hilary Young, 'Hard Man, New Man: re/Composing Masculinities in Glasgow c.1950–2000'. *Oral History* 35:1 (2007), 71–81.

26 Summerfield, 'Dis/composing the Subject', pp. 103–5.

27 Penny Summerfield, *Reconstructing Women's Wartime Lives: Discourse and Subjectivity in Oral Histories of the Second World War* (Manchester, 1998), p. 15.

28 Dawson, *Making Peace with the Past*, p. 123.

29 Ibid., *Soldier Heroes*, p. 23.

30 Alistair Thomson, 'Anzac Memories: Putting Popular Memory Theory into Practice in Australia', in Perks and Thomson (eds), *The Oral History Reader*, pp. 244–54, here p. 245.

31 'London in the Blitz: How Crime Flourished under Cover of the Blackout', *The Guardian*, 29 August 2010; see http://www.guardian.co.uk/society/2010/aug/29/blitz-london-crime-flourish-blackout (accessed 24 September 2010).

32 See Lynn Abrams, *The Orphan Country: Children of Scotland's Broken Homes, 1800 to the Present Day* (Edinburgh, 1998).

33 Interview with Betty by Lynn Abrams, 1997: transcript in Scottish Oral History Centre Archive (SOHCA), University of Strathclyde.

34 Interview with Betty (pseud.) by Lynn Abrams. Transcript in SOHCA.

35 William James cited in Sven-Ake Christianson and Martin A. Safer, 'Emotions in Autobiographical memories', in David C. Rubin (ed.), *Remembering Our Past* (Cambridge, 1995), pp. 218–43, here p. 230.

36 Interview with Arthur (pseud.) by Lynn Abrams. Transcript in SOHCA.

37 Ibid.

38 Ibid.

39 Interview with Christine (pseud.) by Lynn Abrams. Transcript in SOHCA.

40 Interview with Annie (pseud.) by Lynn Abrams. Transcript in SOHCA.

41 Quoted in Craig R. Barclay, 'Autobiographical Remembering: Narrative Constraints on Objective Selves', in Rubin (ed.), *Remembering Our Past*, p. 113.

42 Primo Levi, *If This is A Man* (London, 1959); Sean Field, 'Beyond "Healing": Trauma, Oral History and Regeneration'. *Oral History* 34:1 (2006), 31–42.

43 Antjie Krog, *Country of My Skull* (London, 1999), p. 55.

44 Dori Laub cited in Alison Parr, 'Breaking the Silence: Traumatised War Veterans and Oral History'. *Oral History* 35:1 (2007), 62.

45 K. Stevenson, 'The Lockerbie Air Disaster', unpublished MA dissertation, University of Glasgow, 2010.

46 Stevenson, 'The Lockerbie Air Disaster'.

Further reading

Lynn Abrams, *Oral History Theory* (London, 2010).

Jacob J. Climo and Maria G. Cattell (eds), *Social Memory and History: Anthropological Perspectives* (Walnut Creek, Ca., 2002).

Graham Dawson, *Making Peace with the Past: Memory, Trauma and the Irish Troubles* (Manchester, 2008).

James Fentress and Chris Wickham, *Social Memory* (Oxford, 1992).

Sherna B. Gluck and Daphne Patai (eds), *Women's Words: the Feminist Practice of Oral History* (London, 1991).

Alice Hoffman and Howard Hoffman, 'Reliability and Validity in Oral History: The Case for Memory', in Jaclyn Jeffrey and Glenace Edwall (eds), *Memory and History: Essays on Recalling and Interpreting Experience* (London, 1994), pp. 107–29.

Selma Leydesdorff, Luisa Passerini and Paul Thompson (eds), *Gender and Memory* (Oxford, 1996).

Ulric Neisser and Robyn Fivush (eds), *The Remembering Self. Construction and Accuracy in the Self-Narrative* (Cambridge, 1994).

Robert Perks and Alistair Thomson (eds), *The Oral History Reader*, 2nd edn (London, 1998).

Alessandro Portelli, *The Death of Luigi Trastulli and Other Stories: Form and Meaning in Oral History* (New York, 1991).

—, *The Order Has Been Carried Out: History, Memory and Meaning of a Nazi Massacre in Rome* (Basingstoke, 2007).

David C. Rubin (ed.), *Remembering our Past: Studies in Autobiographical Memory* (Cambridge, 1995).

Penny Summerfield, *Reconstructing Women's Wartime Lives: Discourse and Subjectivity in Oral Histories of the Second World War* (Manchester, 1998).

Alistair Thomson, *Anzac Memories: Living with the Legend* (Oxford, 1994).

Paul Thompson, *The Voice of the Past*, 3rd edn (Oxford, 2005).

CHAPTER FIVE

Generation and memory: A critique of the ethical and ideological implications of generational narration

Wulf Kansteiner

In 2010, *USA Today* launched a series of articles marking the beginning of the retirement age of the first members of the Baby Boomer generation. The coverage features a US-centric online quiz inviting readers to test their generational affiliation in the categories of music, film, TV, news, fashion, technology, toys and sports. Depending on the results of the quiz, readers are assigned to one of the six different generations. Each cohort comprises people born over a period of 25 years ranging from the GI generation which 'fought and won World War II' to the post 9/11 generation 'Z'. A closer look at the quiz reveals that different criteria are brought into play to define each generation. Some are primarily defined on the basis of demographic data (boomer), while others are linked to technological innovations (generation X) or historic events (GI, silent generation). In this way the quiz nicely illustrates the appealing simplicity and useful plasticity of the concept of generation which easily transitions from academic to non-academic contexts.[1]

For most practical purposes, a generation is simply 'any age-defined subgroup within a given wider population which has some recognizable and distinct characteristic'.[2] This notion of generation facilitates communication between Main Street, Fleet Street and Ivory Tower and helps us negotiate many semantic binaries in our lives. Generations mediate successfully between nature and culture, subjective perceptions and social structures, and the continuities and discontinuities of history. Whatever is explained as a result of generational sequentiality and cast into metaphors of family relations appears as inevitable as one's own parents and as pervasive as human reproduction. In this way, generational thinking naturalizes such highly abstract theorems as national history and transnational identity. In its ability to reduce confusing complexities into neat comprehensible information packages, the concept is right up there with class, race and gender and appears all the more natural and innocent because it has never been involved in the kind of withering, divisive battles which the other three categories retain as part of their intellectual heritage.[3]

But there is a price to be paid for considering the world from this intuitively compelling vantage point. The comfortable analytical perspective of generational thinking has important ideological implications. The concept of generation is a tool of intellectual compromise that delegitimizes experiences of relentless homogeneity as well as perceptions of radical discontinuity. Generational thinking advocates for measurable, predictable and manageable rates of social change which might explain its popularity among historians who often imagine the passage of time in similar terms.[4] In fact, as a scholarly explanatory strategy, the concept of political generation is perhaps best described as an intellectual antidote against the upheavals of (post)modernity. In this capacity, it has successfully moderated cultural perceptions of social transformation in many social settings and earned the title, bestowed by Sigrid Weigel, of 'master trope of the twentieth century'.[5]

Halbwachs, Mannheim and narrative templates

In memory studies, the concepts 'memory' and 'generation' are defined by two classical texts from the early twentieth century, published in 1925 and 1928, respectively, long before anybody talked about a field of memory studies.[6] The authors of the two texts, the French sociologist and student of Emile Durkheim, Maurice Halbwachs, and the German-Jewish-Hungarian sociologist Karl Mannheim, belong to the cosmopolitan generation of left-leaning, non-dogmatic intellectuals whose careers thrived in the relatively innovative academic environment of the interwar years. Both gravitated from philosophy to the new discipline of sociology in an effort to augment Marxist theory and develop practical analytical categories for the study of the social dynamics of cultural and political history. In the annals of sociology, they represent the third generation of European sociologists, following in the footsteps of the early nineteenth-century founding fathers Auguste Comte, Karl Marx and Herbert Spencer and the late-nineteenth-century cohort of Durkheim, Georg Simmel, Max Weber and many others.[7] Halbwachs and Mannheim also figure prominently in the ranks of European intellectuals who became victims of Nazi persecution. Halbwachs was arrested by the

Gestapo in July 1944, after his sons had joined the French resistance and after he had vigorously protested against the murder of his Jewish parents-in-law in Lyon; he died in Buchenwald in March 1945 from dysentery.[8] Mannheim lost his professorship in Frankfurt when the Nazis expelled him in 1933. He moved to the London School of Economics and died in London in 1947.[9]

This short biographical sketch of the lives of Halbwachs and Mannheim exemplifies the ordering hand of generational thinking, demonstrating its seductive powers and significant creative potential. The data linked to the names Halbwachs and Mannheim, just like the data linked to the lives of any of us, can be meaningfully inserted into a wide range of generational stories. In the above paragraph, Halbwachs and Mannheim appear in the roles of founding fathers, students, interwar intellectuals, sociologists, family members and victims of Nazism – and one could easily add many more. In each of these roles they are more or less explicitly placed within diachronic and synchronic networks of generational associations providing historians and their readers with a wide range of narrative options and elegantly smoothing over potential contradictions and semantic stumbling blocks. After all, with the help of generational thinking, the text sidesteps a number of intriguing questions: were they philosophers, sociologists, or – unbeknown to themselves – memory studies experts? Are they best described as third-generation sociologists, perhaps even epigones, or visionary founding father? Do the inmate of Buchenwald and the emigrant in London belong to the same trauma generation? This kind of successful reduction of semantic complexity through generational narration depends on a 'generational contract' between author and reader. Both have internalized the generational model and are well equipped for the task of sorting through textual information in an effort to craft and perceive a neatly layered narrative universe in which the different story lines – family history, professional history, political history – can unfold according to their own generational logic despite the fact that these logics are not necessarily internally consistent or compatible with one another.[10]

Halbwachs' work attracted limited attention after World War II, but in the course of the memory boom of the 1980s he ascended to the status of a much-venerated, belatedly appreciated role model of memory studies. His 1925 *Les cadres sociaux de la mémoire* and postwar compilations of his writings on collective memory constitute the most important canonical texts of this young field of study.[11] From the perspective of the late twentieth century, when Western societies reflected about their past in a seemingly endless series of anniversaries and memory initiatives, Halbwachs' remarks struck a chord in an academic community eager to develop critical perspectives on the new obsession with mediated history. The unexpected memory turn in Western culture and the feelings of academic impotence triggered by those developments corroborated Halbwachs' observations from the first half of the twentieth century when he argued in true Durkheimian fashion that individuals have little control over their memory cultures because all forms of individual recollection take place within collectively shaped cultural frameworks of remembrance. Halbwachs illustrated the point with a poignant example. When people remember their childhood, they do not have the ability to differentiate between authentic memories, family lore and memory contents derived from other sources. All recollections, even if pursued in relative social isolation, are facilitated through socially constructed systems of signification (e.g. natural languages) that we can deploy with a great deal of personal ingenuity but cannot invent *ex nihilo* without the help of others.[12]

Mannheim was already an academic star early in his career and his work has found a steady readership ever since.[13] But his publications were always controversial. Before World War II, Mannheim's attempts to develop a comprehensive sociology of knowledge were decried as materialistic by important non-Marxist sociologists and derided as insufficiently grounded in Marxist theory by members of the Frankfurt School. After the war, Mannheim's work received a second lease of life in the context of the rise of the constructivist and post-structuralist history and sociology of science. Once again, however, his ideas failed to reflect predominant academic tastes because his focus on the humanities and social sciences had prevented him from developing path-breaking insights into the social construction of scientific facts in the natural sciences.[14]

In at least one respect, Mannheim has nevertheless attained the status of an undisputed classic. In an effort to identify causal factors of change within his comprehensive sociology of knowledge, Mannheim developed a theory of generational transformation that reflects Marx's thinking about class. Mannheim conceived of generation as a synchronic community of individuals who made similar experiences and encountered similar challenges during their youth and therefore have the chance of developing compatible mentalities, worldviews and styles of action. These individuals share a common generational location regardless of their own consciousness of their collective historical disposition.[15] Mannheim based his ideas on cursory remarks by Auguste Comte and Wilhelm Dilthey who were probably reacting to the French Revolution and German Romanticism in very much the same way that Mannheim's essay reflected the historic cataclysm of World War I. All three intellectuals contemplated the accelerated rate of change in modern societies as they were trying to come to terms with modern signature events that had influenced their own lives. In acknowledging the relative powerlessness of individuals over the past that shaped them, Mannheim initially defined generation as a seemingly objective phenomenon existing independently of its carriers' consciousness. But he was primarily interested in groups whose members were very much aware of their generational context, explicitly defined themselves in generational terms, and, in constituting themselves as historical actors, assumed the role of a political generation intent on changing the status quo. Having recovered a sense of intellectual agency for his and other generations, Mannheim concluded that the members of a specific generation, shaped by watershed events and grappling with similar problems, are often divided into distinct subgroups that pursue more or less radically opposed ideological objectives.[16] From the beginning, Mannheim's theory thus defined generation as both objectively given and subjectively formed and experienced, and that inherent instability contributed to the concept's success.

Mannheim's concept of generation does not play a central role in contemporary sociological theory but enjoys canonical status in the interdisciplinary fields of generation research and memory studies because Mannheim's ideas are beautifully compatible with Halbwachs' notion of social memory. On the one hand, the idea of generation as historically given corresponds to the idea of social memory as facilitated, defined and contained within lasting collective systems of cultural signification. On the other hand, the concept of a political generation with its focus on generational consciousness works on the principle of belatedness. Political generations do not jump into existence during historic events; they are socially constructed after the fact in time-consuming cultural processes of self-definition that allow people of roughly the same age to constitute themselves as a self-conscious generation with the benefit of hindsight. Consequently, political generations only exist as a result of memory activism; the members of a generation come together and maintain a collective identity through the kind of shared narratives, images, institutions and rituals that have long been the empirical and theoretical target of memory studies. All the key concepts of the discipline – for instance, sites of memory (Nora),[17] communicative memory and cultural memory (Assmann)[18] cosmopolitan memory (Sznaider/Levy)[19] – are either based on or easily reconciled with principles of generationality. Mannheim's generation and Halbwachs' social memory thrive off the tension between objective structures and subjective creativity and are therefore inconsistent, instable and versatile in exactly the same ways.

Cohort, 1968, and Pierre Bourdieu

Sociological research about successive age groups differentiates between generations and cohorts. Cohorts are defined by external factors, for instance, educational, military or academic institutions. Cohorts are aggregates of individuals crafted for administrative or scholarly purposes according to more or less objective and arbitrary criteria such as birth years. As a result, cohorts take shape regardless of their consciousness of their existence and in this regard differ from political generations which, following the spirit if not necessarily the letter of Mannheim's intervention, exist first and foremost as self-serving invented traditions and, in that capacity, have attracted considerable scholarly interest.[20] The neat division between generations and cohorts reflects attempts to differentiate between seemingly objective research criteria, on the one hand, and subjective, self-assigned labels adopted in pursuit of strategic political advantages, on the other hand. But this division appears dubious for several reasons. First, administratively set, externally defined cohorts might figure very prominently in subsequent generational myth making. That has, for instance, been the case with the Hitler-Youth-generation whose members, with the benefit of hindsight, cherished the fact they had been too young to partake in the crimes of Hitler's military and were relegated to the far less compromising service in the Hitler Youth – a fact that many members of the applicable age group severely regretted at the time.[21] Second and more important, from the very beginning of modern generation research, that is, from the time that Comte reflected about the age of Napoleon, scholarly interest in cohorts and generations has always also been an exercise in individual and collective self-definition. As a result, research results often played a decisive role in the academic and non-academic constructions of generational identity.

The feedback loop between generation research and generation construction is especially pronounced in the case of the generation of 1968, a particularly rambunctious generation if there ever was one. Pierre Nora has famously remarked about the 68ers that he does not understand all the excitement since nothing really happened to them.[22] Nora's provocation contains more than a kernel of truth if the upheavals of World War II serve as the standard of comparison. Moreover, Nora captured the reasons for the particularly combative style of engagement of the student movement generation. The student activists faced a generation whose members derived legitimacy from having fought on the battlegrounds of World War II. The resulting competitive disadvantage might have prompted the post-war generation to misremember the militancy of their confrontation with the European welfare states and remain deeply ambivalent in their assessment of the crimes committed by left-wing terrorists throughout the 1970s. In their memories, the 68ers also see themselves as the first thoroughly transnational generation capable of maintaining political solidarity across national borders. From a historiographical point of view, those assessments raise pertinent questions about prevalent levels of violence and the precise nature of political consciousness and cross-border communication during a political confrontation that many of the participants still defined in national terms. From a memory studies' vantage point, such epistemological concerns are pointless and misleading. At some point during the long history of the memory of 1968, the real or imagined activists reached a level of agreement about the militancy of their cause and many of them, especially those of the academic persuasion, began to celebrate the accomplishments of their generation within far-reaching transnational networks of exchange. In this sense, collective memories of the twentieth and twenty-first century have exceeded national frameworks of generational remembrance as envisioned by Mannheim. Moreover, in this case as in many others, historical

facts and remembered stories represent reservoirs of knowledge that exist independently of each other. Generations might exist because historical
events or previous or subsequent generations objectively define them but
they most certainly come into existence once people feel and act as members
of a specific cohort.[23] In the latter case they are also a lot easier and more
fun to study.

Since the late twentieth century, the media have pronounced the
emergence of new generations at an ever more rapid pace.[24] The inflationary
deployment of new generational labels might attest to the political
advantages of constituting oneself as a generational player or indicate that
the empirical limits of the generational model have been reached. For Pierre
Bourdieu, the second important sociological theorist of generationality, the
accelerated rate of generational succession is simply a function of advanced
capitalist modes of cultural production. Bourdieu's remarks focus on the
rhythms of exchange and competition which structure the market place
for intellectual and especially artistic products.[25] The struggle for scarce
resources sets into motion a cycle of permanent revolutions which replaces
hierarchies of cherished artistic styles and content in a rapid and generally
unpredictable process of aesthetic innovation. Each paradigm is supported
by a specific generation of artists and intellectuals who define cultural
tastes and accumulate cultural capital until the next cohort eager to enjoy
similar spoils displaces them. In his study of the history of the European
art scene since the early nineteenth century, Bourdieu demonstrates that the
rate of turnover is determined by the market and only vaguely reminiscent
of the succession of natural generations. In fact, revolutions in taste occur
approximately every 10 years and do not necessarily replace biologically
older by biologically younger cohorts. As a result, at any given point in time,
the field of artistic production is crowded with competing social designs
of what it means to be an artist. Each layer is sustained by more or less
clearly separated groups whose members share a common habitus. They
have acquired a common code of generational conduct that structures their
everyday life, including the presentation of their individual and collective
sense of self, through speech, clothing and body language.[26] Bourdieu's
analysis of the art scene thus serves as a particularly vivid example for the
peculiar dynamics of generational competition:

> [G]eneration conflicts oppose not age classes separated by natural
> properties, but habitus which have been produced by different *modes of
> generation*, that is, by conditions of existence which, in imposing different
> definitions of the impossible, the possible, and the probable, cause one
> group to experience as natural or reasonable practices or aspirations
> which another group finds unthinkable or scandalous, and vice versa.[27]

Bourdieu has never attempted to develop a comprehensive, consistent
theory of generationality. His theoretical remarks about the sociology of

generations are dispersed throughout his oeuvre and, as in the case of his predecessors, oscillate between perceptions of generation as naturally given and socially constructed.[28] But in his efforts to grasp processes of social change through categories other than class, efforts that mirror Halbwachs' and especially Mannheim's objectives, Bourdieu very appropriately highlights the element of competition that drives generational turnover. Moreover and more important, he provides particularly compelling illustrations for the phenomenon of contemporaneous non-contemporaneity in modern societies which had already prompted Mannheim, recalling and complicating Dilthey, to reflect about the coexistence of different generations.[29]

Trauma, World War I and two types of political generations

In programmatic reflections as well as empirical studies, the integration of memory and generation is often accomplished by way of the conceptual vehicle of trauma. Traumatic events like the French Revolution, World War I and World War II, the Great Depression, the Holocaust and 9/11 are deemed particularly likely to set into motion enduring processes of remembrance and trigger the formation of political generations.[30] In this theoretical setting, the principle of belatedly crafted collective identities assumes the shape of a powerful psychological metaphor implying that 'injured' societies, like trauma victims wounded by violence on a massive scale, tend to display symptoms of stress after more or less extensive periods of latency. The trauma model also implies the possibility of recovery and improved self-knowledge after appropriate working-through – preferably orchestrated by well-trained memory studies experts.[31]

The transplantation of the trauma concept from the human to the social sciences raises serious empirical and ethical questions regarding the differences between individual and collective experiences and the status of real and imagined victims and perpetrators.[32] The valorization of trauma as a tool of scholarly inquiry with its emphasis on modern catastrophes, belated suffering and insight, and intergenerational contamination also illustrates that 'memory', 'trauma' and 'generation' form a powerful conceptual triangle at the core of memory studies. In this triad, memory represents the most frequently deployed but not necessarily most clearly defined term which retains a very ambivalent relationship to history. In comparison, the term trauma features a more distinct and attractive but also more controversial conceptual profile. Therefore, generation emerges as the least problematic and most reliable and stable conceptual tool in the threesome.

Memory, trauma and generation are suspended in a historically increasingly dynamic matrix of synchronic and diachronic relationships. The diachronic axis of the matrix is grounded in pre-modern and supposedly natural associations of genealogy, as the seemingly straightforward differentiation between cohort and generation suggests. For the longest time, the diachronic axis has been represented by that most conventional and effective of visual aids, the family tree, which, as Judith Burnett has appropriately remarked, is capable of inserting 'unity in the most fragmented of social systems, organising relations into a meaningful continuity, in what is otherwise a discontinuous and meaningless flow of random persons who are born and die'.[33] In this fashion, the more or less artful and imaginative display of lineage has helped bolster the authority of many a dubious noble family and aspiring religion. According to the standard narrative of generational studies, the comforting primacy of diachronicity over synchronicity in social memory fell victim to the long nineteenth century and was finally and thoroughly blown to pieces in the trenches of World War I. According to their postwar self-image, the members of the generation of 1914 ranked synchronic emotional ties forged during the war above family history and social origins. Striving to come to terms with a scale of violence which existing social scripts could not explain, the former soldiers and officers entered an imagined, proto-democratic world of peer solidarity that was maintained by an ever more expansive and successful mass media infrastructure.[34] According to Robert Wohl, who studied the generation of 1914 in the 1970s, the culture of the interwar years formed 'a powerful magnetic field at the centre of which lies an experience or a series of experiences' rendered intelligible by the contemporaries through a 'strange mixture of idealism and biological determinism'.[35]

Wohl's words recall the intriguing generational dialectic with which we are by now very familiar. In highlighting the ambivalent self-perceptions of postwar interpreters of the war experience, Wohl inserts a productive tension in his own writings and anticipates and highlights the flexible, schizophrenic nature of generational reasoning in memory studies. As an empirical historian, Wohl is willing to engage with traditional causal models concerning the genesis of political generations. In some respects, the generation of 1914 might very well have been formed in the trenches of World War I as some of the veterans assumed. After all, the Western front was a site of horrendous, unprecedented mass violence that left severe scars on the bodies and souls of the survivors and perhaps forced into existence, almost by way of a biological reflex, the first radically synchronically oriented age cohort with a distinct psychological, emotional and social profile. But as a cultural historian, Wohl is much more interested in unraveling culture in action and considers the generation of 1914, first and foremost, to be a media invention that only assumed political relevance once it had been successfully propagated in the public sphere of the Weimar Republic and, in the process, homogenized very diverse wartime experiences after the fact. Therefore he concludes, in an ironic reading of the contemporaries' idealistic stories of their heroic service, that the generation of 1914 was fantasized into existence after the war.

The reception of Wohl's important book has set into motion a series of very entertaining and inventive probings of the dialectic of psychological experience versus cultural invention. Some colleagues undertook the task of testing the empirical integrity of lingering notions of psychological-biological imprint, concluding unequivocally that the people who lived through World War I had very different experiences and drew very different conclusions from those experiences. The idea of a homogenous, heroic front generation only emerged after the war as a screen memory for many unpleasant and unheroic events and, even more important, as a formidable political weapon in the fight for limited material and symbolic resources during the postwar years.[36]

However, having settled on invention rather than experience, the field of contemporary history changed tack again and returned to the comforting storyline of psychological imprint and straightforward causality. The generation of 1914 might have been nothing but a useful urban myth but its agenda of wilful misremembering became a hard and fast fact for a postwar generation growing up in the shadow of World War I. In conjunction with a number of pertinent demographic and economic developments and in the ideological crucible of Weimar youth culture, the widely disseminated generational myth of the front generation helped spawn off a real postwar generation replete with a decisive will to action that burst onto the scene with spectacularly destructive consequences in World War II.[37] Thus in the latest historiographical twist of the generational World War I saga of invention versus experience, the dialectic has come full circle, recasting self-serving, inaccurate and often second-hand cultural simulations of history into the role of a more powerful historical force than the war itself. In this emplotment, the media blitz after the war achieved what all the bombs of World War I failed to accomplish, that is, give shape to a bona fide political generation in a direct process of cause and effect.

We will return to the generational origins of World War II and the Holocaust shortly. Suffice it to emphasize at this point that generational thinking is a remarkably flexible discursive machine capable of integrating different historiographical philosophies, story formats and models of causality. In fact, the dialectic of imprint versus invention gives rise to two very different ideal types and storylines of political generations. On the one hand, there are generations of history shaped by hard demographic, military or political facts. They assume historical agency by developing a sense of collective identity, including an explicit vision of their origins, and go on to take control of their own destiny. German social historian Hans-Ulrich Wehler celebrates such a generation of history when he tells his readers the story of his own generation, the Hitler-Youth-Generation, which survived war and dictatorship, drew the appropriate political conclusions from that experience and played a decisive role in crafting the democratic political culture of the Federal Republic.[38] On the other hand, there are generations of memory which only exist as an effect of memory culture, are reluctant to establish themselves as political actors and can only be observed indirectly, for instance, in the way that they craft new collective memories for themselves and future generations. With the '1979ers' cultural historian Harold Marcuse identifies a generation of memory whose historical consciousness was shaped by media events like the American TV series *Holocaust* and who played an important role in creating Germany's Holocaust culture without explicitly claiming the status of a political generation in the way that their predecessors did.[39]

In the practice of generational thinking and writing the two ideal types are constantly combined. There are generations of memory that make history – for instance, the first post-World War I generation discussed above – and generations of history that 'only' produce (memory) culture – for instance, the student movement generation, viewed through the lens of a critical observer like Wehler. As this last example indicates, generations of history and generations of memory are subject to different emotional assessments and projective identifications. Wehler considers generations of history the 'alpha dogs' of generational thinking. They are appreciated and studied by 'real' social (male) historians who have little sympathy left for generations of memory that only produce culture and are best appreciated by cultural historians and media studies experts. But that perception is a highly subjective assessment. Protagonists of generational thinking are constantly negotiating about the status of past and present generations, trying to establish their own generational champions – often identical with their own generations – as powerful collective historical agents while downplaying the historical relevance of other age cohorts. And since generational thinking is a large-scale narrative model with little inherent epistemological integrity, any historian and memory studies expert worth his or her mettle will be able to deconstruct somebody else's generation of history and reduce it to the status of an ineffectual, self-centred generation of memory. After all, it does not take much deconstructive acumen to expose Wehler's celebration of the generation of 1945 as a figment of his egocentric generational imagination. It goes without saying though that given the empirical and conceptual ambivalence of generational narration (and large-scale historical narration in general) neither Wehler nor his critic would be able to prove their case in any intersubjectively and trans-generationally valid sense.

The story of the rise of synchronicity over diachronicity at the hands of a generation that assumed historical velocity after trauma, experienced in the trenches or vicariously imagined after the fact, nicely illustrates that the diachronic and the synchronic axis of the memory-trauma-generation triad represent directly interrelated variables. The fictions of genealogy in any given society play a decisive role in the evolution of synchronic kinship ties – and vice versa. The very success of the generation of 1914 in constituting itself as a social actor indicates that generations imagined in conventional genealogical terms must have already been endangered species before the first shot was fired. In the same vein, the memories of its origin that any political generation invents have a decisive impact on past as well as future generations. The founding of a new generation is always part of a competitive process designed to displace existing generations from positions of power by undermining their successfully propagated self-image. Therefore, the rise of a particularly self-confident generation is prone to trigger 'memory envy' in subsequent and previous age groups, cause the latter to get unduly invested in their precursor's or successor's culture and might even cause them to miss out on the chance of developing a cultural framework of their own. That observation has prompted researchers to describe the sequence of modern generations as alternating between particularly extrovert and decidedly subdued generations.[40] Having taken a passing look at two noisy exemplars – 1914 and 1968 – we will now turn to an initially relatively silent and then exceptionally destructive age group.

The generation of Nazi history

The fabulous versatility as well as the ideological underpinnings of the notion of political generations are perhaps most clearly visible in contemporary German cultural contexts where the concept of generations is particularly frequently deployed as a tool of historical explanation.[41] A case in point is the most infamous generation of twentieth-century German history, the Nazi generation. In important books on Nazi history by Ulrich Herbert and Michael Wildt, the zeal of some of the most committed Nazis is attributed to a specific generational constellation. These Nazis, so the argument goes, had experienced the end of World War I as adolescents and ever since grappled with their fate of having been prevented from joining their older brethren in the trenches. The 'war envy' turned them into particularly merciless technocrats and killers once they received the opportunity of waging a war of destruction and genocide in Eastern Europe.[42]

The causal model powerfully illustrates the dialectical core of generational arguments. Every political generation is defined by how it differs from its predecessor, that is, it is defined by a relational void. According to Herbert, who cites extensively from ego documents of former Nazis and their contemporaries, the essence of the Nazi identity consisted of *not* having fought in the war and therefore not having had a chance to prevent the German defeat. Subsequent generations in German history have rallied around similarly powerful symbolic absences. Both the Hitler Youth and the generation of 1968 were first and foremost defined by what they were not, that is, they were not responsible for Nazism and the Holocaust. On the level of generational self-definition, the self-serving agenda of generational thinking is thus very obvious – even if its proponents do not always publicly celebrate the grace of their late birth in the way that German chancellor Helmut Kohl did in the 1980s.

The moral implications of the scholarly concept of political generation are less obvious but hardly less relevant. Herbert's model, for instance, clearly favours one type of causal explanation at the expense of many others.

It implies that 1918 is a significant, maybe even the most significant point of origin of the relentless criminal energy of key Nazi perpetrators. The explanation highlights the psychological generational dynamics informing Nazi policy and perhaps inadvertently but not arbitrarily attributes less importance to short-term factors linked to the specific social, ideological and psychological context of fall 1941 when the German perpetrators started to commit mass murder and genocide on an unprecedented scale. By deploying the generational model, German scholars born in the 1950s have elegantly located the origins of Nazi inhumanity in the 1910s and thus given themselves a little extra breathing space. As an analytical tool of contemporary history, the generational model does an excellent job in making the immediate past appear less contemporary and more historical by turning it from a pressing current affair into a well-understood and perfectly manageable historical phenomenon. After all, the deeds of a given generation can only be conclusively assessed after a latency period of several decades, once the phase of psychological imprint has run its course.[43] At that point, the unique historical setting that gave rise to the specific generational profile, for instance, the peculiar situation of 1918, can be subjected to scholarly scrutiny but is safely removed from the historian-qua-citizen's realm of political-ethical responsibility.

The ready availability and attractiveness of the generational model might explain why scholars wholeheartedly embrace it despite the fact that their primary sources and relevant secondary literature attest to a multitude of causal explanations and occasionally even resist the imposition of stringent generational interpretations. A sense of that tension might have prompted Michael Wildt to include a series of prolepses in his study of the history of the Reich Security Main Office. Wildt emphasizes that the diversity of Nazi perpetrators requires multi-causal strategies of explanation and that no direct path connects the experiences of the RSHA personnel during their adolescence to their later relentless brutality.[44] But Wildt also concludes that the feelings of the later Nazis at the end of World War I, 'the piercing thorn of missed opportunities',[45] caused them to develop an idiosyncratic generational habitus which in turn represents one of the three necessary preconditions for Nazi genocide:

> Only the combination of a generational experience condensed in a specific world view, the development of a new type of political institution like the Reich Security Main Office, and the conditions of modern warfare may explain the deeds of these historical actors who were fully committed to their racist project and eager to remove any obstacles through ever more radical means.[46]

This conclusion rests on a slim empirical foundation. Wildt quickly whittles down his sample from the entire RSHA staff of 3,000 people to 400 of its leaders and again to 221 individuals who stayed in their positions for a significant amount of time. Roughly three quarters of those fit into Wildt's generational profile. As a result, his relatively far-flung generational arguments reflect biographical data of 170 NS officials. In the light of these numbers, it might be problematic to elevate 'generation' into the position of a key historical-narrative actant and speak of 'the subsequent generation that was later in charge of the RSHA'.[47] Moreover, the precise nature of the generation's experiences and resulting memories remain a bit murky. At one point, Wildt stresses the experience gap between the soldiers of World War I and subsequent generations. On another occasion, he emphasizes the experience gap between World War I soldiers and World War I civilians which could arguably reflect more of a gender division than a generational divide.[48] In any case, the habitus and thought style that Wildt attributes to the post-World War I generation, that is, a future and community-oriented hierarchical elitism combined with relentless, immoral and decisionistic activism, was also embraced by a large number of veterans of the war, including Hitler.[49] In fact, precisely when it comes to defining the dividing line between the World War I and the postwar generation, Wildt's generational model falls victim to his scholarly diligence. As Wildt stresses time and again, there is no indication that the leaders of the Nazi party, the SS, the German military and the German civil service, who were generally older than their peers at the Reich Security Main Office, felt less enthusiastic or proved less efficient in implementing mass murder than their RSHA colleagues.[50] If by some unlikely but hardly impossible strike of NS administrative genius the new institution of the RSHA had been staffed with well-trained older Nazis, the institution would have proven as devastatingly efficient in designing and implementing the 'Final Solution' as it did with its somewhat younger leadership. In the end, there is simply no control group inside or outside the RSHA indicating that relative youthfulness and non-exposure to the actual violence of World War I, combined with emotional investment in fantasies of World War I violence, was a precondition for decisive and relentless genocidal action.[51] With very few exceptions, all Nazi leaders, from the young law student to the aged general overcame whatever qualms they might have entertained in private and became fully functional mass murderers.

Wildt's source material did not 'demand' a generational explanation. Rather, he adopted a generational model because in this way he could turn the relative age homogeneity among RSHA leaders, hardly surprising with a new institution, into a narrative strategy for integrating the dispersive and somewhat overwhelming surfeit of biographical data which he unearthed during his extensive research of the history of the Reich Security Main Office. Or, as Mark Roseman concluded in his reflections on the Nazi generation:

> The fact that the Nazi movement was largely composed of the young should not in itself surprise us; it does not prove that the movement's emergence was caused by a set of experiences peculiar to the young.[52]

The generations of Nazi memory

When it comes to the pitfalls of generational thinking, the memory studies expert seems to be in a better position than the historian. For the historian, applying the concept of political generation triggers more or less welcome commitments to specific models of causality, as above examples illustrate. In contrast, the memory studies expert can contend himself or herself with sticking to a less ambitious plan. He or she may reconstruct prevalent strategies of interpretation as an end in itself without having to explain how these memories shape history. In memory studies, the social relevance of the historical representations under description is often simply assumed and does not have to be demonstrated by way of an explicit cause and effect model.[53] Consequently, political generations can be acknowledged as what they most manifestly are, that is, more or less consciously imagined social networks whose cultural infrastructure provides a great deal of information about the groups under description and the scholars who study the imagined communities within generational parameters.

But before we celebrate the epistemological and moral superiority of memory studies over historical analysis, we should acknowledge at least three serious risks that are linked to the explicit and implicit use of generational thinking in memory studies. All too often histories of memory and the concomitant deconstruction of past generations' strategies of remembrance serve the purpose of legitimizing and naturalizing one's own aesthetic and political preferences. Moreover, highlighting other generations' power of historical representation and manipulation might inadvertently diminish one's own memory agency and political responsibility. But the most serious moral challenge of our scholarly pursuits is linked to the paradigmatic transition from history to memory *per se*.

The ever so subtle yet important shift in perspective is beautifully illustrated in a classic of German memory studies deeply invested in generational analysis. In his magisterial study of the history and memory politics associated with the Dachau concentration camp, Harold Marcuse begins his discussions of German generations and their memories of Nazism with the following statement:

> the first politically relevant cohort in the twentieth century, which I will call the 1918ers, is important in this context only inasmuch as its members created the pivotal event that set the whole dynamic into motion: the Nazi accession to unprecedented political and cultural power after 1930.[54]

The 'only inasmuch' signals the turn away from history to memory and raises the disturbing question as to whether the study of the memory of events like Nazism serves the purpose of not having to engage with its history. Are we developing sustained curiosity about the acts of (mis)representation of postwar generations in order to avoid a direct encounter with the moral depravity of the perpetrator generation? Marcuse does not bear much guilt in this regard because his book contains detailed discussions of Nazi as well as postwar history. But I do not have to look far to find people like myself who have exclusively studied the memory of the Nazi period from generational and other conceptual perspectives.[55] Are we studying how our predecessors have avoided looking at Nazi crimes in order to establish our moral superiority over said predecessors and, at the same time and even more problematically, evade any close encounter with the Nazi crimes and the social dynamics that caused them? Is memory studies a generational aftermath phenomenon that will tell future historians a great deal about our lack of historical curiosity and intellectual courage?

Even if one does not harbour fundamental doubts about the moral integrity of memory studies, one should take note of the important epistemological and narrative stakes involved in the transition from history to memory and, more specifically, in the transition from generations of history to generations of memory. Marcuse, for instance, presents a set of finely tuned and neatly layered arguments that seem to adhere to the principle of generational imprint. As he explains half way through the book, 'in early twentieth-century German history, new cohorts emerged every five to fifteen years', and in these cases as in many others, 'pivotal experiences between the ages of 16 and 26, in certain circumstances from 14 to 30, are critical in shaping lifetime political attitudes'.[56] Marcuse's memory story begins with the generation of the adults of the Third Reich who crafted 'the three founding myths of the Federal Republic', claiming that they 'had fallen victim to developments beyond Germany's control', had 'been ignorant of what was happening in the concentration camps' and had remained loyal to an 'unsullied "other Germany" that had done its best to resist rioting and intruding [Nazi] barbarians'.[57] The three founding myths of victimization, ignorance and resistance were transformed and ultimately dismantled by subsequent age groups in the 1970s, 1980s and 1990s, respectively – with the myth of resistance surviving the longest.[58]

One may raise a number of specific questions about Marcuse's complex and dynamic narrative design featuring three myths and seven political generations and spanning all of the twentieth century. Marcuse gives the members of the first postwar generation a lot of credit for reforming West Germany's historical culture and in this respect confirms that generation's self-perception. Some of that praise could arguably be transferred to the particularly courageous individuals in the ranks of the previous generations who launched the important memory initiatives of the 1960s and thus shaped the historical imagination of the student movement. One may also quibble with Marcuse's conclusion that the former Nazis, in failing to instill in their children an emotional understanding of the complexities and depravity of the Nazi era, are partly to be blamed for the Red Army Faction's descent into violence.[59] Moreover, Marcuse's story of memory progress, reaching from the wilful, self-serving misrepresentation of Nazism in the 1950s to the rise of self-reflexive memory in the 1990s, might have looked very differently if he had published his book a few years later. Since the turn of the century, the myth of German victimization has returned with a vengeance.[60] Finally, as with all generational arguments, there is the fundamental question whether the cultural interventions of a few individuals adequately reflect the attitudes of a significant segment of their cohort peers, most of whom remained silent.

For our purposes, however, it is a lot more important to realize that Marcuse's memory model is effectively detached from history – if we reduce history for a moment to the concrete nuts-and-bolts events of political, economic and military history. Marcuse invokes the imprint theory and labels the generations according to the pivotal events that allegedly shaped their political consciousness. The defeat in World War I, the Nazi seizure of power, Stalingrad, the end of World War II and the currency reform, 1968, the TV series *Holocaust*, and the fall of the Berlin Wall – these events represent the experiential centres of different generations' historical imagination. But in the course of Marcuse's empirically saturated study, we lose sight of the precise connections between the key political events of twentieth-century German history and the political consciousness and collective memories they supposedly shaped. We never learn, for example, what generationally specific experiences of 1933, 1943, 1948, 1968, 1979 and 1989 might have motivated the political protagonists who argued about the design of the memory landscape in Dachau. Can the different attitudes towards the preservation and destruction of the Dachau camp really be attributed to generationally specific experiences of Stalingrad, the Deutsche Mark, or a television broadcast? Are the debates not primarily driven by a basic sense of justice that cuts across a number of different generations pitching the surviving victims of Nazism, a few remorseful bystanders, and their postwar political allies against the vast majority of Nazi fellow travellers, perpetrators and post-1945 opportunists? Or, to take another concrete example from the book, how do the publications of a Hitler-Youth historian like Martin Broszat differ from the writings of the 1979ers historians Norbert Frei and Michael Brenner and in what respect are these differences the result of generational experiences and not other factors? Can the dominant themes, metaphors and explanatory strategies of their complex oeuvres really be reduced to their perceptions of 1945/48 and 1979, perceptions which they share with other members of their age cohort but not with other Germans who lived through these times? Does it make sense to equate these two sets of experiences on a functional level in assuming that living through total national defeat, years of deprivation and miraculous recovery have structurally comparable effects on the worldview of a young adult than 'surviving' years of public television programming about the Nazi past?

Rather than integrating political, sociological and cultural viewpoints, as the generational model implies, Marcuse's study is first and foremost a self-contained cultural history of a multitude of competing and overlapping gestures of memory politics.[61] The complex story of cultural change is grafted onto a structural model of political generations but not in any way effectively causally linked to the pivotal historical events that allegedly shaped these generations. As in the case of Wildt, Marcuse adopts the inherently compelling generational storyline to bring order into a bewildering surfeit of data. In this way, he avoids having to resort to more conventional and less innovative and attractive narrative strategies focusing, for instance, on ideological conflicts between left and right or the memory clashes between the victims, bystanders and perpetrators of the Nazi regime. Even in the realm of professional historiography, generational thinking, along with many other narrative explanatory strategies, is primarily an invented tradition.

Postmemory and the future of generational narration

Generational narration and generational research appear to be inextricably linked to self-serving political and intellectual agendas. In theory, that observation does not preclude the possibility that generational narrations have objective collective validity and that generational experiences place hard limits on the range of possible generational self-stylizations.[62] In practice, however, generational narration always seems to fall into the trap of postmemory as described and practised by Marianne Hirsch. In her classical study about the transmission of Holocaust memory in families of Holocaust survivors, Hirsch demonstrates with great precision how subsequent generations become emotionally and intellectually invested in their parents' lives:

> [P]ostmemory is distinguished from memory by generational distance and from history by deep personal connection. Postmemory is a powerful and very particular form of memory precisely because its connection to its object or source is mediated not through recollection but through an imaginative investment and creation. This is not to say that memory itself is unmediated, but that it is more directly connected to the past. Postmemory characterises the experience of those who grew up dominated by narratives that preceded their birth, whose own belated stories are evacuated by the stories of the previous generation shaped by traumatic events that can be neither understood nor recreated.[63]

In other publications, Hirsch developed the concept into an extended matrix of diachronic and synchronic relations suggesting that the close proximity to the belatedly unfolding trauma of the survivor generation might turn the members of the second generation into surrogate sites of memory for their parents and allow them to work through traumatic experiences which the parents have often not been able to assimilate into functional memories.[64] Hirsch further extends the model of trans-generational witnessing and working through by arguing that the members of the second generation can themselves become objects of 'intra-generational horizontal identification' that would make their Holocaust knowledge available to their generational peers in a process of 'affiliative postmemory'.[65]

The concept of postmemory partakes in the aestheticization and valorization of trauma that has played an important role in literary criticism, media studies and Holocaust memory since the 1990s and, as we have seen, attracted significant criticism in recent years. In the current context, the concept of postmemory is particularly noteworthy for the politics of memory that inform its web of familial and affiliative memory relations. Hirsch has designed a blueprint for a culture of Holocaust remembrance that places the second generation, her own generation, in a position of remarkable interpretive control. In her model, the members of the second generation emerge as pivotal, powerful memory brokers who conclude the memory work that their parents were unable to accomplish and share the extraordinary insights derived from the proximity to trauma with people who did not grow up with the burden and benefit of vicarious trauma access. Second-generation memory appears to be the most authentic form of Holocaust memory that can be cast into conventional formats of historical reflection. In this regard, it represents a symbolic victory over the survivors and all protagonists of Holocaust culture who are not graced with the privilege of affiliative birth.

Hirsch's reflections on postmemory are a form of intellectual self-indulgence – but that criticism seems to apply to many forms of generational thinking. Apparently, the academic terrain circumscribed by the terms memory and generation with its close affiliation to family history offers a particular fruitful and transparent arena for projective and transferential encounters with our own past. One would hope that the experience of consuming self-serving forms of academic memory helps set into motion self-critical reflections about one's own academic pursuits. In the end, the celebration of the proximity to trauma in postmemory as well as the genealogical expulsion of Nazi perpetrators into the more distant past – but also the decisive indictment of cultural trauma theory –[66] are all more or less obvious examples of generational acting out. The theories and empirical studies of generational memory only make sense if they are read against the grain and placed in a critical dialogue with each other. Consumed in that fashion they offer some information about the past and a lot of intriguing insights into contemporary contexts of cultural and scholarly production.

It is difficult to predict the future of generational memory. Claus Leggewie tried to do just that in 1995 when he argued that the teenagers of 1989 were poised to become a powerful, well-defined political generation. In his mind, all the ingredients were present: a crucial central event, as well as new values, ideas and challenges linked to globalization, European integration and the reform of the welfare state in pursuit of intergenerational economic justice. Leggewie expected that generation would emerge as a key social category while other organizing principles such as class, confession, social origins and gender were losing relevance.[67] Leggewie's predictions have not yet materialized. Political generations might still exist but accelerated patterns of social fragmentation, global exchange and media consumption appear to prevent age cohorts from auto-poetically constituting themselves as self-conscious political generations.[68] And that might not be such a bad thing since some of the most self-conscious age cohorts in modern history also count among the most destructive.[69] Perhaps we should hope for a future dearth of generational ego documents and an absence of researchers who feel as members of political generations and are therefore particularly inclined to study them?

Notes

1   'Which generation do you belong to?', *USA Today.com* (see http://projects. usatoday.com/news/generations/quiz/, accessed 1 March 2012).

2   Mark Roseman, 'Introduction: Generation Conflict and German History 1770–1968', in Roseman (ed.), *Generations in Conflict: Youth Revolt and Generation Formation in Germany 1770–1968* (Cambridge, 1995), pp. 1–46, here p. 5.

3   Ulrike Jureit, 'Generation, Generationalität, Generationenforschung, Version: 1.0', in *Docupedia-Zeitgeschichte*, 11 February 2010. See http://docupedia.de/ zg/Generation (accessed 1 March 2012), pp. 6–7.

4   For a comprehensive survey of the use of generational narration in historical studies since the 18th century see Josef Ehmer, 'Generationen in der historischen Forschung: Konzepte und Praktiken', in Harald Künemund and Marc Szydlik (eds), *Generationen: multidisziplinäre Perspektiven* (Wiesbaden, 2009), pp. 59–80.

5   Sigrid Weigel, 'Family, Phantoms and the Discourse of "Generations" as a Politics of the Past: Problems of Provenance – Rejecting and Longing for Origins', in Stefan Berger (ed.), *Narrating the Nation* (New York, 2010), pp. 133–50, here p. 140.

6   Karl Mannheim, 'Das Problem der Generationen', *Kölner Vierteljahreshefte für Soziologie* 7 (1928), pp. 157–85, 309–30; reprinted in Mannheim, *Wissenssoziologie: Auswahl aus dem Werk* (Berlin, 1964), pp. 509–65; Maurice Halbwachs, *Les cadres sociaux de la mémoire* (Paris, 1925).

7   Reinhard Müller, 'Maurice Halbwachs' and 'Karl Mannheim', *Internetlexikon: 50 Klassiker der Soziologie* (Universität Graz), http://agso.uni-graz.at/lexikon/ index.htm (accessed 5 February 2012). Consider in this context the very helpful proto-generational chronology of Müller's *Internetlexikon*, always present in its right-hand margin.

8   Wolf Lepenies, *Deutsch-Französische Kulturkriege: Maurice Halbwachs in Berlin* (Berlin, 2004), 15; Annette Becker, *Maurice Halbwachs: Un intellectuel en guerres mondiales 1914–1945* (Paris, 2003).

9   Müller, 'Karl Mannheim'.

10 Björn Bohnenkamp, Till Manning, Eva-Maria Silies (eds), *Generation als Erzählung: Neue Perspektiven auf ein kulturelles Deutungsmuster* (Göttingen, 2009).

11 Halbwachs, *Les cadres sociaux de la mémoire*; Halbwachs, *The Collective Memory*, ed. by Mary Douglas (New York, 1950); Jeffrey Olick, Vered Vinitzky-Seroussi, Daniel Levy, 'Introduction', in Olick, Vinitzky-Seroussi and Levy (eds), *The Collective Memory Reader* (Oxford, 2011), pp. 3–62, here pp. 16–25; and Jean Christoph Marcel and Laurent Mucchielle, 'Maurice Halbwachs' mémoire collective', in Astrid Erll and Ansgar Nünning (eds), *A Companion to Cultural Memory Studies* (Berlin, 2008), pp. 141–50.

12 Olick, Vinitzky-Seroussi and Levy, 'Introduction', pp. 18–19. For a fitting example of culturally induced intergenerational misremembering, see Harald Welzer, Sabine Moller and Karoline Tschuggnall, *'Opa war kein Nazi'. Nationalsozialismus und Holocaust im Familiengedächtnis* (Frankfurt, 2002).

13 See especially Mannheim's 1929 bestseller *Ideologie und Utopie* (Frankfurt, 1995) [1929].

14 David Kettler and Volker Meja, 'Karl Mannheim and the Sociology of Knowledge', in G. Ritzer and B. Smart (eds), *Handbook of Social Theory* (London, 2001), pp. 100–11.

15 Mannheim, *Wissenssoziologie*, pp. 542, 550.

16 Ibid., pp. 544, 548. Mannheim deploys a number of terms traversing the spectrum from generation as objectively given to subjectively experienced/ constructed, including 'Generationslagerung' (generational location), 'Generationszusammenhang' (generational cohesion), 'Generationseinheit' (generational subunit), 'Generationsstil' (generational style), and 'Generationsentelechie' (generational entelechy).

17 Pierre Nora, *Les lieux de mémoire*, 3 vols (Paris, 1997 and 1998), vol. 1.

18 Jan Assmann, *Cultural Memory and Early Civilization: Writing, Remembrance, and Political Imagination* (Cambridge, 2011), pp. 34–7.

19 Daniel Levy and Natan Sznaider, *Holocaust and Memory in the Global Age* (Philadelphia, 2005), esp. pp. 23–38.

20 Judith Burnett, *Generations: The Time Machine in Theory and Practice* (Farnham, 2010), p. 42 and passim.

21 Bude, *Deutsche Karrieren: Lebenskonstruktionen sozialer Aufsteiger aus der Flakhelfer-Generation* (Frankfurt, 1987).

22 Pierre Nora, 'La generation', in Nora (ed.), *Les lieux de mémoire*, vol. 2 (Paris, 1997), pp. 2975–3015, here p. 2978.

23 Nina Leonard, 'Generationenforschung', in Christian Gudehus, Ariane Eichenberg and Harald Welzer (eds), *Gedächtnis und Erinnerung: Ein interdisziplinäres Handbuch* (Stuttgart, 2010), pp. 327–36, here p. 335.

24 Weigel, 'Family, Phantoms and the Discourse of "Generations"', pp. 133–4.

25 Pierre Bourdieu, *Homo Academicus* (Stanford, 1988); and Bourdieu, *The Field of Cultural Production: Essays on Art and Literature* (Cambridge, 1993).

26 Bourdieu, *The Field of Cultural Production*, esp. pp. 52–71 and passim.

27 Bourdieu, *Outline of a Theory of Practice* (Cambridge, 1977), p. 78.

28 June Edmunds/Bryan Turner, *Generations, Culture and Society* (Buckingham, 2002), p. 15.

29 Beate Fietze, *Historische Generationen: Über einen sozialen Mechanismus kulturellen Wandels und kollektiver Kreativität* (Bielefeld, 2009), p. 40.

30 Therefore some proponents of generational analysis conclude that the category can only be applied with precision in the aftermath of particularly violent and disruptive events, see, for example, Bude, *Deutsche Karrieren: Lebenskonstruktionen sozialer Aufsteiger aus der Flakhelfer-Generation* (Frankfurt, 1987), p. 36.

31 On trauma as a category of cultural studies and memory studies see Jeffrey Alexander et al. (eds), *Cultural Trauma and Collective Identity* (Berkeley, 2004); and Roger Luckhurst, *The Trauma Question* (London, 2008).

32 For a critique of the trauma paradigm, see, for example, Anne Rothe, *Popular Trauma Culture: Selling the Pain of Others in the Media* (New Brunswick, 2011), and Wulf Kansteiner and Harald Weilnböck, 'Against the Concept of Cultural Trauma or How I Learned to Love the Suffering of Others without the Help of Psychotherapy', in Astrid Erll, Ansgar Nünning (eds), *Cultural Memory Studies: An International and Interdisciplinary Handbook* (New York, 2008), pp. 229–40.

33 Burnett, *Generations*, 16.

34 Jay Winter, *Sites of Memory, Sites of Mourning: The Great War in European Cultural History* (Cambridge, 1995).

35 Robert Wohl, *The Generation of 1914* (London, 1980), pp. 210, 237.

36 Richard Bessel, 'The "Front Generation" and the Politics of Weimar Germany', in Roseman (ed.), *Generations in Conflict*, pp. 121–36, here pp. 133, 135.

37 Jürgen Reulecke, 'The Battle for the Young: Mobilising Young People in Wilhelmine Germany', in Roseman (ed.), *Generations in Conflict*, pp. 92–104, here pp. 102–3.

38 Hans-Ulrich Wehler, 'Wolfgang J. Mommsen 1930–2004'. *Geschichte und Gesellschaft* 31 (2005), 135–42, here p. 135. Wehler's extraordinarily frank remarks were made in the inherently nostalgic and emotionally charged genre of the 'Nachruf' (obituary) but they correspond to similar remarks in his social history, see Wehler, *Deutsche Gesellschaftsgeschichte*, vol. 5 (Munich 2008), p. 187.

39 Harold Marcuse, *Legacies of Dachau: The Uses and Abuses of a Concentration Camp, 1933–2001* (Cambridge, 2001), p. 291.

40 Burnett, *Generations*, p. 49.

41 Ulrike Jureit, *Generationenforschung* (Göttingen, 2006).

42 Ulrich Herbert, *Best: Biographische Studien über Radikalismus, Weltanschauung und Vernunft 1903–1989* (Bonn, 1996), pp. 42–5, also pp. 282–3; Michael Wildt, *Generation des Unbedingten: Das Führungskorps des Reichssicherheitshauptamtes* (Hamburg, 2002), p. 848 (available in English as *An Uncompromising Generation: The Nazi Leadership of the Reich Security Main Office*, trans. by Tom Lampert (Madison, 2010)).

43   Burnett, *Generations*, p. 35 and passim.

44   Wildt, *Generation des Unbedingten*, pp. 22–3, 137.

45   Ibid., p. 848.

46   Ibid., p. 847.

47   Ibid., p. 45.

48   In both contexts Wildt uses the term 'Erfahrungsdifferenz' (pp. 45, 68). The gender limits of the generational habitus also become obvious when Wildt briefly discusses the wives of the RSHA perpetrators (pp. 190–203).

49   Wildt, *Generation des Unbedingten*, pp. 137–42.

50   Ibid., pp. 415, 451, 532, 634, and especially p. 846.

51   At some point during his research Wildt encountered an interesting control group whose profile and actions unfortunately do not lend support to his analytical model. The leading staff members of the division V of the RSHA, the department of the criminal police, turned out to be significantly older on average than their peers in other RSHA divisions. Almost half of the leaders of division V was born before 1900, already served as police officers before the Nazis came to power, joined the party after 1933, and, for several years thereafter, retained church memberships. Wildt very appropriately concludes, however, that 'none of this means in the least that the leaders of division V were any lesser perpetrators' (p. 311).

52   Roseman, 'Generation Conflict and German History', p. 28.

53   For the shift from causality to representation that accompanies the paradigmatic transition from history to memory see also Kansteiner, 'Finding Meaning in Memory'. *History & Theory* 41 (2002), pp. 179–97.

54   Marcuse, *Legacies of Dachau*, p. 291.

55   Wulf Kansteiner, *In Pursuit of German Memory: History, Television, and Politics after Auschwitz* (Athens, Ohio, 2006), pp. 77–81 and passim.

56   Marcuse, *Legacies of Dachau*, pp. 291, 294.

57   Ibid., p. 74.

58   Ibid., pp. 327, 372.

59   Ibid., p. 203.

60   See, for instance, Stuart Taberner and Karina Berger (eds), *Germans as Victims in the Literary Fiction of the Berlin Republic* (Rochester, 2009), and compare to Marcuse, *Legacies of Dachau*, pp. 382, 402–6.

61   That integration would have required an explicitly developed psychological model concerning the correlation between social experience and the evolution of political attitudes in early adulthood. Any such explicitly acknowledged model would have smacked of psychohistory and might have been received critically by a historical profession that has held a decidedly negative view of psychohistorical explanation since the 1980s.

62   Heinz Bude, 'Soziologie der Generationen', in Georg Kneer and Markus Schroer (eds), *Handbuch spezielle Soziologien* (Wiesbaden, 2010), pp. 421–36, here p. 432.

63   Marianne Hirsch, *Family Frames: Photography, Narrative, and Postmemory* (Cambridge, MA, 1997), p. 22.

64   Marianne Hirsch, 'Surviving Images: Holocaust Photographs and the Work of Postmemory'. *The Yale Journal of Criticism* 14:1 (2001), 5–37, here p. 12.

65   Marianne Hirsch, 'The Generation of Postmemory'. *Poetics Today* 29:1 (2008), 103–28, here pp. 114–15.

66   Kansteiner and Weinböck, 'Against the Concept of Cultural Trauma', and, more subdued, Kansteiner and Weinböck, 'Provincializing Trauma? A Case Study of Family Violence, Media Reception, and Transcultural Memory'. *Journal of Literary Theory* 6:1 (2012), 149–75.

67   Claus Leggewie, *Die 89er: Portrait einer Generation* (Hamburg, 1995), esp. pp. 302–5.

68   Consider in this context Barbara Fietze's contention that the rise of self-conscious political generations depends on structural compatibilities and partial amalgamations between individual-biographical and collective-historical concepts of time (Fietze, *Historische Generationen*, p. 241).

69   Lutz Niethammer, 'Die letzte Gemeinschaft: Über die Konstruierbarkeit von Generationen und ihre Grenzen', in Bernd Weisbrod (ed.), *Historische Beiträge zur Generationsforschung* (Göttingen, 2009), pp. 13–38, here pp. 37–8.

Further reading

Pierre Bourdieu, *The Field of Cultural Production: Essays on Art and Literature* (Cambridge, 1993).

Judith Burnett, *Generations: The Time Machine in Theory and Practice* (Farnham, 2010).

June Edmunds/Bryan Turner, *Generations, Culture and Society* (Buckingham, 2002).

Beate Fietze, *Historische Generationen: Über einen sozialen Mechanismus kulturellen Wandels und kollektiver Kreativität* (Bielefeld, 2009).

Marianne Hirsch, 'The Generation of Postmemory'. *Poetics Today* 29:1 (2008), 103–28.

Ulrike Jureit, *Generationenforschung* (Göttingen, 2006).

Nina Leonard, 'Generationenforschung', in Christian Gudehus, Ariane Eichenberg, Harald Welzer (eds), *Gedächtnis und Erinnerung: Ein interdisziplinäres Handbuch* (Stuttgart, 2010), 327–36.

Karl Mannheim, 'Das Problem der Generationen'. *Kölner Vierteljahreshefte für Soziologie* 7 (1928), 157–85, 309–30; online at: http://www.1000dokumente. de/pdf/dok_0100_gen_de.pdf.

Mark Roseman (ed.), *Generations in Conflict: Youth Revolt and Generation Formation in Germany 1770–1968* (Cambridge, 1995).

Sigrid Weigel, 'Family, Phantoms and the Discourse of "Generations" as a Politics of the Past: Problems of Provenance – Rejecting and Longing for Origins', in Stefan Berger (ed.), *Narrating the Nation* (New York, 2010), 133–50.

Robert Wohl, *The Generation of 1914* (London, 1980).

CHAPTER SIX

Writing the history of national memory

Stefan Berger and Bill Niven

Introduction

'We must respect the multiplicity of ways in which the past is performed in our societies, and, in our scholarship, work to make such performances as honest and accurate as we can. Above all, we must acknowledge that we too engage in a kind of performance. In all our writing . . . we unfold the past to the public, to our readers, and ask them to go with us on a voyage of the mind. Recognising that it is a voyage, and a shared voyage at that, will not only enhance our scholarship, but also make it more imbedded in, and more responsible to, the world in which we live.'[1] Jay Winter, one of the foremost historians of the memory of the First World War, speaking in the first person plural for historians in general, warns his fellow historians with these words not to overstate the divide between memory and history and to accept that their histories, however much they must strive to be 'honest and accurate', contain subjective elements which have a lot to do with subjective memories of the historians who are speaking.

In this chapter we would like to expand on this theme by exploring the diverse ways in which memory has been related to history and by asking specifically to what extent histories of memory have impacted on the writing of national histories from the nineteenth century to the present day. We will trace the recent boom in nationalism and national identity studies back to the 1980s and ask about its impact on the constitution of the relationship between national memory, national history and national identity. Under the impact of postmodernism, national memories have not only multiplied, but they have also become much more diverse. In addition, the foregrounding of spatial and non-spatial 'others' (e.g. regional or European memories as well as class, religious, ethnic/racial or gender memories) as well as the blurring of the borders between national memory and national history, we shall argue, had by the 2000s produced a deep crisis of national master narratives, which in turn has led to various attempts by nation states to strengthen national history as a means to provide a greater sense of national cohesion and togetherness. This tension produced by the parallel developments of the dissolution of fixed national memories and the attempt to recreate them have led to a strong politicization of the history of national memory. This can be observed both in history politics and in the importance attached to 'anniversarism'.

The relationship between history, memory and the nation

The rise of history as a professional discipline in the nineteenth century was intimately connected with the rise of the idea of the modern nation.[2] History became national history and the task of the historian was to compile this history as truthfully as possible, using a particular methodology and training that would make professional historians speak about the past with a special authority unrivalled by novelists or anyone else speaking about this past. The past was to be reconstructed out of the sources that came from that past, and although historians realized from early on that only fragments of this past survived, and that it was difficult to talk about the past without taking into account the particular normative, political perspective of the historian in the present and without accounting for the historian's own subjective memories, the aim remained, in Leopold von Ranke's famous words, to extinguish the historian's self, or, in Jules Michelet's equally famous words, to breathe the past through the dust of the archives and to reconstitute that past as objectively and truthfully as possible.[3]

Professional history distinguished itself from personal or collective memory in that it was neither selective nor subjective. Perspectivity in historical writing was accepted as early as Johann Martin Chladenius (1710–59),[4] but even where it was accepted (and it was by no means accepted everywhere), the idea was to declare this perspectivity from the outset and then still try to be as balanced in one's judgement as possible. Partisanship in historical writing was much less accepted, except for Marxist-Leninist scholarship where partisanship for the leading Communist Party and its alleged representation of working-class interests was perceived to be in line with historical objectivity.[5] But professional historians of all political and theoretical persuasions tended to perceive memory as the 'other' of history – characterized precisely by its selectivity and its subjectivity. Or, to put it another way, history was perceived as the methodologically objectified memory of larger collectives, in the nineteenth century especially nations. Historians did not doubt that nations had forms of collective national memory. Take, for example, Ernest Renan and his famous lecture on 'what is a nation', where he argued that 'the possession in common of a rich legacy of memories' was the precondition for the formation of national identity.[6] And who better to objectify this memory than the professional historian, who, through his professionalism could draw a distinction between the merely subjective memory of individuals and collectives, the false collective memory peddled by historically untrained amateurs and the true national memory as authenticated by history. Most nineteenth-century national histories, conceptualized as national master narratives, were in effect seeking to authenticate the national memory in the singular.[7]

The first major theoretician of collective memory in the twentieth century and a kind of intellectual father figure of all historians of memory today, Maurice Halbwachs, confirmed this juxtaposition between memory and history. Collective memory, while it was based on the past, had a very different function from history. Collective memory came in the plural – there were as many collective memories as there were groups within society, but history, Halbwachs argued, always came in the singular. The historian, he insisted, was after all 'not located within the viewpoint of any genuine and living groups of the past or present'.[8] Halbwachs thus confirmed the nineteenth-century historist desire to find a more truthful perspective than the one provided by competing collective memories.

Halbwachs was loosely associated with the Annales circle of French historians in the interwar period, but his concern with collective memory as the basis of collective identity, including national identity, was not picked up in a major way until the 1980s, when Pierre Nora turned national memory into a major concern for historians, first in France and then worldwide.[9] Nora, like Halbwachs, started from the assumption of a clear difference between national history and national memory. History started where the living and organic memory of a collective had stopped. For Nora, a unified collective memory of the French was under threat by the 1980s. The nation seemed to him to have come apart at the seams with too many different sectional interests and groups underpinning and promoting different and often mutually incompatible forms of national memory. The end of a unified collective national memory, he argued, had led to the demise of the French national master narrative; French history could no longer be narrated from a standpoint that would unify and homogenize the different groups and interests. In response, Nora came up with an ingenious idea: national history could be rewritten as the history of national memory. Historians had to trace the places or 'realms of memory' ('lieux de mémoire') that were constitutive of the nation. In seven volumes, all under his direction, he tried to provide the French nation with a canon of its realms of memory. As Benoît Majerus exemplifies in his chapter to this book, Nora's concept was adopted by and adapted to many different national contexts in Europe throughout the 1990s and 2000s.[10]

There is a striking correlation between the willingness to reconstitute the national history through a codification of histories of national memory and the relative instability of national master narratives. Where the latter have been particularly contested, rivalled, fractured or divided, as in countries like France, Belgium, Germany, Austria and Italy, Nora's notion of memory realms was eagerly picked up, whereas in countries where the national master narrative was relatively stable and uncontested, such as in Britain or Sweden, we do not find 'lieux de mémoire'-type projects. Nevertheless, as Lutz Niethammer has recently argued, the 'realms of memory' concept might have one key advantage over the 'identity' concept in that identity is essentially defined through exclusion of 'others', while 'realms of memory' are more open, plural and allow for greater contestation.[11]

What Nora is to France, in terms of establishing national memory studies, Jan and Aleida Assmann are to Germany. As an Egyptologist and an archaeologist, Jan Assmann had no particular interest in the national dimension of memory studies. In fact, he came to Halbwachs and to memory through his interest in religion and religious identity.[12] It was his theoretical interest in the concept of memory that made him and his wife, the literary scholar Aleida Assmann, pen a range of seminal books and articles which also deeply influenced historical conceptions of national memory.[13] Jan Assmann's distinction between 'communicative memory', ranging up to 100 years and associated with the memory of the living, and 'cultural memory', which is based on various forms of memorialization and can last for centuries, has been reproduced in endless histories of memory. And Aleida Assmann's many explorations of the forms and functions of cultural memory across a wide variety of different arts and histories have rightly acquired the status of canonical texts. Their subtle and complex conceptualization of the relationship between memory and history has been an inspiration to many historians of memory. And yet, Jan Assmann's idea of 'cultural memory', like Nora's postulate of 'lieux de mémoire', can easily be misconstrued as an attempt to homogenize memorial processes in society. Arguably, Jan Assmann himself has been very much aware of this. He has repeatedly warned against overemphasizing any notion of consensus underlying the idea of collective identity. The contestation of any social reproduction of the past, according to Assmann, has to be the starting point of any exploration of collective memory. And yet, what are we to make of the following statement?

> The concept of cultural memory comprises that body of reusable texts, images, and rituals specific to each society in each epoch, whose "cultivation" seems to stabilize and convey that society's self-image. Upon such collective knowledge, for the most part (but not exclusively) of the past, each group bases its awareness of unity and particularity.[14]

Can it really be said that societies ever had a self-image in the singular? Was there ever any agreement about the body of reusable texts, images and rituals that were supposed to be part of the collective memorialization of nationally constituted societies? Memory does not only unite, it also divides, and different conceptualizations of history stand for different cultures of memorialization in any one given society. As Christopher L. Hill has recently reminded us, the past has been an important resource in memory discourses, in order to situate particular projects, such as nation-building, in the framework and under the new conditions of modernity.[15] It has been all too easy to slip into assumptions of a unified collective memory, and this has also been a danger that histories of collective memory have to guard against. As we shall argue in the following, the constructivist turn in nationalism and national identity studies was a great help in this respect.

New perspectives on national identity and nationalism studies since the 1980s and its impact on memory studies

Nora's idea of using notions of collective national memory in order to reinvent a canon of national history fell in the same decade as a new boom in histories of nationalism and national identity. This boom took its starting point from the publication of three highly influential books, published between the early 1980s and the early 1990s. John Breuilly's *Nationalism and the State* was influenced by Weberian notions of power relationships and their impact on nationalist ideologies and movements.[16] Breuilly essentially argued that it was state power which promoted nationalism and made it a force to be reckoned with in nineteenth- and twentieth-century politics. Taking up ideas of Ernest Gellner,[17] he linked notions of nationalism to forms of capitalist modernization in which states played a crucial role in nineteenth-century Europe.

The second important intervention came from Benedict Anderson. In his book *Imagined Communities*, Anderson offers a far more culturalist interpretation of nationalism.[18] Emphasizing the importance of print capitalism to the initial spread of nationalism, Anderson argued that nations hung together not because their inhabitants had anything real in common but because they were presented with imagined commonalities, but the imagining was not necessarily a top-down state-driven process. Instead it was rooted in the midst of civil society and nascent national movements.

Anderson's argument was congenial to the third important publication in the realm of nationalism studies, Eric Hobsbawm's and Terence Ranger's *The Invention of Tradition*, which, like Anderson's book, stressed the elements of construction in national traditions.[19] Even authors such as Anthony D. Smith, who has been more willing than others to lend credence to the thought that nations cannot be invented out of nothing, has left no doubt that much of national collective identity has been constructed.[20] This constructivist turn of nationalism studies, in its culturalist or power-political variants, led to innumerable studies across Europe and the wider world emphasizing the invention and construction of national traditions. The Berlin exhibition *Myths of the Nations*, curated by Monika Flacke for the German Historical Museum in 1998, can be seen as an example of how much this paradigm influenced not only professional history writing but also the wider, more popular perception of national history.[21]

Overall, we can see that an important departure for the revival of nationalism studies since the 1980s was built on assumptions that collective national identity is not a given, perennial and unchanging value but that it is constructed and in its constructedness forever fragmented, contested and changing. National history as an important part of national identity was perceived as equally constructed, contested and part and parcel of a perennial power game over which constructions of the past gained hegemony over others.

These perspectives from nationalism studies brought history and memory much closer together and made earlier juxtapositions look far more dubious. National memory just as much as national history now appeared as constructed and invented with memories, myths and histories all being located on an interconnected sliding scale of appropriations of the past. Under these premises, the writing of national memory became not so much a way of reconstituting a unified national history as a means of showing up the contestation and plurality of constructions of national pasts.

From the history of the one national memory to the history of the many sub-national memories

This move from homogeneous understandings of national memory to heterogeneous, mutually contradictory and pluralist understandings of national memory counteracted Nora's ingenious reinvention of national history through memory. Many historians writing on national memory now wanted to contribute to a higher self-reflexivity about the constructed or even invented nature of national identity. Many historical studies on national memories no longer contributed to the reformulation of national master narratives; rather, they undermined them. They encouraged a kaleidoscopic understanding of nation, according to which a variety of different perspectives on the nation produced many different memories and understandings of national history. One turn of the kaleidoscope and the pieces of the puzzle fell into an entirely different but equally beautiful order. Take, for example, the recent comparative study by Patrick Finney on how national historiographies, guided by collective memories, constructed the road to the Second World War in ways which had a decisive impact on national identities in countries such as Britain, France, Italy, Germany, Japan and the United States. Finney's book emphasizes how 'history, identity and memory are bound up together in a shifting discursive relationship, constantly feeding off and speaking to each other'.[22] Memory histories have not only undermined notions of homogeneous national narratives, but have also exploded the idea of the one history by showing that the distinction between memory and history, maintained so strongly ever since Halbwachs first put collective memory onto the map of historians, was arbitrary. The border between history and memory, as a result, became more and more blurred.

The net results of these developments were two-fold: first, particularist groups within the nation wrote their histories seeking to reinforce their identities within the nation. This was true especially for ethnic or national minorities, for the working classes and for women. In so far as these particular histories were at odds with existing homogenizing national master narratives, they further undermined those narratives. Gender historians have argued convincingly that national memory has been highly gendered for a very long time. The most active elements in national master narratives tended to be male, whereas women at best played a symbolical role for national memory. While historians of women have managed to foreground the role of women in national pantheons across Europe, historians of gender have shown how national master narratives were often framed around the duality of male strength and the female need for protection. The representation of women in national memorial cultures has been investigated over recent years.[23] Existing studies have underlined that, in political allegories, in war and other forms of collective violence and in the role of the family for the welfare of nations, women always played a crucial role for national memory cultures. Hence the examination of national memorial cultures under gender aspects has certainly enriched our knowledge about the workings of national memory.[24]

National memories were not only fractured by issues of gender. Concerns of ethnicity and race were perhaps even more important in undermining notions of homogeneous national master narratives. Thus many ethnic minorities found themselves not at all represented by existing national master narratives, and so set about reconstructing themselves as ethnic/racial groups with their own collective memories. From the Saamis in Scandinavia to the Jews of Europe, from a variety of national minorities in nation states across the world to the hyphenated identities of migrants in settler societies from the United States to Canada and Australia, ethnicity and race came to fracture national master narratives. It is, however, interesting to note how many of these ethnic histories were themselves prone to producing homogenized notions of collective memory for their particular group. While histories of Scandinavian nations have been increasingly willing to concede that the collective memory of their nations excluded the Saamis for a very long time, they nevertheless tend to homogenize the Saami collective memory – a tendency fostered by a nascent Saami national history based on the construction of a fairly homogeneous Saami collective memory.[25] The same development can be observed in Norman Davies' history of the 'Isles', a national history of Britain which explodes the myths of a unified national memory and instead posits the existence of four national memories. But whereas the English construction of Britain is deconstructed, the Welsh, Scottish and Irish national memory is too often taken at face value.[26]

Furthermore, unified histories of national memories were increasingly undermined by explorations on how religion underpinned but also divided national master narratives. Historians of religion pointed out how secular national memories had been locked into battle with religious ones, how different denominational narratives shaped national memories and resulted in rival national memories. In Poland and Spain, historians could point to the symbiotic relationship between Catholicism and constructions of national identity. Similar arguments could be made about Lutheranism and national identity in Scandinavia or Orthodoxy and national identity in Romania and Russia. In confessionally divided nation states, such as Germany or Switzerland, confessional national master narratives were based on different collective memories within one and the same nation state. Almost everywhere, secular national master narratives struggled with and against religiously infused ones. And the very concept of national identity, was, as Anthony D. Smith has shown, built on Judeo-Christian principles of 'chosen peoples'.[27]

Last, but by no means least, class, or to be more precise, the division of society into diverse social classes, has also undermined assumptions about collective national memories underpinning homogeneous national identities. Memories of class and histories of class constructed alternative national master narratives rather than rejecting those national narratives altogether, but they nevertheless constituted rival cultural memories, highlighting the contested character of national memory and national history. Under the influence of neo-Marxism, class histories in the 1960s and 1970s, across the Western world, produced cultural memories of class which fractured existing national master narratives.[28]

Historians of memory, then, in their exploration of issues of gender, ethnicity/race, religion and class, have contributed significantly to a re-evaluation of the whole idea of homogeneous national memories and histories. Many studies on national memory came to the conclusion that the concept of 'collective memory' in the singular was unsustainable.[29] The more the official memorial culture of nations was challenged by diverse public memories coming from the midst of a highly diverse civil society, the more it became impossible to write a unitary history of national memory. Totalizing visions of the nation gave way to kaleidoscopic ones.

This was particularly marked in the USA, where histories of national memory almost disappeared behind the many hyphenated histories that established and foregrounded the memory of collectives below the national level.[30] The many divisions of national memory were also highlighted in the case of Israel by Yael Zerubavel who contrasted a 'master commemorative narrative' of the Israeli past with several counter-memories challenging this master narrative from the perspective of various marginalized positions. National memory and national history thus become a prime site of contestation over different ideas of the nation.[31]

The fall of Communism in Eastern Europe after 1989 provided several prominent examples both of the fracturing of notions of collective national memories and of attempts to reify those collective memories.[32] The peaceful break-up of Czechoslovakia provided a relatively benign example of the fracturing of constructions of a Czechoslovak memory in favour of reified Czech and Slovak memories, respectively.[33] Far less benign was the splintering of notions of collective memory in Yugoslavia, where Yugoslavism, arguably never particularly strong, gave way to virulent exclusivist and violent constructions of national memories in the individual republics constituting Yugoslavia. The Yugoslav civil war was to a considerable extent the direct outcome of such attempts to construct homogeneous national memories at the level of the previous Yugoslav republics.[34] The splintering of the Soviet collective memory and the accompanying reification of unified collective memories in newly independent nation states in post-Soviet space mirror the processes which led to the explosion of Yugoslav collective memory.

The latter example from Eastern Europe draws our attention to the fact that previously homogeneous histories of national memory were threatened not only by non-spatial memories of class, religion, ethnicity/race and gender, but also by rival spatial memories. This phenomenon was not restricted to Eastern Europe. In fact, the examples of Britain, Spain and Belgium in Western Europe also show clearly how the reification of regional memories as unified national memories has gone hand in hand with the questioning of constructions of homogeneous national memories on the level of the composite nation state. As we already referred to Britain above, we can perhaps take a closer look here at the examples of Spain and Belgium.

In Spain, no subject has been given greater attention than the memory of the civil war and its role in the reconstitution of the Spanish national master narrative after the transition from Francoism to democracy.[35] Those who masterminded that transition attempted consciously to draw lessons from the memory of the civil war in order to avoid a repetition of history and the collapse of the peaceful transition into another clash of opposing political cultures. While this was by and large successful, it also came at a price; on the one hand, many of the gruesome episodes of the civil war had to remain under the carpet, and it is only within the last 10 years that research has been trying to deal with the many skeletons still in the cupboard. And in the wake of the transition, regionalisms raised their head as new nationalisms, so that not only in Catalonia but in other regions of Spain as well, memory discourses now serve directly the purpose of nation-building below the level of the Spanish state.[36] It is characteristic that much of that nation-building jumps directly from sub-state national history and memory to Europe.[37] National memory discourses in places such as Catalonia, the Basque Country, Flanders and Scotland are inextricably linked with the commitment to European memory landscapes, conveniently forgetting about the Spanish, Belgian and British nation state as a locus for an altogether different memory discourse. In Belgium, the ethnic master narrative of the Flemish population has for some time now been threatening the unity of the Belgian nation state. While Henri Pirenne's masterly narrative of the history of Belgium from the interwar period, stressing the telos of the country as bridge between Germanic and Romanic cultures, is out of print, Flemish memory histories are intent on constructing a Flemish national history that has little in common with the Walloon part of Belgium.[38]

The challenges, both non-spatial and spatial, to ideas of homogeneous national memories and histories that we discussed above produced notable counter-reactions in a number of nation states. For a start, historians were unwilling to let go of the established distinction between memory and history, as this would have made it impossible to carve out any claim of a higher authority or even of intersubjective validation for professional historians when speaking about the past. In many parts of the world, where historians were still willing to make themselves the prophets of the nation, such authority was important to legitimate their particular national master narratives. But, perhaps even more importantly, historians unwilling to accept such abuse of their professionalism still felt that precisely their professionalism needed some way of distinguishing between memory and history. They were deeply influenced by Paul Ricoeur's call on historians to understand their profession as one that can support, correct or refute collective memories. Through archival work, explanation and interpretation, historical knowledge, itself forever subject to revisions and rewritings, can, according to Ricoeur, provide a more truthful perspective on the past than collective memories.[39] Ricoeur's important work on history and memory sought to re-enforce the boundaries of the profession that had become all too porous in the 1990s.

And politically, the question moved to the fore as to how national solidarities could be sustained, if national memories and histories were entirely dissolved into a plurality of incompatible and contested group identities. This question acquired a much sharper edge under the impact of three different political developments. First, the emergence of new nation states in the post-Communist societies of East-Central and Eastern Europe led to a revival of homogeneous national master narratives as discussed above.[40] The frantic search for a 'normal' national identity in the reunified Germany was ultimately to produce a new national master narrative in the form of Heinrich August Winkler's *The Long Road West*. Here the story of the modern German nation was retold through the lens of a prominent normalization discourse, that is, the notion that 'national normality' for the Germans had only become possible after 1990, when the democratic political consciousness of the West Germans could unite with acceptance of a unified German nation state legitimated by the democratic revolution of the East Germans.[41]

Secondly, the declaration of 'ever closer political union' among the member states of the European Union and the resistance this provoked within individual member states also produced tensions between, on the one hand, the move to transnational histories and their supranational memory cultures and, on the other hand, the re-enforcement of national histories and their localized memory cultures. Transnational processes, such as Europeanization and globalization, perceived as an opportunity for highly mobile, educated elites, is seen as a threat by the vast majority of locally, that is, nationally rooted people in Europe and elsewhere. At a time when the European Union is conceptualizing a house of European history virtually in secret, without public debate and discussion, it is exactly a debate surrounding the content and contestations of a European historical memory which could inject the European project with new life and vigour.[42] So far, transnational European memory cultures only exist among small sections of the population. It needs, in order for those memory cultures to become more widespread, more public controversy and more public debate about the historical contents of those memory cultures. Some scholars have begun to call for a more thorough examination of memory discourses in an increasingly globalized world and have warned about restricting these discourses to the national or even European realm.[43] Events such as the Holocaust, the Second World War and the transitions from dictatorship to democracy do indeed have the potential to become part and parcel of a globalized memory discourse. The Holocaust is perhaps the one event in twentieth-century history which has come closest to a concrete event in history that is discussed in global terms and has been able to set global standards.[44] And yet, despite such moves towards transnational, potentially global memory cultures, the overwhelming evidence is that memory cultures across Europe remain highly nationalized.[45]

Finally, in the wake of the 9/11 attacks on the United States and the global rise of Islamic and religious fundamentalism, the idea of multiculturalism has come in for a good deal of sustained criticism across the Western world. It is no longer widely upheld as a panacea for increasingly heterogeneous societies in Europe. In fact, many nation states have adopted measures to strengthen common national identities. Popular among them was the introduction of guidelines for the teaching of national history at school, which stressed the importance of national memory for creating national cohesion. It would appear that a new search is on for the construction of national memory via histories that can create a sense of national solidarities across increasingly diverse citizens.[46]

Developments therefore seem to have come full circle: we started with scholarship that used memory theory to retell unified national histories and we have seen how scholarship moved away from this to use memory theory to undermine the notion of unified national histories only to find that there has been a revival in attempts to construct national memories as basis of national histories that can hold nationally constituted societies together. Altogether, all of these developments demonstrate the strong link between national politics, national memory and national history. This link can be seen most clearly in the importance of what one might term anniversarism and in the politics of memory which is associated with it.

Anniversarism, 'founding moments' and national memory

The term 'anniversarism' we use here to refer to the tendency to actualize national memory around anniversaries. Each nation has its own mental historical calendar, on which the days, months or years considered significant for national history are marked. Celebrating, or mourning, the associated past events at regular annual, biannual, quinquennial or decennial intervals – the usual patterns – has long served as a way of rallying the nation around whichever national self-image is enshrined and evoked in the rituals of anniversarial remembrance. Often, such anniversaries cluster around what are envisioned as 'founding' moments in the history of a nation: Bastille Day in the case of France, for instance, or the 4th of July in the United States. The national project requires, it seems, the anthropomorphic notion of a point of birth or emergence – or, following catastrophe, the divine one of rebirth or re-emergence.[47] For countries such as Germany, with its volatile twentieth-century history, the concept of a 'founding moment', while retaining its appeal, has been subject to reinterpretation over time. Anniversary celebrations such as the Day of Sedan, associated with German victory in the 1870 Franco-Prussian war, or the 'Memorial Day for the Movement' which focused on Nazi 'martyrdom' in the 1923 Munich Putsch, were unthinkable after 1945. Yet not all dates or symbols loaded with national significance from the pre-1945 era were rejected. It was often more a question of reframing.

Take, for example, the anniversary of the Battle in the Teutoburg forest in 9 AD, where Germanic tribes defeated Roman legions. Nationalists in Germany, historians among them, had long celebrated this event as confirmation of the superiority of the German over the Roman nations. The monument to the victor, known as 'Hermann, der Cherusker', or by his Roman name, Arminius, which still stands today, was inaugurated in 1875 to underline the military prowess of the German nation, its victory in 1871 over a Roman nation, the French, and its essentially Protestant and anti-Catholic character. The sword, that Hermann holds was, after all, directed against Rome. After 1945, Hermann rather went out of fashion: in the 1970s, the views of historian Dieter Timpe, who claimed that Hermann was in reality a Roman officer and hardly a popular Germanic hero, found wide circulation in West Germany.[48] Yet even if the 'Varus battle' no longer acted as focal point for aggressive nationalist sentiment, understandings of it as symbolizing the historical right of Germans to national unity continued. In the 1960s, the monument was used to stage protests against the Berlin Wall by the West German Free Democratic Party; when the 100th anniversary of its construction was celebrated in 1975, local politicians sought to interpret it as a symbol of the need for German reunification.[49] Centuries of nationalist framing of the Teutoburg forest battle came to an end in 2009, when the celebrations, for the first time ever, were focused not on Hermann but on the loser, the Roman general Varus. He had been depicted by nineteenth-century nationalist historians, like Heinrich von Treitschke, as an effeminate, incompetent and cowardly individual – in stark contrast to the manly, cunning and courageous Hermann. Now, the anniversary celebrations and the historians working towards and for them, stressed a different picture and demasked the nationalist legends that had characterized the celebrations for so long.[50] What one could observe clearly in Germany in 2009, during the Varus year celebrations, was how the impact of the higher self-reflexivity of national history produced a very different framing of national memory, which in turn contributed to a different historical understanding.

The anniversaries of foundational events for nations have a particularly strong pull for collective memory, and historians have worked tirelessly over the centuries to establish beyond reasonable doubt the validity of events at those national junctures. Over the past three decades, however, under the impact of the constructivist turn in historical writing and of national memory studies, these careful constructions of foundational moments have come undone. Historians, increasingly, seek to expose how images of a foundational moment depend on particular, often deeply questionable assumptions about what actually happened at these moments. In the case of the 'Varus Battle', for instance, as historian Kirstin Buchinger has shown in her discussion of the way it has been narrativized and remembered, we don't know for sure when the battle began, let alone the precise course of events.[51]

Informed by theories of the constructed nature of collective memory, Israeli sociologist and historian Nachman Ben-Yehuda uses the terms 'deviant belief system' and 'mythical narrative' to describe the generally accepted version within Israel of events at Masada, the isolated rock plateau in the Judean dessert (66–73 AD), which was the site of a mass suicide of its Jewish defenders who chose death rather than surrender to the besieging Roman troops. The retrospectively heroicizing view of these events as a 'revolt', which can be traced back to the times of the Yishuv, served the purpose of strengthening Jewish national resolve in the present. In fact, until recently, Israeli paratroopers took their oath of allegiance at the site of Masada. But, as Ben-Yehuda shows, such actualization does little justice to history: in his view, neither was there a revolt, nor was it Zealots who held out at Masada, but the marauding Sicarii (Jews, at the time, were split into factions).[52]

The constructed nature of foundational moments to which historians draw our attention becomes even more visible through studies which emphasize the 'updating' of commemorative frames to fit the exigencies of the present. To stay with the example of Masada: in her book on collective memory in Israel, Yael Zerubavel points out that, in the early decades of Israel's existence, the collective suicide at Masada was largely forgotten. Instead, Masada was remembered as a heroic revolt, and functioned as a 'countermetaphor' to the Holocaust, supposedly representing a 'dignified alternative to the European Jews' response to the Nazi persecution'.[53] But as the Holocaust moved more to the forefront of Israeli memory, so the collective suicide at Masada came to feature in Israeli remembrance of events there. In line with increased national identification with victimhood during the Holocaust, the commemorative focus has shifted 'from armed resistance to the Romans to the situation of utter helplessness and despair, epitomized by the suicide'.[54]

It is not necessarily the case, though, that diverging interpretations of founding moments only emerge over time. Studies which have focused on various forms of commemorative activities tend to highlight the contested nature of commemorations which can be traced back to divisions and contestations over national memory and history.[55] In recent years, for instance, a number of historical studies have appeared which explore the dichotomous character of the anniversary commemorations of 8 May 1945 in Germany, dichotomous because the day was regarded as symbolizing both liberation and defeat; overlaying this was a difference between East and West Germany, with East Germany emphasizing the positive role of the Soviets, and West Germany tending to reserve the notion of 'liberation' for the Western Allies.[56] The relative emphasis on liberation and defeat shifted back and forth over time, with the former gradually coming to dominate over the latter in commemoration. But this dominance remains contested. Anniversaries of 8 May are not merely played out at the level of high-level political ritual and speechmaking, they are often accompanied by new television films, documentaries, books and extended newspaper articles, producing a certain 'multivocality'.[57]

Undoubtedly, then, historians – inspired by insights into the complex, shifting and multifaceted character of collective memory – have recently done much to uncover not just the presentist agendas of national anniversarism as practised by high politics, but also the disputed nature of the memory and meaning of past events which is often papered over by political speechmakers in their attempts to conjure a consensual view of history. At the same time, one wonders if this thorough exploration of the instable and contested character of anniversaries, especially those of 'founding moments', is not also a celebration of this very contestedness. On the horizon of such studies, we see the notion emerging that agreeing to disagree might be a kind of umbrella under which the nation could come together to protect itself from the travails of difference. Taking this a step further, such studies imply that the ability of the nation to contain a plurality of images of the past, of histories and memories, and to mediate between them becomes the measure of its maturity.

Many national histories also have to deal with traumatic events in the past which are difficult to memorialize, for example, genocides, civil wars or revolutions. Over the past decades, studies on national memory have frequently focused on such national traumas, thereby contributing to what Jeffrey K. Olick has termed a 'responsible politics of regret' that he sees as sign of our time.[58] Some national histories share the same trauma: the Second World War, for instance, or the Holocaust. Just as the Holocaust itself has become the subject of ever more intensive research in recent years, so memory of the Holocaust has become the subject of scrutiny by scholars of all kinds, including historians.[59] Frequently, such studies point to a long reluctance to confront the topic: not just in the states which inherited the legacy of the perpetrators, East and West Germany, but also in the new state of Israel which emerged from the suffering of the Holocaust. Some studies have sought to expose the way in which countries invaded by Hitler, such as Poland and France, sought to build a postwar national identity based on memory of victimhood and resistance, occluding from view difficult questions of collusion and complicity in anti-Semitic measures. The critique of past national memory by historians appears to underpin national commemorative trends in the present towards a stance of acknowledgement of past wrongs – well evidenced, for instance, by French President Jacques Chirac's 1995 apology for the role of French policemen in the 1942 round-up of Parisian Jews (Chirac was speaking on the 53rd anniversary of the round-up). While critiquing the memorial national master narratives was an achievement of historians, then, such deconstruction has in recent years been absorbed into political acts of commemoration. While this seems laudable, one might ask whether it does not simultaneously represent an attempt to co-opt self-critical memory, raising it to the level of a new national master narrative (according to which the nation has 'learnt' from its mistakes to progress morally) and robbing it of its critical potential. Hence anniversarism might well be characterized by the same tension that is a hallmark of studies on national memory more generally – they tend to be uneasily poised between confirming national master narratives and questioning them.

More recently, scholars working on national memory have emphasized the performative character of forms of national memory and national history which is particularly visible during anniversaries, when the need for diverse forms of historical enactment is pressing. The very act of performance further dissolves the tight boundaries between national memory and national history. History and memory are both crucial to a variety of different cultural practices that constitute the past.[60] In this sense one can perhaps say that national memory has almost subsumed national history, as the latter is increasingly seen as a particular type of cultural memory.[61]

The politics of national memory – the West German historians' controversy as a case study

Anniversarism impacts vitally on national memory and history. Which anniversaries are celebrated, and how, is often connected to particular political conjunctions. The impact of politics on national history and memory can also be seen from a whole range of historical controversies. History politics is sometimes also referred to as memory politics, and the conflation of the two terms and the confusion over if and how they should be kept apart is in itself a sign how close together history and memory have moved from a position in the early twentieth century where they were still kept very much apart.

It is striking, for a start, to what an extent history/memory politics are still national in character. Most of the debates take place within nationally constituted societies, and even transnational debates, such as the one on the impact of communism or the Holocaust are conducted overwhelmingly within those national parameters. It is a clear sign of the continuing strength of the nation state as a container for collective memory in the contemporary world.

One of the most famous instances of history/memory politics was the West German historians' controversy of the mid-1980s about the singularity of the Holocaust.[62] It was started not by a historian, but by a philosopher, Jürgen Habermas, one of the best-known West German public intellectuals at the time, who accused a troika of conservative historians, Ernst Nolte, Andreas Hillgruber and Michael Stürmer, of wanting to relativize the importance of the Holocaust and of National Socialism as the anchor of West German historical identity in order to strengthen positive national feeling in West Germany. Instead Habermas insisted on the need to abandon positively accentuated national identity and replace it with postnational constitutional patriotism. In 1982 a centre-right government under Chancellor Helmut Kohl had programmatically demanded a return to more positively accentuated national history and announced plans for two national history museums in Bonn and Berlin. Michael Stürmer was a close advisor of Kohl and stressed, time and again, that German history could and should not be reduced to the 12 years of National Socialism. Nolte, who had pioneered the comparative history of fascism in the 1960s, argued in the 1980s that National Socialism was a part-legitimate response to Bolshevism, and that the Gulag preceded the Holocaust. The latter, he argued, was partly a response to Bolshevist class warfare with its millions of dead. Perhaps the most interesting case, from the perspective of memory, was that of Andreas Hillgruber. He had authored a little booklet comparing what he called 'two downfalls' (*Zweierlei Untergang*), the murder of European Jewry and the downfall of the German East. Hillgruber came from the German East and had personal and family memories of the east. He repeated the myth of the Wehrmacht defending unprotected civilians from the Soviets (when, in fact, the German military command had for far too long prevented the civilian population from evacuating the areas threatened by the Red Army), and his own personal experiences and memory of those experiences at the end of the war clearly influenced his writing.

For Habermas, all three authors were writing apologetic forms of history seeking to relativize the catastrophic civilizational break of National Socialism in the desire to move the German people back to normalized forms of positive national identity. The divide was as much political as it was historiographical – those who were close to the Social Democrats backed Habermas, those who were close to the Christian Democrats backed Nolte, Stürmer and Hillgruber. The historians' controversy was as much a debate about politics as it was about history. But insofar as it was about history, it was also about the collective memory of the Germans and the lessons the German people drew from their history. What should be memorialized, and how it should be memorialized was at the centre of the debate. And yet the debate was still very much a debate about history and its consequences for national memory. History and memory were not yet conflated, the boundaries were not yet blurred; it was a debate about the correct interpretation of history on which basis a particular national memory could develop. The idea that different forms of memorialization were just the result of different conceptualizations of history and therefore part and parcel of a pluralistic and essentially contested history and memory culture in a democratic society was not yet part of the debate.

Conclusion

The construction of collective national memories has been crucial to attempts to define national histories. The purpose of those constructions has varied over time – for many decades in the nineteenth and twentieth centuries, nation states played a crucial role in trying to shape those definitions, because it gave the elites governing those states power over their nationally constituted societies. However, they were never the only show in town. Alternative readings of the past were based on counter-memories derived from various sections of a plural civil society. Power struggles over collective memory characterized the attempts to fix memory cultures and national histories. However, as we have tried to argue, from the 1980s a more self-conscious reflection of the role of collective memory for the construction of national histories impacted massively on the historical profession. Maurice Halbwachs's theories of collective memory were picked up by Pierre Nora in order to underpin a new sense of national identity in France, while in Germany, Jan and Aleida Assmann also began to theorize the importance of memory for group identities. With the revival of nationalism and national identity studies since the 1980s, the history of national memory has become somewhat of a boom industry. As we have shown above, it has been poised uneasily between the desire to reconfirm forms of national master narratives and attempts to deconstruct those very master narratives. Its strong links to forms of anniversarism and its vital role in kick-starting debates surrounding history/memory politics showed how contested a terrain the history of national memory has been over the past 30 years in a variety of different countries around the world. The theoretical perspectives on memory have certainly been used by a variety of authors in very different ways in either underpinning or questioning dominant national master narratives.

Notes

1   Jay Winter, 'The Performance of the Past: Memory, History, Identity', in Karin Tilmans, Frank van Vree and Jay Winter (eds), *Performing the Past: Memory, History and Identity in Modern Europe* (Amsterdam, 2010), p. 21f.

2   Stefan Berger, Christoph Conrad and Guy Marchal (eds), *Writing the Nation*, 8 vols (Basingstoke, 2008–2014).

3   On Ranke, see Georg G. Iggers (ed.), *The Theory and Practice of History: Leopold von Ranke* (London, 2011); on Michelet, see Carolyn Steedman, *Dust* (Manchester, 2001).

4   On Chladenius, see Frederick C. Beisser, *The German Historicist Tradition* (Oxford, 2011), Chapter 1.

5   Heiko Feldner, 'History in the Academy: Objectivity and Partisanship in the Marxist Historiography of the German Democratic Republic', in Patrick Major and Jonathan Osmond (eds), *The Workers' and Peasants' State. Communism and Society in East Germany under Ulbricht 1945–1971* (Manchester, 2002), pp. 262–79.

6   Ernest Renan, 'What is a Nation?', in John Hutchinson and Anthony D. Smith (eds), *Nationalism: A Reader* (Oxford, 1994), p. 17.

7   Stefan Berger and Chris Lorenz (eds), *The Contested Nation. Ethnicity, Class, Religion and Gender in National Histories* (Basingstoke, 2008).

8   Maurice Halbwachs, *The Collective Memory* (New York, 1980), p. 83.

9   Pierre Nora, *Les Lieux de Mémoire* (Paris, 1984–1992); selected articles were also published in English as *Realms of Memory: Rethinking the French Past*, 3 vols, ed. by Lawrence D. Kritzman (New York, 1996–1998).

10   See the chapter by Benoît Majerus in this volume.

11   Lutz Niethammer, 'Regionale Identität – ein Plastikwort', paper given at the conference 'Zwischen Gedächtnis, Geschichte und Identitätskonstruktion: was ist ein Erinnerungsort und wie entsteht er?', Institute for Social Movements, Ruhr-Universität Bochum, 13/14 Dec. 2012.

12   Jan Assmann, *The Search for God in Ancient Egypt* (Ithaca, NY, 2001); idem, *Religion and Cultural Memory* (Stanford, California, 2006).

13   See, among many others, Jan Assmann, *Cultural Memory and Early Civilization: Writing, Remembrance and Political Imagination* (Cambridge,

2011); Aleida Assmann, *Cultural Memory and Western Civilization. Arts of Memory* (Cambridge, 2011).

14 Jan Assmann, 'Collective Memory and Cultural Identity'. *New German Critique* 65 (1995), 125–33, here p. 132.

15 Christopher L. Hill, *National History and the World of Nations: Capital, State and the Rhetoric of History in Japan, France and the United States* (Durham, NC, 2009).

16 John Breuilly, *Nationalism and the State* (Manchester, 1993).

17 Ernest Gellner, *Nations and Nationalism* (Oxford, 1983).

18 Benedict Anderson, *Imagined Communities: Reflections on the Origins and Spread of Nationalism* (London, 1983).

19 Eric Hobsbawm and Terence Ranger (eds), *The Invention of Tradition* (Cambridge, 1983).

20 Anthony D. Smith, *The Ethnic Origins of Nations* (Oxford, 1986).

21 Monika Flacke (ed.), *Mythen der Nationen: ein europäisches Panorama* (Munich, 1998). Unfortunately there is no English translation to date.

22 Patrick Finney, *Remembering the Road to World War Two. International History, National Identity, Collective Memory* (London, 2011), quote on p. 310.

23 One example among many is: Sylvia Paletschek and Sylvia Schraut (eds), *The Gender of Memory. Cultures of Remembrance in Nineteenth and Twentieth Century Europe* (Frankfurt/Main, 2008).

24 On the gendering of German national master narratives, for example, see Patricia Herminghouse and Magda Mueller (eds), *Gender and Germanness: Cultural Productions of Nation* (Oxford, 1997); Karen Hagemann and Jean H. Quataert (eds), *Gendering Modern German History: Rewriting Historiography* (Oxford, 2007).

25 Trond Thuen, 'Samis and Norwegians: Symbols of Peoplehood and Nationhood', in Tania Das Guptas (ed.), *Race and Racialization: Essential Readings* (Toronto, 2007), pp. 132–43.

26 Norman Davies, *The Isles: A History* (London, 1999); for a close analysis, see Stefan Berger, 'Rising Like a Phoenix: The Renaissance of National History Writing in Britain and Germany since the 1980s', in Stefan Berger and Chris Lorenz (eds), *Nationalizing the Past: Historians as Nation Builders in Modern Europe* (Basingstoke, 2010), pp. 426–51.

27 Anthony D. Smith, *Chosen Peoples. Sacred Sources of National Identity* (Oxford, 2003).

28 The chapters in Stefan Berger (ed.), *Writing the Nation: a Global Perspective* (Basingstoke, 2007), give many concrete examples of this trend, which was the same across all Western historiographies in the 1960s and 1970s and also inspired post-colonial historians in non-Western societies.

29 Bill Niven, 'On the Use of "Collective Memory"'. *German History* 26 (2008), 427–36.

30 On the developments of American national history since the 1980s, see in particular Thomas Bender (ed.), *Rethinking American National History*

(Berkeley, 2002); Bender was one of the main critics of the disappearance of American national history in the 1990s and wrote a much-acclaimed national history of the USA which sought to incorporate both sub- and transnational aspects of national history. See Thomas Bender, *A Nation among Nations. America's Place in World History* (New York, 2006).

31   Yael Zerubavel, *Recovered Roots: Collective Memory and the Making of Israeli National Tradition* (Chicago, 1995), pp. 10–12.

32   See also Attila Pók's contribution to this volume.

33   Michael Kraus and Allison Stanger (eds), *Irreconcilable Differences? Explaining Czechoslovakia's Dissolution* (Lanham/Maryland, 2000).

34   Wolfgang Hoepken, 'War, Memory and Education in a Fragmented Society: the Case of Yugoslavia'. *East European Politics and Societies* 13 (1999), 190–227.

35   Paloma Aguilar, *Memory and Amnesia. The Role of the Spanish Civil War in the Transition to Democracy* (Oxford, 2002).

36   Xosé Manuel Núñez Seixas, *Historiographical Approaches to Nationalism in Spain* (Saarbrücken, 1993).

37   See, for example, Josep R. Llobera, *Foundations of National Identity: From Catalonia to Europe* (Oxford, 2004).

38   Kas Deprez and Louis Vos (eds), *Nationalism in Belgium: Shifting Identities, 1780–1995* (London, 1998).

39   Paul Ricoeur, *Memory, History, Forgetting* (Chicago, 2004).

40   Sorin Antohi, Balázs Trencsényi and Péter Apor (eds), *Narratives Unbound: Historical Studies in Post-Communist Eastern Europe* (Budapest, 2007).

41   Heinrich August Winkler, *Germany: The Long Road West*, 2 vols (Oxford, 2007).

42   Claus Leggewie und Anne Lang, *Der Kampf um die europäische Erinnerung. Ein Schlachtfeld wird besichtigt* (Munich, 2011).

43   Aleida Assmann and Sebastian Conrad (eds), *Memory in a Global Age. Discourses, Practices and Trajectories* (Basingstoke, 2010).

44   Daniel Levy and Natan Sznaider, *Erinnerung im globalen Zeitalter. Der Holocaust* (Frankfurt/Main, 2001).

45   Christoph Cornelissen, 'Die Nationalität von Erinnerungskulturen als ein gesamteuropäisches Phänomen'. *Geschichte in Wissenschaft und Unterricht* 62:1/2 (2011), 5–16.

46   Maria Grever and Siep Stuurman (eds), *Beyond the Canon: History for the Twenty-First Century* (Basingstoke, 2007).

47   Gabriella Elgenius, *Symbols of Nation and Nationalism: Celebrating Nationhood* (Basingstoke, 2011).

48   See Klaus Bemmann, *Deutsche Nationaldenkmäler und Symbole im Wandel der Zeiten* (Göttingen, 2007), p. 129.

49   See W. Stölting, *1875–1975: 100 Jahre Hermannsdenkmal* (Detmold, 1976), pp. 70–2.

50   Tillmann Bendikowski, 'Mythos einer Schlacht'. *Die Zeit*, 45, 30 October 2008.

51 Kirstin Buchinger, 'Teutoburger Wald 9 n. Chr.: Der Hermannsschlacht – ein Erinnerungstag?', in Etienne Francois and Uwe Puschner (eds), *Erinnerungstage: Wendepunkte der Geschichte der Antike bis zur Gegenwart* (Munich, 2010), pp. 25–40.

52 Nachman Ben-Yehuda, *Collective Memory and Mythmaking in Israel* (Madison, 1995), esp. pp. 3–26.

53 Zeruvabel, *Recovered Roots*, p. 71.

54 Ibid., p. 192.

55 John R. Gillis, *Commemorations. The Politics of National Identity* (Princeton/ NJ, 1992).

56 Relevant studies include Peter Hurrelbrink, *Der 8. Mai 1945: Befreiung durch Erinnerung* (Bonn, 2005), and Jan-Holger Kirsch, 'Wir haben aus der Geschichte gelernt': Der 8. Mai als politischer Gedenktag (Vienna and Cologne, 2002). See also Bill Niven, *Facing the Nazi Past* (London, 2002).

57 A term used by Zeruvabel in reference to Masada, see *Recovered Roots*, p. 196.

58 Jeffrey K. Olick, *The Politics of Regret. On Collective Memory and Historical Responsibility* (New York, 2007), p. 15. On the fascinating case of Ireland see Graham Dawson, *Making Peace with the Past? Memory, Trauma and the Irish Troubles* (Manchester, 2007). From a more theoretical perspective, see also Elazar Barkan, *The Guilt of Nations: Restitution and Negotiating Historical Injustices* (Baltimore, 2001), and Melissa Nobles, *The Politics of Official Apologias* (Cambridge, 2008).

59 See Peter Carrier's chapter in this volume. Studies on memory of the Holocaust include Peter Novick, *The Holocaust and Collective Memory* (London, 1999); Jonathan Huener, *Auschwitz, Poland, and the Politics of Commemoration, 1945–1979* (Athens, Ohio, 2003); and Harold Marcuse, *Legacies of Dachau: The Uses and Abuses of a Concentration Camp, 1933–2001* (Cambridge, 2001).

60 Tilmans, van Vree and Winter (eds), *Performing the Past*.

61 Wulf Kansteiner, *In Pursuit of German Memory: History, Television and Politics after Auschwitz* (Athens, Ohio, 2006), p. 15.

62 Charles Maier, *The Unmasterable Past: History, Holocaust and German National Identity* (Cambridge/MA, 1988); Richard J. Evans, In *Hitler's Shadow: West German Historians and the Attempt to Escape from the Nazi Past* (London, 1989); Geoff Eley, 'Nazism, Politics and the Image of the Past: Thoughts on the West German Historikerstreit 1986–87'. *Past and Present* 121 (1988), 171–208.

Further reading

Benedict Anderson, *Imagined Communities: Reflections on the Origins and Spread of Nationalism* (London, 1983).

Jan Assmann, *Cultural Memory and Early Civilization: Writing, Remembrance and Political Imagination* (Cambridge, 2011).

Stefan Berger and Chris Lorenz (eds), *The Contested Nation. Ethnicity, Class, Religion and Gender in National Histories* (Basingstoke, 2008).

Eric Hobsbawm and Terence Ranger (eds), *The Invention of Tradition* (Cambridge, 1983).

Charles Maier, *The Unmasterable Past: History, Holocaust and German National Identity* (Cambridge/MA, 1988).

Pierre Nora, *Les Lieux de Mémoire* (Paris, 1984–1992).

Ernest Renan, 'What is a Nation?', in John Hutchinson and Anthony D. Smith (eds), *Nationalism: A Reader* (Oxford, 1994), pp. 17–18.

Yael Zerubavel, *Recovered Roots: Collective Memory and the Making of Israeli National Tradition* (Chicago, 1995).

CHAPTER SEVEN

Lieux de mémoire – A European transfer story

Benoît Majerus

Introduction

If an imaginary European History Academy had to choose the word of the last 20 years in historiography, then undoubtedly *lieux de mémoire* – realms of memory, or *Erinnerungsorte* in German – would be on the short list. The writings of Pierre Nora on *lieux de mémoire* have successfully created a meta-concept able to unite the growing studies on memory. Rarely has a notion coined by one person spread so rapidly through the Western academic world. But the homonym of the translations can be treacherous, hiding a heterogeneity of meanings. The following chapter tries to answer three questions. In which intellectual context did the original *lieux de mémoire* emerge? What was the discursive subtext of the whole enterprise? And how was the theoretical frame translated into practice? In a second step, I will try to trace the European success of the concept by analysing how the French paradigm of *lieux de mémoire* was introduced into other national historiographic traditions.

French spaces

The *lieux de mémoire* project developed during an academic course organized by Pierre Nora in the late 1970s at the École des Hautes Etudes en Sciences Sociales in Paris. Nora, the initiator, was at that moment already a well-established historian and publicist. His starting point was a pessimistic one: 'the rapid disappearance of our national memory seemed to call for a list of these places'.[1] Collective memory seemed to have ceased to exist at the beginning of the 1980s. Nora's initial purpose was thus to establish an inventory of a fading memory. Ten years later, after the *bicentenaire* of the French revolution and the debates about the Vichy regime, Nora complained that French society was saturated by too much memory. The wish to chart national history/national memory was accompanied by a desire for a history of the 'second degree'. Such a history was not so much interested in examining reality itself as in how this reality was remembered. The project should however not be qualified as postmodernist, since Pierre Nora maintained a strict distinction between (subjective) memory and (objective) history.

The original *lieux de mémoire* project emerged from within the framework of French national historiography. In his introduction of 1984, Pierre Nora spoke of 'our national memory' ('notre mémoire nationale'), not of the 'French national memory', illustrating the historian's proximity to the subject of his analysis.[2] The subdivision of the books – *La République*, *La Nation*, *Les France* – further 'nationalised' the whole undertaking. This configuration, which structured the whole project, seemed rather difficult to export to other historiographies. It is interesting to note that no other country has tried to bind its narrative to a similarly rigid structure. Moreover, the vast majority of the participating historians in the writing of the *Lieux de mémoire* were of French nationality. The whole undertaking was evidently written for a French readership (and) in a French context.

The constructivist approach towards the nation which shaped the project was at that time a common paradigm within French historiography (Le Goff, Furet, Joutard). What is astonishing is the almost complete absence of any theoretical background besides the work of Maurice Halbwachs.[3] Maurice Halbwachs had published in the interwar period on the social construction of memory, taking issue with Sigmund Freud and Henri Bergson, who explained memory on an individual level. The French sociologist stressed the importance of the collective frames in which memory is organized and is expressed.

The seven-volume *Les lieux de mémoire* constitutes a heterogeneous collection of articles on different (im)material places of memory. Indeed, and this a probably one of the more attractive aspects of the project, Pierre Nora defined the *lieux de mémoire* as identity projection screens that could be a place like the Eiffel Tower, a book like *Le tour de France par deux enfants* or a more abstract concept such as *Le génie français* or *Le local*. All three elements, at different levels, played an important role in the definition of French identity. Nora defines *lieux de mémoire* on three levels: a material one, a functional one and a symbolic one. But despite this rather loose and open definition, the more than 130 articles more often provide a specialist's view on a given subject rather than inscribing it into this broader theoretical framework.

The influence of international historiography on the French project was rather limited. Classics on nationalism such as Anthony Smith's

The Ethnic Revival or Karl Deutsch's *Nationalism and Social Communication* were not mentioned, neither was the influential work of Aby Warburg, a cultural theorist from the interwar period.[4] When reading the 132 articles, the absence of a common methodological background is very obvious. Nevertheless, the *Lieux de mémoire* were very well received by national newspapers and academic journals alike. Almost 100,000 copies were sold, and Pierre Nora was made a member of the Académie française.

Despite the unmitigated French character of this undertaking, the concept of the *lieux de mémoire* became one of the major export products of recent French historiography. Yet the historian who had developed the terminology took a rather ambiguous view of the internationalization of the *lieux de mémoire*. In an article from 1993, entitled 'La notion de "lieu de mémoire", est-elle exportable?', he expressed his scepticism. Several elements he adjudged to be problematic. First of all, the word *lieu de mémoire* itself, taken from Cicero's *locus memoriae*, could not be translated into English, German or Spanish, according to Pierre Nora. Secondly, Nora was convinced that the undertaking had been born in a specifically French context: the evolution from history to memory, and the triumph of the latter. In no other country, he believed, had the role played by historians been so important in the nation-building process. Finally, the structure of the undertaking was genuinely French. In no other country, would the tripartite distinction – *La République*, *La Nation*, *Les France* – make any sense.[5] Even if Pierre Nora's opposition weakened in the following years, his scepticism remained. In 1994, he pleaded for a comparative history of memory and concluded that 'en matière de mémoire, il n'y a pas d'"exception française"' ('in terms of memory, there is no "French exception"'). Yet only a few pages further on, he speaks of a 'surdétermination mémorielle' ('overdetermination by memory') specific to the French model.[6] By 2001, his opposition had further weakened: the differences between Germany and France he no longer considered to be of a conceptual nature, but rather related to the contents.[7]

Several developments prove the international success of the *Lieux de mémoire*: translations into other languages, the presence of the seven volumes in all major European national libraries and the transfer of the concept into other national historiographic discourses, for instance. Although the original *Lieux de mémoire* were never translated in their entirety, there are partial translations in English and German. In most Western European national libraries, it is possible to find the seven French volumes. But, with the exception of Poland and Serbia, no national library in the former Eastern bloc countries has acquired the original *Lieux de mémoire*. Despite the importance of social memories for the reconstruction of Eastern European societies, to which many French historians pointed at a very early stage,[8] it was only recently that Pierre Nora's ideas entered historiographical discourse on Eastern Europe, be it at conferences,[9] or in academic journals.[10]

The English edition, which regroups 46 of the original 132 articles in three volumes, was published by an academic publisher in the United States (Columbia University Press) 4 years after the last volume had been printed in France. *Realms of Memory* were co-edited by Lawrence Kritzman, a specialist of French cultural history. His role as a French-American mediator had already been important prior to this translation: in 1990, he had been made *chevalier* by the French government,[11] and the research centre that is directed by Kritzman is partly financed by the French government.[12] Even if the French version had received some reviews in the Anglophone press, it was only through the translation that it became accessible to a wider readership. The English version was reorganized around three themes: *Conflict and Divisions, Traditions* and *Symbols*. While the newspaper reviews were largely positive, the major historical journals proved to be rather critical. The opinion expressed by Hue-Tam Ho Tai in the *American Historical Review* may be considered representative: 'the contents and conflicts that are so amply documented in the collection are not about France per se but about the nature of its national identity. . . . This is a France that is indivisible':[13] thus regionalism is absent, as are the colonies, gender, etc. Finally, only the masculine *France profonde* is present in the *Realms of Memory*. The same could be said about the original *Lieux de mémoire*. As far as the availability of the English translation in European libraries is concerned, the situation is similar to that of the original *Lieux de mémoire*: it can be found in most of the Western European national libraries, but only in very few of the Central and Eastern European national libraries.

In Germany, Pierre Nora's ideas were translated even before all the volumes of the *Lieux de mémoire* had been published. In 1990, the small but well-known Wagenbach publishing house edited a short book with three articles and a new preface by Pierre Nora. Eight years later, one of the major paperback publishers in Germany, the Fischer Verlag, republished this version,[14] and most of the larger German libraries hold a copy of this book. It was only in 2005 that 16 articles from the *Lieux de mémoire* were translated into German. While the original French *Lieux de mémoire* are frequently cited in German works, it is evident that most authors mainly used the abridged translation from 1990. In a book anticipating the German *Erinnerungsorte*, Editor Constanze Carcenac-Lecomte refers in the first footnote of her introduction to the *Lieux de mémoire*. On the following pages, however, there is only one single reference to the original edition, but 23 to the translation.[15] In general, the only articles from the *Lieux de mémoire* that seemed to have been read – not only in Germany – are those written by Pierre Nora himself.

European spaces

In addition to the impact of these translations, Nora's topography of French collective memory inspired numerous similar undertakings in several European countries. In Italy and Germany, two large projects were launched that deserve a closer look.[16]

Even if the Italian undertaking is on a somewhat smaller scale than the *lieux de mémoire* – 'only' three volumes and 60 authors – it follows the French example very closely. At the end of the first volume, the editor, Mario Isnenghi, clearly refers to the influence of Pierre Nora, writing that 'la prima . . . dalle stimolazioni venute dal grande progetto portato a termine de Pierre Nora a dai suoi collaboratori inventando e divulgando anche il concetto dei "lieux de mémoire"' ('the first motivation . . . came from the great project realized by Pierre Nora and his colleagues who invented and disseminated the concept of the *lieux de mémoire*').[17] Two key sources of methodological inspiration can be traced back to Pierre Nora's introduction: Maurice Halbwachs and the duo Hobsbawm/Ranger. Neither the editor nor the authors – with the exception of Marco Fincardi, who had studied at Pierre Nora's home institution, the *Ecole des Hautes Etudes en Sciences Sociales* – had any direct link with France or French historiography. But the Italian historical sciences are generally very French-oriented. Moreover, several authors, in contrast to their German colleagues, referred directly to the *Lieux de mémoire* in their articles, illustrating the widespread diffusion of the book in Italy. The *Luoghi della memoria* were relatively well reviewed by the academics,[18] but were not a great success for the publisher: there was no second edition, and no paperback version. The publication of the *Luoghi della memoria* was however overshadowed by a conflict between Isnenghi and Nora. Pierre Nora himself had plans to launch a collection of Italian *lieux de mémoire*, which he had to abandon once the Isnenghi project was published.[19] This clash revealed two things. On the one hand, the term *lieux de mémoire* quickly developed a market value for publishers. On the other hand, this raised the issue of who actually holds the 'copyright' for the concept. Pierre Nora did not just want others to acknowledge their indebtedness to his work: he wanted to enforce a certain right of supervision over any similar project. This seems a rather unusual wish, but surprisingly, several of the other project coordinators involved Pierre Nora directly in their work as it was progressing.

Apart from the French *lieux de mémoire*, the German edition was without any doubt the biggest and commercially most successful undertaking. As was the case with the French project, the project was launched through an academic course. This was co-organized by Hagen Schulze, former director of the German Historical Institute in London and a specialist on the German nation-building process, and Étienne François. François, professor at the University of Paris I, had been director of a French-German research centre in Berlin, the *Centre Marc Bloch*, and was the director of the *Frankreichzentrum* at the Technical University in Berlin at the time when the *Erinnerungsorte* were published. His personal contacts with the French and Parisian academic field as well as his access to institutional resources proved to be an ideal background for the transfer of the French concept to a German context. Several preliminary conferences were thus organized at the *Centre Marc Bloch*, confronting German social scientists with the concept of the *lieux de mémoire*.[20]

The German *Erinnerungsorte* placed themselves in a rather a-critical genealogical relation to the initial French project, as is illustrated by Pierre Nora writing the afterword. Whereas Nora is acknowledged as one of their major inspirations from page one already, François and Schulze do not openly refer in their methodological introduction to any of the critical reviews the *Lieux de mémoire* had triggered. On the other hand, and contrary to the French model, the editors try to elaborate a broader theoretical background. They discuss quite extensively the work of the French sociologist, Maurice Halbwachs, stressing the importance of collective frames in organizing memory. The French historian Henry Rousso and the German cultural scientist Aleida Assmann constitute the two other major reference points. Rousso pointed out the important tension between memory and oblivion, an oblivion that allows for the existence of memory. Assmann provided the tools to deal with the opposition between history and memory. For Assmann, history leads a double life: as science and as memory. Both do not necessarily compete, nor are they contradictory: rather they are two different ways by which to link the past to the present.[21] In trying to open up the concept, *Erinnerungsorte* offered a far more eclectic approach, including articles, for instance, on the *Bundesliga* (the German Premier League), the *Schrebergarten* (allotment garden), but also on Goethe and the Berlin Wall.

The reception of the *Erinnerungsorte* was however quite critical; the result was seen as too essayistic, too 'museal' (antiquated), as too arbitrary in terms of the selection made – and as not popular enough. Even if the German contributions attempt to underline the discontinuity of national history, some observers still condemn what they see as a too homogeneous presentation of German history in the *Erinnerungsorte* volumes.[22]

A comparative analysis of the French and the German undertakings reveals much that is significant. Both projects are more or less of the same scale. Both projects clearly had national ambitions, and this is certainly how they were understood in academic circles. Both projects tried to address the scientific community and the larger educated public (*Bildungsbürgertum*). But contrary to the French project, which was clearly part of a larger project of nation building, the German *Erinnerungsorte* was not so much defined by a sense of the continuity of history.[23] A comparison of the authors, even if the samples are rather small, produces some interesting hypotheses concerning the historiographical fields in both countries. For some aspects, figures relating to the somewhat smaller Italian project are included in the comparison.

The first difference is gender-related. While female authors made up 12 per cent of those involved in the *Lieux de mémoire* project, every fifth author of the *Erinnerungsorte* contributions was a woman. More important is the dissimilarity concerning the citizenship of the authors. In the French undertaking, the participation of foreign historians was limited: the non-French authors came from five countries (United States, Israel, Italy, Poland,

Switzerland, Germany) and represented 8 per cent of all authors. François and Schulze asked twice as many foreigners, hailing from four countries (France, Great Britain, Israel and Poland). Four-fifths of the foreign historians in the *Erinnerungsorte* project originate from France, which shows the importance of the personal links – Étienne François – and institutional networks – *Centre Marc Bloch* and *Frankreichzentrum/TU Berlin* – within the context of which the German project was conceived. The German undertaking was also clearly placed within a broader European framework, not only due to the international composition of the authors, but also because the scope of the articles often stretched beyond the German borders. But this framework is nonetheless characterized by the old French-German axis which defined (Western) Europe in the 1950s and the 1960s, but which no longer defines Europe at the beginning of the twenty-first century. The complete absence of any foreign involvement in the *Luoghi della memoria* project seems to indicate a certain sealing off of national Italian historiography from foreign participation – despite the numerous foreign historical institutes in Rome.

The German *Erinnerungsorte* project was not only more open to foreign authors, but it was also informed by a greater methodological openness. One third of the authors were non-historians; in the French case, this percentage was lower at 25 per cent, and in the Italian case, it was under 20 per cent. In Germany, most of the non-historians came from literary studies, in France they were mostly philosophers and art historians. François Audigier, the only historian who has hitherto tried to write the history of the *lieux de mémoire*, was therefore perhaps a little bit hasty when declaring that the French project was characterized by its multidisciplinarity and openness to foreign historians.[24]

The biggest difference between the French and German enterprises evidently relates to the importance of the political capital of the country. The *Lieux de mémoire* were not only a predominantly male undertaking, but also a Parisian one. Two thirds of the authors were working in Paris, 20 per cent of them based at the Ecole *des Hautes Etudes en Sciences Sociales*. In Germany and Italy, the reverse is the case. The *Luoghi della memoria* seemed to be a project of the universities of Northern Italy and united many historians specializing in Italian fascism. In Germany, even if both editors came from Berlin, most of the authors did not. Finally, the German project was realized by a younger group of historians than the French one.

The dissimilar nature of these editorial projects reveals much about the historiographical fields in both countries and about the place of the project in the context of both national historiographies. As the above analysis shows, the French project was more of a national undertaking, written by male, well-established historians, whereas the *Erinnerungsorte* project, while not existing at the margins of the guild, clearly could not (pretend to) speak for the majority of German historians. It seems as if the comparison between the *Lieux de mémoire* and the *Erinnerungsorte* projects provides further proof of Pierre Nora's assertion that in France, historians have played a more fundamental role in the construction of the nation's master narrative than in other countries.

In addition to these two larger projects, numerous smaller ventures dealing with the construction of national identities referred to Pierre Nora. The only exception to this is the *Dansk Identitetshistorie*, published between 1991 and 1992 in Denmark.[25] It is not the intention of this chapter to present a complete overview of these smaller projects, but consideration of some of them will reveal how the *lieux de mémoire* circulated in the European world of ideas.

The first country in which the *lieux de mémoire* were adapted, were the Netherlands. One of the Dutch editors of the *Lieux de mémoire et identités nationales*,[26] Pim den Boer, wrote his thesis on nineteenth-century French historians: this methodological and geographic proximity on the part of one of the initiators explains the rapid transfer. In the end, however, the book had little in common with the French *Lieux de mémoire* besides the title. It is an edition of papers presented at the *Institut Néerlandais* in Paris in 1991 on the construction and invention of the French and Dutch nations. Half of the participants were French historians who had participated in the *Lieux de mémoire* project, including Pierre Nora himself, while the other half were Dutch historians. Their articles provide not so much an analysis of one specific *lieu de mémoire* as a general overview, as is demonstrated by Nicolas van Sas' article on 'La nation néerlandaise au dix-neuvième siècle: mythes et représentations'. Nevertheless, the book testifies to the attractive character of the spatial metaphor at a very early stage.

If the Dutch, the Italian and the German projects remained confined to a national framework similar to the one developed by Pierre Nora, there have recently been several undertakings that tried to 'downgrade' the *Lieux de mémoire* to subnational levels or 'upgrade' them to a supranational one.

In several French regions, there have been attempts to write regional *Lieux de mémoire*. A search of *Opale*, the catalogue of the *Bibliothèque Nationale*, shows that the concept seems to have been particularly 'successful' in the Lorraine, where four books have been published in the last 20 years with *Lieux de mémoire* in their title.[27] The same publications also illustrate the speed with which the word was transferred from an academic to a wider, more popular context. Indeed, only one of the four books has a clear academic ambition, the three other are popular or touristic in character. In the last volume of the *Lieux de mémoire*, Pierre Nora shows himself overwhelmed by this 'success' and seems distressed by the popularization of the concept, which, however, had been facilitated by the nostalgic character with which Nora himself had invested the project.[28] The academic *Mémoire et lieux de mémoire en Lorraine*, edited by two professors of the University of Nancy, is interesting in several regards. First, it demonstrates that smaller social groups can have their own *lieux de mémoire* and that they can construct their identity in similar ways. Secondly, one of the editors, Philippe Martin, made two important contributions that are too rarely taken into account: on the one hand, he introduced a kind of scale (according to the number of people who can relate to a *lieu*) by distinguishing between 'le lieu de souvenir, le lieu d'identité [et] le lieu de mémoire' (realm of remembrance, realm of identity and realm of memory). On the other hand, he also made some pertinent remarks about those events, persons, places that had never become or no longer were *lieux de mémoire*.[29] Both perspectives had been overlooked in Nora's *lieux de mémoire*, whose vision was clouded by the national approach and who did not take enough account of the variations in scale.

At the same time, however, his project is clearly being utilized by the local political elite of the *région*. In France, these administrative units have gained a greater importance since decentralization started in the 1980s and *conseillers régionaux* (regional councillors) were elected directly by their constituencies. Numerous regions have been engaged in a process well known to the historians of nineteenth-century nation-building, namely desperately looking to history to legitimate their existence.[30]

In Austria, a transnational approach was chosen, a transnationality resting on a common history, namely that of Habsburg rule. The avowed aim was to take a first step towards a European history of national constructions,[31] a project Pierre Nora had always regarded with great scepticism. One of the three editors of the Austrian project was Jacques Le Rider, a French specialist on the Habsburg monarchy. Similarly to the German *Erinnerungsorte*, the Austrian *Orte des Gedächtnisses* project refers to Pierre Nora etymologically, but on a methodological level, they rely more on German scholars such as Aleida and Jan Assmann. In the Austrian project, the contributions are not limited to one specific *lieu de mémoire*, but are focused more on a long process of nation building. One of their core aims is to analyse how 'transnational' persons/elements were renationalized and instrumentalized to invent national identity. Austria and Vienna appear in this approach as a meeting point of different identities: this is a perspective that breaks with a national perspective, but that seems at the same time to participate in shaping a new metaphor for this region as the 'heart' of the new, enlarged Europe. In parallel to this transnational project, the University of Vienna has launched a specifically Austrian project on realms of memory that tries to integrate results from empirical evidence gathered by the social sciences, such as representative polls.

Other *lieux de mémoire* have been written for countries that no longer exist, such as the GDR,[32] and countries that seem doomed to disappear, such as Belgium.[33] Moreover, it is interesting that the Belgian project was the last one to be launched by the six EU founding members. In 2011, the European Institute in Mainz (Germany) launched a multi-volume work on European *lieux de mémoire*. Up to now, however, the British Isles and the Iberian Peninsula have proven quite resistant to the concept.[34]

Hypothetical spaces

First coined in a quintessentially French context at the beginning of the 1980s, the *lieux de mémoire* have become within 25 years one of the most successful export concepts of French historiography. A first general analysis leads us to the following remarks and hypotheses:

(1) The success of the 'image' of *lieu de mémoire*.

While there are evidently problems translating the French term *lieu de mémoire* into other languages, one cannot deny that the metaphor 'invented' by Pierre Nora has functioned effectively in a wider European context. Even if the approach is not always comparable to the *lieux de mémoire*, as in the Dutch or Austrian case, the editors choose to maintain this term in their title. The apparent methodological openness of the concept explains the numerous national and local adaptations the idea was submitted to. Presenting national history as a labyrinth, as Aleida Assmann has called the French *lieux de mémoire*, rather than under the rubric of totality was in line with a larger European movement that was looking for new ways of writing national histories.[35] The resurgence of nationalism after 1989 made a critical approach all the more necessary. Only recently has the concept begun to extend beyond issues of spatially defined national identities and been applied to language or to political parties.

(2) The limited expansion of the concept.[36]

Without any doubt, the *lieux de mémoire* concept swiftly crossed the borders of French historiography, but originally the scope of the transference remained relatively limited. Indeed, despite the fact that the Berlin Wall had fallen 3 years before the last volume of the *Lieux de mémoire* was published, the concept did not cross this old political frontier quickly. Most of the national libraries of the former Eastern bloc countries hold neither the French nor the English version. For 20 years, the concept was not implemented systematically in the former communist republics. An exception to this general thesis are countries which used to belong to the Habsburg monarchy. They did not develop their own realms of memory, but were 'colonised' by Austrian historians. It is thus revealing that there is only one Romanian historian involved in the transnational Central-Europe project. Only recently did a German-Polish project see the light of day, with German and Polish historians working together on German-Polish realms of memory. The history of the transfer of the concept demonstrates that the 50-year division of Europe into two parts still poses an obstacle to processes of globalization and cultural interpenetration. On the other hand, it is interesting that all six founding countries of the European Community have their realms of memory projects, perhaps an indication of the academic interdependence that has developed in the last decades.

(3) From passive reception to active appropriation.

The usage of the French concept varied greatly in Western Europe. The arguments in circulation and the interpretations within different national contexts were very heterogeneous in character. In Italy, one can speak of a one-to-one transference. There was no methodological transformation of the original *Lieux de mémoire*: Maurice Halbwachs and Eric Hobsbawm remained the only methodological reference points. In Germany, however, there was a partial transformation, reflecting a wider theoretical investment. The French concept was enriched by the scholarly discussions conducted at that time in Germany. Other countries just used the 'magic words' *lieux de mémoire*, following only very loosely the method proposed by Pierre Nora.

(4) The importance of personal vectors.

Without wanting to fall into the trap of writing a mechanistic history in which developments are attributed to individuals, it is interesting to observe that in almost every national publication, one finds among the editors a French historian or an academic with links to France. The spread of the *lieux de mémoire* was and still is facilitated by these people and institutions who act as mediators between the French culture and the rest of world. The *Lieux de mémoire* benefited from a particular well-developed French cultural network. This is particularly obvious in the case of the English translation by Kritzman or of the role played by Étienne François and the *Centre Marc Bloch* in the German case. A final example is the recently published version of the Dutch *Lieux de mémoire*, edited by Henri Wesseling, a Dutch historian who has worked on France and whose books have been translated into French.[37]

(5) The importance of the national *habitus* of the respective historical guild.

As the comparison between the *lieux de mémoire*, the *Erinnerungsorte* and the *Luoghi della memoria* has demonstrated, national habits still played an important role. Even if these undertakings shared numerous similarities, there were quite significant differences in the composition of the participating authors. The geographic distribution shows the central role played by Paris in the field of French historiography, which is but one of the numerous elements that demonstrate the strong centralization of French intellectual life despite the decentralization introduced since the 1960s. The fact that the French team of authors was primarily composed of older men, was less interdisciplinary and included fewer foreigners are factors that support, in my view, the hypothesis that the *lieux de mémoire*, as a critical analytical tool, still operates within the long genealogy of French history writing, starting with Ernest Lavisse and ending with Marc Ferro's *Histoire de France*.[38] This difference is also visible in the way both works have been received by their peers: in France, the reception has been relatively positive across the board, while in Germany the reception has been more ambiguous and critical.

(6) A one-way transfer until recently.

Only one of the other projects has been translated into French or English, while none received a larger coverage in academic journals in other countries.[39] The German school of memory studies around Jan and Aleida Assmann, which played an important role in the German and Austrian undertaking, has had little impact in Italy or France. In his new introduction to the paperback edition of the *Lieux de mémoire*, Pierre Nora does not refer to the discussions that were already taking place at that moment in the Netherlands or in Germany.[40] This is a final example of the lasting impermeability of intellectual frontiers, something I did not anticipate when I began analysing the apparent success story of the Europeanization of the French *Lieux de mémoire*.

(7) The difficulty in not acting as identity creator.

Even if the *lieux de mémoire* projects inspired by Nora's writings claim to adopt a critical approach towards the legitimating role of the historians of the nineteenth century, they all had to face the reproach that they were doing precisely what they were trying to deconstruct. Neither the more eclectic German method nor the regional approach adopted in Lorraine nor the transnational Austrian perspective can prevent the potential creation of new identities and profess merely to deconstruct older ones.[41]

Notes

1 'la disparition rapide de notre mémoire nationale m'avait semblé appeler un inventaire des lieux'.

2 Pierre Nora, 'Présentation', in Pierre Nora (ed.), *Les lieux de mémoire*, vol. I (Paris, 1984), p. 15.

3 An exception is Eric Hobsbawm and Terence Ranger (eds), *The Invention of Tradition* (Cambridge, 1983), which is mentioned in Piere Nora, 'Présentation', in P. Nora (ed.), *Les lieux de mémoire*, vol. III (Paris, 1984), p. 3043.

4 See Anthony Smith, *The Ethnic Revival* (Cambridge, 1981) and Karl W. Deutsch, *Nationalism and Social Communication* (Cambridge, 1983).

5 Pierre Nora, 'La notion de 'lieu de mémoire est-elle exportable', in Pim den Boer, Willem Frijhoff (eds), *Lieux de mémoire et identités nationales* (Amsterdam, 1993), pp. 3–10.

6 Pierre Nora, 'La loi de la mémoire'. *Le débat* 78 (1994), 188 and 190.

7 Pierre Nora, 'Nachwort', in Étienne Francois, Hagen Schulze (eds), *Deutsche Erinnerungsorte*, vol. 3 (Munich, 2001), pp. 681–6.

8 Alain Brossat, Sonia Combe, Jean-Yves Potel and Jean-Charles Szurek, *A l'Est, la mémoire retrouvée* (Paris, 1996).

9 'Die baltischen Städte Riga und Tartu als Erinnerungsorte' ('The Baltic Cities Riga and Tartu as Realms of Memory'), held on 28 and 29 June 2006.

10 See *Tabula* (a Hungarian ethnographic journal) 7:2 (2004), or *Neprikosnovenny Zapas. Debaty o politike i kulture* (a Russian literature journal) 2005, pp. 2–3, which was a special number dedicated to the memory of the Second World War and included an article by Pierre Nora.

11 In 2000, Lawrence Kritzman was awarded the Order of National Merit, the second highest civilian award accorded by France.

12 http://www.thedartmouth.com/article.php?aid=1995013101050 (accessed 21 February 2006).

13 Hue-Tam Ho Tai, 'Remembered Realms: Pierre Nora and French National Memory'. *American Historical Review* 106:3 (2001), 906–22, here p. 910.

14 Pierre Nora, *Zwischen Geschichte und Gedächtnis* (Berlin, 1990); Pierre Nora, *Zwischen Geschichte und Gedächtnis* (Frankfurt a.M., 1998).

15 Constanze Carcenac-Lecomte, 'Pierre Nora und ein deutsches Pilotprojekt', in Constanze Carcenac-Lecomte (ed.), *Steinbruch. Deutsche Erinnerungsorte* (Frankfurt a.M., 2000), pp. 13–26.

16 A Dutch undertaking, the first volume of which has recently been published, has not been taken into account here. In the absence of the other volumes, it is impossible to provide a substantial analysis.

17 Mario Isnenghi, 'Conclusione', in Mario Isnenghi (ed.), *I luoghi della memoria – Simboli e miti dell'Italia unita*, vol. 1 (Roma, 1996), p. 559.

18 Thanks to Irene di Jorio (Université libre de Bruxelles) for this information.

19 On the conflict between Nora and Isnenghi, see N. Weill, 'Démarquage sauvage des "Lieux de mémoire" en Italie', *Le Monde*, 3 January 1997, VIII (supplément littéraire).

20 Étienne François (ed.), *Lieux de mémoire – Erinnerungsorte. D'un modèle français à un projet allemand* (Berlin, 1996); Rudolf Speth, Edgar Wolfrum (eds), *Politische Mythen und Geschichtspolitik* (Berlin, 1996).

21 Étienne François, Hagen Schulze, 'Einleitung', in Étienne François, Hagen Schulze (eds), *Deutsche Erinnerungsorte*, vol. 3 (Munich, 2001), pp. 9–24.

22 For a critical presentation of the major German reviews of the *Erinnerungsorte*, see Nicole L. Immler, '"Gedächtnisgeschichte" – Ein Vergleich von Deutschland und Österreich in bezug auf Pierre Noras Konzept der *lieux de mémoire*', in Ian Foster and Juliet Wigmore (eds), *Neighbours and Strangers. Literary and Cultural Relations in Germany, Austria and Central Europe since 1989* (Amsterdam/New York, 2004), pp. 173–96.

23 Stephen Legg, 'Contesting and Surviving Memory: Space, Nation, and Nostalgia' in '*Les Lieux de Mémoire*'. *Environment and Planning D: Society and Space* 23 (2005), 481–504.

24 François Audiger, 'Les lieux de mémoire: un concept, son invention, sa mise en œuvre et sa réception', in Philippe Martin and François Roth (eds), *Mémoire & lieux de mémoire en Lorraine* (Sarreguemines, 2003), pp. 31–2.

25 Ole Feldbaek (ed.), *Dansk Identitetshistorie*, 4 vols (Copenhagen, 1991–92).

26 Pim den Boer, Willem Frijhoff (eds), *Lieux de mémoire et identités nationales* (Amsterdam, 1993).

27 Marcel Cordier, *Hommes et lieux de mémoire en Lorraine* (Sarreguemines,

1991); René Bastien, Colombe Puhl and Véronique Reato, *Lieux de mémoire en Lorraine* (Metz, 1997); Martin and Roth (eds), *Mémoire & lieux de mémoire en Lorraine*; Jacques Didier, *Lorraine 1914: Guide des lieux de mémoire* (Louviers, 2004).

28 See Legg, 'Contesting and Surviving Memory'.

29 Philippe Martin, 'Jalons pour une approche des lieux de mémoire en Lorraine', in Martin and Roth (eds), *Mémoire & lieux de mémoire en Lorraine*, pp. 29–44.

30 Préface written by the Président du Conseil Régional de Lorraine, in Martin and Roth (eds), *Mémoire & lieux de mémoire en Lorraine*, pp. 9–12.

31 Jacques Le Rider, Moritz Csaky and Monika Sommer, 'Vorwort', in Jacques Le Rider, Moritz Csaky and Monika Sommer (eds), *Transnationale Gedächtnisorte in Zentraleuropa* (Innsbruck, 2002), p. 8.

32 Martin Sabrow (ed.), *Erinnerungsorte der DDR* (Munich, 2009).

33 Johan Tollebeek et al. (eds), *België, een parcours van herinnering* (Amsterdam, 2008).

34 See however Raphael Samuel, *Theatres of Memory* (London, 1996–98).

35 Aleida Assmann, 'Im Zwischenraum zwischen Geschichte und Gedächtnis: Bemerkungen zu Pierre Noras "Lieux de mémoire"', in François (ed.), *Lieux de mémoire*, p. 22.

36 On the difficulties of creating a European memory space see Étienne François, 'Ist eine gesamteuropäische Erinnerungskultur vorstellbar?', in Bernd Henningsen, Hendriette Kliemann-Geisinger and Stefan Troebst (eds), *Transnationale Erinnerungsorte: Nord-und südeuropäische Perspektiven* (Berlin, 3009), pp. 13–30.

37 Henk Wesseling (ed.), *Plaatsen von herinnering* (Amsterdam, 2006).

38 Marc Ferro, *Histoire de France* (Paris, 2001).

39 Étienne François et al. (eds), *Mémoires allemandes* (Paris, 2001).

40 Pierre Nora, 'Préface à l'édition "Quarto"', in Pierre Nora (ed.), *Les lieux de mémoire*, vol. 1 (Paris, 2001), pp. 7–8.

41 Benoît Majerus, Sonja Kmec, Michel Margue and Pit Peporte (eds), *Dépasser le cadre national des 'Lieux de mémoire': innovations méthodologiques, approches comparatives, lectures transnationales* (Brussels, 2010).

Further reading

Aleida Assmann, *Cultural Memory and Western Civilization* (New York, 2011).
Pim den Boer, Heinz Duchhardt, Georg Kreis, and Wolfgang Schmale (eds), *Europäische Erinnerungsorte 1: Mythen und Grundbegriffe des europäischen Selbstverständnisses* (Munich, 2011).
Pim den Boer and Willem Frijhoff (eds), *Les Lieux de mémoire et identités nationales* (Amsterdam, 1993).

François Dosse, *Pierre Nora: homo historicus* (Paris, 2011).

Ariane Eichenberg, *Gedächtnis und Erinnerung: Ein interdisziplinäres Handbuch* (Stuttgart, 2010).

Astrid Erll and Ansgar Nuenning (eds), *Cultural Memory Studies: An International and Interdisciplinary Handbook* (Berlin, 2008).

Richard Holbrook, 'Pierre Nora (1931–)', in Philip Daileader (ed.), *French Historians 1900–2000* (Chichester, 2010), pp. 444–60.

Patrick Hutton, 'Recent Scholarship on History and Memory'. *The History Teacher* 33/4 (2000), 533–48.

Marie-Claire Lavabre, 'Historiography and Memory', in Aviezer Tucker (ed.), *A Companion to the Philosophy of History and Historiography* (Oxford, 2009), pp. 362–70.

Pierre Nora (ed.), *Les lieux de mémoire* (Paris, 1984).

—, *Realms of Memory: Rethinking the French Past* (New York, 1996).

Adam Piette, 'Contesting Realms of Memory in Early Cold War France'. *Theory, Culture & Society* 27:5 (2010), 86–106.

Susannah Radstone (ed.), *Memory: Histories, Theories, Debates* (New York, 2010).

Helke Rausch, 'Staging Realms of the Past in 19th-Century Western Europe: Comparing Monumental Strategies of Middle-Class Nationalists'. *East Central Europe* 36:1 (2009), 37–62.

Huetamho Tai, 'Remembered Realms: Pierre Nora and French National Memory'. *The American Historical Review* 106:3 (2001), 906–22.

CHAPTER EIGHT

On the memory of communism in Eastern and Central Europe

Attila Pók

Following the intention of the editors of this volume, the present chapter deals with the memories of communism in the historiographies and historical thought of the countries of the Soviet Bloc during the last two decades, contrasting these memories with the impact of communism on historical scholarship in the same region. The legacy of communism will also be addressed as memory can hardly be separated from legacy: what and how individuals or smaller or larger groups of people remember is very much shaped by the layers of surviving traditions.

The literature to be surveyed examines how communist politicians and political thinkers were trying to combine communist proletarian internationalism with powerful nationalism in the countries of the Soviet Bloc between the late 1940s and the late 1980s. The failure of this 'blending' of nationalism and internationalism is frequently defined as one of the causes of the collapse of communist regimes in Central Europe and as a decisive factor in shaping the memory of communism there. Other selected issues in the historical works to be discussed include problems relating to the roots or 'embeddedness' of communism in Eastern and Central Europe. Are the 40 years of communist rule part of the 'normal course' of national histories in the region, or were the communist political system and ideologies just imposed on these societies by Soviet imperialism without substantially transforming them? A closely related question is the interpretation of the causes of the collapse of the communist regimes. Was it the consequence of the struggles for liberty of these freedom-loving nations or just the result of a deal between the US and the declining USSR? The chapter also critically analyses the historiographical discussions around continuities and discontinuities of historical tradition in the countries of the former Soviet Bloc.[1] In addition to written sources, the chapter is also based on the author's experiences as a participant in a number of international historical research projects, most of which resulted in substantial publications.[2] Some related works of sociologists and political scientists have also been utilized.[3] The majority of the examples have been taken from the works of Hungarian and Polish historians.

The Marxist-Communist interpretation of history

When does 'contemporary history' start? When members of my '1968 generation'[4] in the countries of the Soviet Bloc went to university during the late 1960s and early 1970s, we did not speak of contemporary history. We used other chronological concepts to describe most recent history, such as the translations of the Russian term *novaja i novejsaja istorija* coined by our Soviet colleagues. *Novaja* meant the period following the English 'glorious revolution', while *novejsaja* referred to the time following the period that began with the 1917 Great October Revolution (celebrated on 7 November). We were educated in a spirit in which revolutions arising from class struggles were defined as the most decisive turning points in history. The first bourgeois revolution started the age of capitalism, the first major socialist revolution the age of socialism. It was assumed that all societies go through the evolution of the basic modes of production, that is, from slave-holding via feudalism, capitalism and socialism (the preliminary stage to communism) to communist society. According to the basic teachings of 'scientific socialism', the fundamental difference between socialism and communism on the one hand and all the other (slave-holding, feudal and capitalist) social formations on the other is that the former eliminate private property and consequently both class struggle and exploitation.[5]

In all the countries of the Soviet Bloc, the interpretation of the main course of human history as being the road from various forms of exploitation to socialist and communist societies without exploitation of any kind was a mandatory element of dealing with history in any form and on any level. This ideological axiom was combined with the teachings on how the economic basis determined the formation of the social, political, cultural suprastructure and on how class struggles informed historical processes.[6]

According to the interpretation of communist ideologists, historical laws and not great power games or the intricacies of domestic politics made the rise of communist parties to power possible. The teachings of Marx, Engels and Lenin (and, up to about 1956, Stalin) were the sources defining the fundamental laws that governed the lives of human societies. The 'constantly developing' doctrine of scientific socialism and scientific communism incorporated the more recent historical experiences. They proved the inevitable, ultimate victory of communism (socialism being the first step of this process). The memory of the origins of communism as interpreted by communist ideologists in the countries of the Soviet Bloc was less an analysis of what actually happened in the past and more of an anticipation of the inevitable future. This 'memory' reflected how 'progressive' ideologies, movements and personalities paved the road towards the victory of the international working class movement led by the Soviet Union. Both in political rhetoric and education, the emphasis was on presenting the 'objective laws' of history, and the carefully selected historical events served to illustrate these laws. 'Shallow empiricism' was considered to be one of the worst mistakes of 'bourgeois' philosophers and ideologists.[7]

National identities and European historical consciousness

A tremendous amount of Marxist-Communist literature addressed the 'national question'. Communism as a political ideology based on the philosophical teachings of Marx, Engels, Lenin and Stalin targeted the worldwide victory of the proletariat in the global class struggle against the bourgeoisie. This struggle, however, also had to be reconciled with presenting communists as the best patriots of all nations of the world. Still, class conflicts were considered to be much more important than disputes among nations: basic Marxist manuals argued that if the proletariat of the world were to unite, the conflicts among bourgeois national interests would be automatically resolved.

The memory of communism is therefore closely connected to the national momentum. If we are trying to find one core issue, a major point of reference in the voluminous literature of the last two decades on the communist memory of the past and on the post-communist memory of communism, this issue is the relationship between national histories and regional and global developments. In other words: do the fundamental changes in the Soviet Union and the countries of the former Soviet Bloc in 1989–90 reflect some general pattern of 'progress' from authoritarian dictatorships to well-functioning democracies, or are they to be interpreted as a series of singular cases, incidentally showing some striking similarities due to the changes in the international balance of power?

Socialist in content, national in form

The 'principle' in the above subtitle was set down by Stalin,[8] and it permeated all fields of life in the countries of the Soviet Bloc. The official master-narratives sought to prove that in spite of the regional peculiarities, the societies of all socialist countries go through all stages of social, economic and political development, and socialism is basically the same social-economic-political formation in all the countries building socialism from Bulgaria to Poland.[9] The potential of national creativity can best flourish in the brotherly community of peace-loving socialist countries under the wise guidance of the Soviet Union: the worldwide victory of communism under the leadership of the Soviet Union was an indispensable component of communist teleology. The concept of historical progress involved the milestones leading to this ultimate point of human development. This is how international solidarity, the superiority of class solidarity versus national conflict was to be reconciled, with communists presented as the best possible patriots.

Hungary

This doctrine was challenged in various scholarly and non-scholarly forms already during communist times, the most spectacular example being a big historical-political controversy initiated by Erik Molnár in Hungary during the aftermath of the 1956 revolution in the early 1960s. Erik Molnár was a lawyer by training and acted as the defender of several Hungarian underground communists who were tried during the interwar period. He wrote a number of social scientific works in the dogmatic Marxist spirit of the time. After the Communist takeover in Hungary, he held a number of top-level political positions, but after 1956 he focused on his scholarly work as the director of the Institute of History of the Hungarian Academy of Sciences. In a series of articles published between 1959 and 1961, he challenged the dominant 'revolutionary progressive' interpretation of history, that is, the view that presented the Hungarian past since the collapse of the powerful mediaeval Hungarian kingdom in the middle of the sixteenth century as a series of failed revolutionary struggles for independence. These failures were attributed to external (Turkish, Habsburg, Czarist, German) interventions. The resistance against invaders was said to have given cohesion to Hungarian society, and in this sense the struggle for 'social progress' and for national sovereignty were correlating aspirations. Molnár and his followers criticized this interpretation as unhistorical, naive and non-scholarly, disregarding as it did the ethnic and social diversity of Hungarian society. In the atmosphere of the post-1956 anti-nationalist campaign, Molnár pointed out the 'class-contents' of these struggles for independence, that is, that in fact the leaders of these struggles came from the upper layers of the nobility and were driven more by concern over losing financial and political privileges than by some abstract patriotism. This view was in sharp opposition to the assumption that a unified Hungarian people with a strong community consciousness was defending the 'national interests'. Though clearly politically motivated, Molnár's initiative was echoed by serious Hungarian historical scholarship in at least three areas: studies on the mediaeval origins of Hungarian national consciousness and national identity;[10] comparative studies of sixteenth–eighteenth-century Eastern and Western European agrarian developments, exploring the origins of the peculiarities of agrarian development east of the river Elbe;[11] and, finally, scholarly reassessments of Hungary's place within the Dual Austro-Hungarian Monarchy (1867–1918).[12] The results of research and the scholarly discussions from the late 1960s onwards showed just how complex 'progress' really was. For example, Hungary could be seen to have profited from being part of the Habsburg Monarchy; there also existed a non-communist, both intellectually and politically creative Left; moderate reforms arguably served the 'national interest' just as much, if not more, than radical revolutions; and frequently used concepts such 'the toiling masses' or the 'feudal bourgeois exploiters' were but empty rhetoric without any analytical value.

Poland

Communism as the defender of the integrity of the nation played a very important role in Polish communist propaganda as well. Here, there was a pressing political need to prove that, following World War II, the Soviet-supported Lublin government was the true representative of Polish national interests, not the Polish government in exile in London. Similarly, communist propaganda insisted that it was the Russian revolution, not Pilsudski's efforts which had made Poland's resurrection as a sovereign state in 1918 possible.[13] Professor Wandycz aptly summarizes the geographic-historical reorientation, as he calls it, of Polish historical studies during the aftermath of World War II, following the country's shift to the west as a result of losing eastern and acquiring western territories: 'emphasis was to be placed on German-Polish relations and the medieval Polish *(Piast)* character of these "western lands". By contrast, the Jagiellonian period of Polish-Lithuanian union and eastward expansion was to be treated more critically and Slav unity stressed.'[14] The dogmatic emphasis on the economic determinants of history paradoxically helped the continuation of an established 'bourgeois' tradition of economic history (Franciszek Bujak, Jan Rutkowski). The Institute of History of the Polish Academy of Sciences created in 1952 encouraged respective research projects. During the 1960s, as in Hungary, Marxist-Leninist-Stalinist dogmas were challenged in Polish historical scholarship. Even most sensitive topics, such as the nineteenth-century anti-Russian revolts, were on the agenda of scholarly exchanges. The orthodox Marxist doctrine that 'the masses had always to be progressive and patriotic and the gentry reactionary and unpatriotic was at least partially abandoned'.[15]

Czechoslovakia

These Polish and Hungarian tendencies were paralleled – *mutatis mutandis* – in Czechoslovakia. Here, the 'peculiar mixture of old romantic nationalism and the theory of class struggle'[16] of the early 1950s gradually gave way by the late 1960s to more sophisticated approaches concerning the interdependence of Czech and Central European history, including the Czech-German and Czech-Slovak relationships. It was during the 1960s, for instance, that Miroslaw Hroch of Prague University emerged as an influential personality in international research into the making of modern nations. In contrast, however, to Hungary and Poland, the August 1968 Soviet intervention in Czechoslovakia caused a substantial backlash. Nevertheless – especially when we take into account the impact of the works of émigré historians on both the historians' 'guild' and the broader intellectual public opinion in Czechoslovakia – there could be no return to the dogmatic national and orthodox Marxist way of writing history.

Romania

Keith Hitchins offers us a succint overview of developments in Romania:

> . . . history and social thought between 1947 and 1989 evolved in three broad stages. The first was the period of mobilisation, lasting until about 1960, and was characterised by a more or less strict adherence to the tenets of Marxism-Leninism, as interpreted by the party and a general uniformity of views about Romania's past. The second period, between the early 1960s and 1971, was one of relaxation corresponding to the modest trend of liberalisation in cultural life and a slight softening of political and conomic rigidity. It allowed historical inquiry and discussion to diversify and flourish in ways unknown during the previous twenty years. Then, in 1971, the situation changed dramatically, when Nicolai Ceausescu demanded a return to strict ideological conformity in the humanities and social sciences. At the same time, his so-called July theses signaled the beginning of party-sponsored nationalism in historiography, which soon became interwoven with an oppresive cult of personality unique in modern Romanian history.[17]

The traditional dilemma of Romanian intellectuals over whether Romanians belonged more to the Eastern or Western cultural hemisphere certainly lingered on throughout all these periods. As a peculiar Romanian development, the officially supported hostility towards the Soviet Union during the second half of the 1980s was just as much a defence against Gorbachev's reforms as an element of 'protochronism'; this was the historical doctrine that, on the evidence of the Dacian state (especially at the time of Buresbista), attached a worldwide pioneering role to the Romanians in state building. By sheer chance, the commemoration of the 2050th anniversary of the foundation of the unified and centralized state of Burebista coincided with the World Congress of Historians in Bucharest in 1980. Both during communist times and following 1989, Romanian collective memory was strongly permeated by historical myths: such, for example, as the idea that Romanians have never been aggressive, rather they made great efforts to defend the West from the Ottoman Turkish conquest and this effort has never been properly rewarded by the ungrateful West Europeans.

Bulgaria

The stages in the transformation of historical studies in Bulgaria are very similar to those in Romania. Following the Communist takeover in 1946, the Marxist-Leninist-Stalinist axioms on the laws of historical development had to be echoed by the profession, emphasis being placed on the reactionary role of the imperialist powers and the Bulgarian bourgeoisie, and on the heroism of the various revolutionary movements. From the end of the 1950s on, although lip-service was still paid to these doctrines, 'a continuous escalation took place in the national feelings of all groups within the intelligentsia, but primarily among the liberal arts and particularly acutely among historians and writers. . . . Historians . . . took upon themselves the voluntary task of protecting and promoting the "national interests" and the "national cause" which enabled them to espouse the false but self-satisfying illusion that they were taking a dissident position. . . . This project was perfectly acceptable to the Communist leadership because it saw in such historiography the ideal legitimation of its authoritarian and, often, totalitarian ambitions'.[18] This did not mean that no serious works based on extensive archival research were prepared and published, but that theoretical-methodological innovations within the historical profession were much less in evidence than in Poland or Hungary at the time. More powerfully than in those countries, in Bulgaria there emerged a continuity of pre-communist, communist and post-communist historiography 'according to the precepts of what was considered to be its duty to shape the national conciousness and thus fulfill an important social function'.[19]

Yugoslavia

In Yugoslavia, most obviously of all the socialist countries, the place and significance of national identitites and histories in relation to forms of federation, as well as religious and class affiliations were the key issue for communist historiography and historical-political thought. It is well known to what a great extent, following Slobodan Milosevic's coming to power in 1989, 'the conclusions of political historiography became fully operational in Serbia's confrontation with the autonomous provinces of Kosovo and Vojvodina'.[20] Vasilije Krestic, a prominent historian of the history of the Serbs in the Habsburg Monarchy, was a key figure in what one might call the 'academic inspiration' behind the hostilities between Serbs and Croats. In a 1986 article, for example – based on just a few, randomly selected quotes – he wrote: '. . . genocide against the Serbs in (Ustasa) Croatia is a specific phenomenon in our (Serb) centuries-old common life with the Croats. The protracted development of the genocidal idea in certain centers of Croat Society . . . did not necessarily have some narrow – but rather a broad – base, took deep roots in the consciousness of many generations.'[21]

The Yugoslav case takes us on to the memory of communism in the post-communist societies. We will look first at the institutional carriers of this memory.

Institutions as carriers of memory

There is by now a substantial literature[22] examining the institutional background of the memory of communism: this literature covers History Commissions, Institutes of National Memory, museums set up on the premises of former terror sites and statue parks. Given this wealth of publications, in this chapter we can only point out some 'creative tensions' in the various forms taken by the institutional representations of the memory of communism. First, these institutions convey the message that communism just as much as fascism is a matter of the past; it has been defeated and has no chance of returning. Still, they consider remembering absolutely necessary in order to re-educate post-communist societies and counteract the successful survival strategies of communist elites and their influence. Secondly, this historical rhetoric can be in sharp contradiction with daily politics. When, for instance, the Chinese Prime minister visited Hungary in June 2011, his Hungarian counterpart, famous for his powerful anti-communist rhetoric since 1989, said that 'in the past 24 years, ever since the last Chinese head of government paid a visit to Budapest, the world and Hungary had undergone big changes, but the friendship between the two countries had remained unbroken . . . .we respect one another's politics and this is a principle underpinning our cooperation . . . we wish China to continue the policies which have produced fantastic achievements over the past decade . . . we raise our hats to this fantastic success . . .'.[23] Thirdly, most of these institutions give the impression that communism was aggressively and violently imposed on the societies of the countries of the Soviet Bloc; as soon as the external conditions allowed, these societies successfully threw off the communist yoke. At the same time they emphasize how extensively the communist dictatorship ruined and destroyed these societies. The best example of this institutional but controversial condemnation of the Communist past is the work of the Presidential Commission in Romania. The president who set up this commission, Traian Basescu, was a successful merchant marine officer during communist times, a position that could not be occupied without ties to the communist secret service. A second-tier communist party member, after the revolution he became a prominent figure among the reform communists spearheading the new leading political power, the National Salvation Front. According to Romanian political scientists, around the beginning of the new millennium '63 per cent of the current political elite had held positions in the Communist Party prior to 1989'.[24] The 18 members of the commission included both professional historians and politicians. They focused on presenting how Romania and its citizens became victims of communism: 'the Communist regime . . . was a regime of foreign occupation which liquidated the Romanian elite and its institutions of democracy, its market economy and private property. All this was annihilated for forty-five years, a false turn on the path of true modernization . . . it was a giant step backward, which led us to chronic poverty, the isolation of the country, the wasting of human and material resources, the alienation of the individual and the destruction of our traditions and national culture'.[25] On the other hand, the report contains the names of numerous Romanians who bore responsibility for the vices of communism, and it warns of the attempts at hijacking the revolution after 1989, naming among many others Ion Iliescu, the leader of the National Salvation Front, and a surviving communist agent. The use of the first-person plural ('our traditions') creates a unity that never existed in Romanian society. Far right anti-communists, dissident communists, protesting students and workers all appear as freedom fighters against communist dictatorship. In spite of both the spectacular timing of its presentation by president Basescu – just two weeks before Romania's accession to the European Union on 1 January 2007 – and the inclusion of its conclusions in school textbooks, local experts argue that the report did not achieve its aims. It did not succeed in creating a solid consensus on the existence of a dominant and prevailing political tradition of liberal democracy in Romania to which communism was presented as a major but successfully defeated threat.[26]

Most post-communist countries have institutions dealing with the 'management' of the memory of communism, but their political influences and scholarly significances vary. They include the Institute of National Remembrance in Poland, the Office of the Federal Commisioner for the Records of the National Security Services of the former GDR (Germany), the Nation's Memory Institute (Slovakia), the Institute for the Study of Totalitarian Regimes (the Czech Republic), the National Council for the Study of Securitate Archives (Romania), the Institute for the Investigation of Communist Crimes (Romania), the Historical Archives of State Security Services in Hungary and the Archives of the Security Service of Ukraine. There exists a co-operation among the respective authorities of seven countries (Germany, the Czech Republic, Slovakia, Romania, Bulgaria, Hungary and Poland) under the name of 'European Network of Official Authorities in Charge of the Secret-Police Files'. This organization works in scientific, educational and informational fields.

The memory of communism: The national interest

Historiography on the legacy and memory of communism pays special attention to the place of communist rule in respective national histories. It seeks to answer the question: how do the decades of Soviet Bloc membership 'fit' into the 'organic' course of national history?

Communism as a deviation

A very influential tendency in historiography and historical-political thought presents both communism as an ideology and especially the communist social-political system as the brainchild of criminals – as a deviation, in other words, from a hypothetical 'normal' course of development.[27] According to this argumentation, communism was imposed on various societies by an alien power, the Soviet Union, the communist power that in its murderous character did not differ from Nazi Germany. The military strength of this power, reinforced by the subversive activities of a small number of domestic traitors, tried to incorporate the conquered lands into an empire of evil. The societies under attack, however, turned out to be much more resistant than originally assumed by the oppressors. Finally, encouraged and enabled by the the decline of the Soviet Union, these societies succeeded in getting rid of this brutal yoke. This idea of undue suffering inflicted on unfortunate peoples is an old stereotype of Eastern and Central European historical thought. It contrasts the unfortunate state of affairs of the age of the historian with some hypothetical past or future 'golden age' and looks for the causes of the decline and/or the potential of recovery. The golden age was frequently connected to great historical personalities such as Jan Hus in the Czech case. In Romania, it was connected to figures such as Burebista (and the whole issue of the Roman origins of Romanians),[28] Stephen the Great (1457–1504 in Moldavia), Vlad Dracul III (1456–62 in Wallachia) and Mihai Viteazul (1558–1601; in 1600 Viteazul had temporarily united Moldavia, Wallachia and Transylvania under his control). With slightly changing emphasis, these personalities could be integrated into both communist and anti-communist historical narratives.

Communism in the social fabric

Another interpretation of the making and breaking of the communist systems in Eastern and Central Europe seeks to establish to what extent communism permeated the social fabric of these societies and, when explaining the collapse of the system, focuses more on the interaction of internal problems and external factors. External factors in this interpretation do not simply mean the Soviet Union but, much more broadly, include the economic and geopolitical restructuring of the global world system. A Hungarian political scientist argues that the 'the system change did not so much have aims as in first instance causes, and the international factors going beyond the local conditions both in terms of power politics and the economy determined the changes much more than the actors of changes would have assumed . . . it is to be questioned whether the meaning and substance of the changes as perceived by their actors are identical with the scholarly interpretation of the presumably inescapable changes'.[29] Ralf Dahrendorf summarizes the respective views of a key figure of the Polish transition as follows: 'Adam Michnik likes to emphasize that the revolution of 1989 had no utopia, "no society or state ideal", though it had its dreams of freedom and rights and openness and the pursuit of truth. The dreams were and are justly cherished, but even they were not enough to create the elements of a liberal order.'[30] Public opinion, argues Prof József Bayer, hardly notices the results of historical scholarship: '. . . the analysis of the past in today's public discourse is basically limited to listing the crimes of communism or moral hysteria in connection with the (communist secret police) agents.'[31]

Victims and perpetrators

The pattern of the oppressed and exploited working people and nations in communist historiography is mirrored in some post-communist historiography of communism and in symbolic manifestations of the interpretation of the communist past. Such a pattern of thought assumes that there always exists a clearly defined borderline between victims and perpetrators, and the perpetrators are responsible for 'derailing' history. The communist train was derailed by various bourgeois counter-revolutionary enemies of progress, whereas an influential post-communist interpretation of communism blames communists for derailing the train carrying the peoples of the Soviet Bloc along the 'normal' track of history heading towards communism. The same pattern applies when the culprits for the nations' failures and great tragedies are named. The role of communists in the 1918–19 Central European revolutions is thus a heroic one from a communist perspective, and a key cause of all later disasters from a post-communist, anti-communist perspective. In the official and semi-official communist representations of Hungarian history in the twentieth century, the period of the Republic of Councils between 21 March and 1 August 1919 played a key role. After the collapse of the Habsburg Monarchy and following a short-lived democratic republic, a Communist-dominated coalition between Communists and Social Democrats took power in Hungary. According to the communist view, this proved the fact that communism was deeply rooted in Hungary. In the collective Hungarian memory and the post-communist master narrative, however, this event was described as a conspiracy and has been linked to the tragic territorial losses of the country after World War I. It is assumed in the post-communist memory of communism in Hungary that the victorious Entente powers sanctioned the dismantling of Hungary only out of fear that the country's communism would spread all over Europe. Results of decades of extensive research pointed out that this was not the case, but the myth that in fact the communists, and not the traditional elites, had led the country into a lost war, survived and was rekindled with particular intensity around the time of the post-communist transition in the early 1990s. In the political struggles of the early post-communist period, liberals (a number of them children of former Communist officials) were frequently presented as the direct personal and political descendants of the communist 'squanderers of the country'. This phenomenon was closely connected to the fact that numerous military and political leaders of the countries of the Soviet Bloc could be and actually were blamed and sued for their anti-internationalist, anti-communist and anti-Soviet policies in the course of their trials following World War II. After 1989–90, quite a number of them were rehabilitated and praised for their clearsightedness in recognizing the criminal nature of communism. In this way, for example, the attack on the Soviet Union in June 1941 could be presented as a highly legitimate preventive measure, as part of an anti-communist 'crusade'.[32]

Refighting past battles

Spectacular events were organized to emphasize the post-communist view of national history: symbolic (re)burials, the removal of old monuments and the erection of new ones and the choice of new national holidays. In Yugoslavia, the 1989 commemorations of the 600th anniversary of the death of Prince Lazar at the battlefield of Kosovo meant a return to the founding myth of the Serbian Kingdom, a myth that was to replace the cult of the Yugoslav partisans in World War II. The Croatian struggle for independence was fought not only on the battlefields, but to a very great extent in quite successful attempts at reshaping collective memory by symbolic steps, such as reerecting the monument dedicated to Jelacic[33] on the main square of Zagreb. First erected in 1866, it was removed in 1947 and, as it had been preserved, reerected at the original location as part of huge festivities in 1990.[34]

The use of fascism and National Socialism as non-analytical concepts, even as terms of abuse was quite common in both communist historiography and post-communist historical-political discourses. A random example: the front page of the Belgrade daily *Politika* argued on 9 June 1990 that Serbia's answer to the pro-fascist, rightish orientation in the north-west of Yugoslavia is a democratic, leftish, socialist orientation.[35] It is remarkable that the German Minister of Foreign Affairs, Joschka Fischer, found no better way to describe Milosevic in 1999 than to argue that he was a new Hitler.[36] In the post-communist Serbian discourse, the traditional subjects such as World War II and the struggle against Fascism did not disappear, but were given new, nationalist interpretations. The ethnically, nationally neutral dichotomy of collaboration and resistance was substituted by the 'atavistic' struggle of the nations.[37] These ideas had well-known, tragic practical consequences: at the beginning of the 1990s, large groups[38] within former Yugoslavia's population believed that they had to refight the battles of previous centuries and thus correct their outcomes.

The return to his homeland of the heart of of the Bulgarian Tsar Boris (who died in 1941 under unclarified circumstances) was a symbolic break with the communist legacy of Bulgaria (that defined Boris' rule as monarchofascism),[39] and by 2001 gave Simeon II, the son of Boris, a chance to enter the political arena of Bulgaria and achieve a sweeping victory for his party, the National Movement Simeon II. Myth, however, in the longer run, did not aid his political cause. Although his party still ranked second at the 2005 elections and was part of a big coalition from 2005 to 2009, it was not elected into parliament in 2009. Still, Bulgaria is the country where communist history propaganda in this respect most conspicuously failed. Boris, labelled a fascist oppressor of his people by communists, changed into the responsible, conscientious father of his people, and the saviour of Bulgarian Jews in post-communist Bulgaria. Parallel with the re-emergence of Simeon, the long-term Communist leader Zivkov's power and prestige collapsed more dramatically than that of any other Soviet Bloc leader – with the exception of Romania's Ceausescu.[40] Communism in mainline discourses of the memory of communism turned out to be a term of abuse in the same way fascism was in communist historical terminology and political rhetorics (and not only in Bulgaria).

The message of public spaces

More efficiently than by speeches and publications, collective memories are shaped and mobilized frequently through the use of public space and by creating special sites of memory. This includes removing, reerecting and erecting monuments and the building of museums on sites of former terror. In his extremely well-documented and most inspiring book, James Mark points out that the most successful Communist memorial museums contain 'multiple histories of suffering'. Thus the Sighet memorial in Romania marks the location of a jail under numerous successive regimes, namely the Austro-Hungarian Empire, then the Romanian state between 1919 and 1941, followed by the Hungarian state from 1941 to 1944, and finally the Romanian communist state following World War II. The House of Terror Museum in Budapest is located at the former torture centre used by the Hungarian Nazis during late 1944, after which it became the headquarters of the Communist-controlled state security.[41] At such memorial sites, communist sins and offences are shown to provide the climax of a criminal process, as the latest and most extreme example. The greatest difficulty here is posed by placing communist guilt next to fascist, Nazi crimes, and comparing the suffering of Holocaust victims with that of victims of Communism. James Mark provides an excellent example of the use of the Holocaust imaginary to demonize Communism: the Vojna Memorial in the Czech Republic (near Pribram, south of Prague). The site at which the memorial stands was originally used as a prisoner-of-war camp following its construction by German soldiers after World War II. Under communist rule, it became a political prisoners' camp from 1949 to 1960. In 1999, the Czech government decided to transform it into a museum site,[42] and at the entrance a board with the Czech equivalent of 'Arbeit macht frei' was put up. Here, the message was much more important than the originality of the exhibits (otherwise, a guiding professional principle in museums): '. . . the sign was able to tap into the power of globally recognizable imagery drawn from the Holocaust in order to alert visitors to the continuities between fascist persecution and that of Communism after the war.'[43] Over the last two decades, many books and documentaries have examined the fate of deportees to the Soviet Gulag camps. As Gulag history was hardly known in the countries of the Soviet Bloc, explanation and interpretation are in most cases also related to the Holocaust. It is frequently argued that, although the victim toll of the Holocaust and that of the Gulag terror are comparable, much less attention was paid to the latter.[44] There is some confusion in properly identifying the victims of communist terror, as war criminals and ordinary criminals could easily be mixed together with real targets of destructive terror among the participants of the loosely defined national resistance against communism.[45] A bad scandal broke out in Budapest when a researcher proved that in the special section of the largest Budapest cemetery, dedicated to people who have sacrificed their lives for their homeland, a number of war criminals executed in the aftermath of World War II were also buried.[46] The graves of the victims of the post-1956 revolution terror are also located in a section of the cemetery where people executed for war crimes or manslaughter can also be found. As a result, official tributes to the victims of communism can be seen to honour simple criminals as well – albeit quite unintentionally. When the present followers of Hungarian Nazis realized that some of their 'heroes' were buried on this site, they started using it as a meeting place of their own.

Comparing Hitler, Stalin and Truman

Recently, both politics and scholarship have been looking for new frameworks of interpretation of the murderous nature of communism, Nazism and fascism. In the course of this search, reassessing the significance of 1945 as a chronological borderline has taken on great significance. In other words, if the Stalin regime is as murderous as the Nazi one, the real turning-point comes not with the end of the war but with Stalin's death. As Jan T. Gross put it: 'In one part of the continent, the Nazi-instigated war and the Communist-driven postwar takeovers constituted one integral period. We could note this by pointing out the continuities in the transformation of the social fabric, as well as the affinities in the deployed strategies of subjugation.'[47] If we broaden the scope and take into account mass murders and other crimes in other regimes as well, including those committed by all the victors of World War II, the analysis becomes even more difficult. The broader the horizon, the larger the number of case studies, and the harder it becomes to apply the intellectually and politically comfortable and reassuring separation of victims, perpetrators and onlookers. If we analyse the memory of communism in this broader context, we should pay attention to Daniel Goldhagen's warning: 'The difficulty of keeping distant the three tasks of definition, explanation, and moral evaluation muddles considerations of mass murder. The passions of assigning guilt, blame, or moral responsibility hijack the other two usually cooler enterprises. This happens constantly in discussions of the Holocaust . . . we can, as a matter of fact, call Truman's annihilation of the people of Hiroshima and Nagasaki mass murder and the man a mass murderer, putting Truman and his deeds into the same broad categories of Hitler and the Holocaust, Stalin and the Gulag, Pol Pot, Mao, Saddam Hussein, and Slobodan Milosevic and their victims, without giving the same explanation for Truman's actions as we do for theirs, and without judging them morally as being equivalent.'[48]

Do personalities change with regimes?

A comprehensive approach to the memory of communism, as one type of authoritarian rule, can hardly do without taking into account individual and social psychological factors as well. Did the collapse of the communist, authoritarian regimes lead to a decrease in people's inclination towards authoritarianism as well? Do authoritarian personalities vanish with the demise of authoritarian regimes? One recent and intriguing investigation into these questions is based on the methods of empirical sociology and social psychology. In 1998, a group of Central European social scientists decided to contrast the classical work of Adorno and his colleagues on the authoritarian personality of 1950[49] with their new empirical research.

The essays seek out correlations between the mindset and psychological traits of individuals and their political behavior in various regions. One of the articles is based on the answers of about 10,000 students from 44 countries (the interviews were conducted between 1991 and 1997), analysing their democratic, authoritarian and multiculturalist attitudes. Of the eight world regions (Western Europe, the Pacific Islands, Latin America, Africa, North America, Asia, Eastern Europe, Russia and the CIS), Russia and the CIS had the least support for democracy and the highest level of authoritarianism. The East European respondents also showed strong inclinations towards authoritarianism, but rejected dictatorships. The strongest support for democracy could be detected on the Pacific Islands and in Western Europe, surpassing the USA! Popular attitudes towards authoritarianism were thus stronger in regions formerly under communist rule, so the results of this research support the point that the transformation of mentalities does not follow the pace of political changes.

A theoretically very well-grounded project of 1993 with a small but representative sample of 30 interviewees was based on Bourdieu's interpretation of human *habitus* and Halbwachs'collective memory concept.[50] According to this group of Hungarian researchers, what the two concepts have in common is that in spite of the fast pace of social and political changes in modern societies, *habitus* as defined by Bourdieu and collective memories as defined by Halbwachs set limits to the autonomy of the individual's reactions to these changes. The surprising conclusion of the project was that the mechanisms of collective memory structure post-communist societies more than economic factors. In other words, the boundaries among the major social groups identified by this research were defined less along the lines of wealth and income than they were by differences in the way the collective communist past is perceived. This, of course, does not mean that the differing economic positions did not matter, but rather that social background and family roots shaped attitudes towards communism more than current positions in the income hierarchy. On a much broader scale, a careful analysis of election results at a neighbourhood level can also confirm that the supporters of parties cannot be differentiated according to wealthier or poorer neighbourhoods.[51]

Another small-scale empirical Hungarian research project (2003) is also worth mentioning because of its unique starting hypothesis: being successful in terms of individual performance was alien to the value system of socialism. Success could only be promoted by the caring socialist state that on the one hand protected its citizens from the vicissitudes of the free market, but on the other set firm limits to creativity. In principle, the system change cleared away the political and ideological obstacles to rapid self-assertion and, indeed, impressive careers were launched. Strangely enough, however, this did not change mentalities. These research results show that in comparison with the immediate aftermath of the system change, egalitarianism became stronger, while meritocratism weakened among the members of the major target group cited by the research project, young male professionals, as well as in other sections of society.[52]

The memory of communism: Backwardness

It was especially Polish and Hungarian sociologists, social and economic historians[53] who, during the 1960s, started looking into the peculiarities of regional economic and social development 'east of the river Elbe'. It was along the river Elbe that Europe was divided into the two groups of liberal democracies on the one hand, and peoples' democracies on the other after World War II. As a consequence, the historical question was politically highly charged: to what an extent is this river the border between historically defined regions and not just a line of division arbitrarily imposed on Europe by the US and the Soviet Union?

Charlemagne, Churchill, Roosevelt and Stalin

As the outstanding Hungarian mediavelist, Jenő Szűcs, put it in a very influential essay on the regions of Europe: 'a very sharp line of demarcation that was in fact to cut Europe into two parts from the point of view of economic and social structure after 1500, divided off the far larger, more easterly part as the scene of the second serfdom. Moreover Europe in our time (the turn of the 1970s and 1980s), another 500 years later still, is divided more clearly than ever before into two "camps" almost exactly along that same line (with a slight deviation in Thuringia). It is as if Stalin, Churchill and Roosevelt had studied carefully the status quo of the age of Charlemagne on the 1130th anniversary of his death.'[54] This raises another fundamental issue: the origins of the backwardness of the societies of the Soviet Bloc. It was mainly Gerschenkron's and Immanuel Wallerstein's works that helped in putting this problem into a global context. Both social scientists of communist countries and researchers into the legacy and memory of communism had to confront a challenging question: did the socialist–communist systems aggravate the gap between the regions East and West of the river Elbe (the river understood as a symbolic borderline between socialist and capitalist Europe), or was it the other way round? In other words, were the communist systems a monumental attempt at catching up, accelerating the modernization process in the traditionally underdeveloped Eastern and Southeastern parts of Europe? Perhaps, as some researchers have argued, this question is misleading, because rather than there being one standard pattern of development (i.e. the one shaped by the French political and the British industrial revolutions),[55] there exist several alternative modes of European (and global) economic, social and political development. Any attempts at imposing a 'Western' model onto 'Eastern' societies can lead to disasters. From the early 1980s on, the search for a definition of a transitory 'Central European' region[56] seemed to prove fruitful, but following the collapse of the Soviet Bloc, this search for an 'in-between' area lost its relevance.

Enforced path or free choice?

The new, very topical question concerning the regions of Europe is: to what an extent are the possibilities, pace and methods of the Eastern enlargement of the European Union and NATO determined by deeper-lying, historically determined 'hard facts' of long-term economic, social and political development? Do the various 'circles' of EU expansion just reflect unfortunate developments in current affairs and the arbitrary decisions of uninformed, uneducated 'Eurocrats' and NATO officials, or is the truth very different? In fact, the pessimistic hypothesis argued, despite the best intentions and the great efforts of responsible politicians, the ghost of history has not been laid and continues to force East and Central European societies down a 'set path'. In search of the factors that make it possible for the societies of the former Soviet bloc to join the European Union, both scholarly and political analyses focus more on intellectual and cultural legacies (with special emphasis on religion and churches) than on economic and social structures, or political institutions. Here, the unity of Western civilization is more apparent: numerous scholars argue that communism could be destructive in terms of ruining the economy and terrorizing society, but it was unable to cut off cultural roots. As part of this continuing discussion, in the post-communist political climate a number of historians who started their careers during the 1970s suggested that evidence for the early modern origins of the gap between Eastern and Western Europe presented by the previous generations, that is, the founders of Marxist historical scholarship in the countries of the Soviet Bloc,[57] served political more than scholarly interests. It sought to supply historical arguments to legitimate the post-World War II division of Europe. However, the ensuing discussion revealed that understanding the history of East and West as one of economic and social divergence had been part of the agenda of German, Hungarian and Polish economic history long before the Yalta Conference. Still, with the Soviet Bloc seemingly consolidated for all eternity, it was inevitable that research into the various aspects of European regionalism and 'backwardness' would have political implications. Defining the 'backwardness', underdevelopment, peculiarities and origins of regional differences in Europe is still on the research agenda of historians of the post-Soviet region, but this agenda is embedded more within a global context, within research into world systems. This research looks at the fall of the European communist systems not just from the perspective of the victory of democracy over authoritarianism but at the same time also focuses on the emergence and decline of neoliberal ideologies and political movements.

The decades from the early 1980s through to the present crisis had witnessed the strengthening of East Central European alternative civilian movements and their development into political factors. This long-term and multifaceted process reached a climax in 1989–91 with the fall of the Berlin wall, the collapse of the Yalta system and the disintegration of the Soviet Union. The same decades, however, also saw the rise and fall of neoliberal illusions connected to the global process of democratization, the termination of the division of Europe and the capacities of the welfare state.[58]

Conclusion

The dismantling of the communist view of history and/or the communist approach to the past in the countries of the Soviet Bloc was not an abrupt, unexpected change (unlike the political transformation) but rather an extended process. There are essential stereotypes, patterns of thought and key issues that connect the communist view of history with the memory of communism in post-communist societies. The widest bridge here connects to national identities: according to the communist view, the peak of the progress of national societies is reached with the ultimate (and inescapable) victory of socialism and then communism in every single country. In post-communist societies, there are many conflicting views of the legacy of communism, in terms of the good or harm it did to the national interest. A common trend in the literature presents the revival of nationalism in the countries of the former Soviet Bloc as a key issue: it is seen as a strong political force, even a severe danger. Zbigniew Brzezinski and Adam Michnik agreed that nationalism is the last, unavoidable stage of communism. A contrary, more traditional view argues that the resurgence of radical nationalism is a reaction to its having been suppressed during communist rule; it filled the ideological vacuum after the fall of communism. The third, in my view, most convincing interpretation points to the ongoing presence of nationalism in Eastern and Central Europe since the early nineteenth century: in spite of the internationalist rhetoric of communist ideology, most of the time and in most places, nationalism and communism merged. After 1989, as Iván T. Berend puts it, this 'new-old nationalism, a consequence of "unfinished nation building" in peripheral Central and Eastern Europe, became visible, unmasked and open'.[59]

These issues hardly fit into the mainstream of present-day historical scholarship, as research interests focus more and more on supra- and subnational problems. The nation, of course, remains a point of reference for historians, as 'national history has been a dominant genre of history writing in Europe for almost two centuries'.[60] The national narratives, however, are being challenged more and more not only by other national narratives but also by various types of comparative and transnational approaches (with respect to religion, class, ethnicity, race, gender, peculiarities of regions and empires) and by explorations of the relationship between man and his natural and built environment. The role of the state remains a major research issue, though not so much as the conduit of national interests, but as a servant or oppressor of the citizen. Recalling the memory of communism from the perspective of national interests is not a key issue of the mainstream historiography of the last 20 years. This memory has been and is being dealt with more from the perspectives discussed above: what influence did communism have on the environment, on the modernization of infrastructures, on the quality of modern life? The most visible issue in exchanges over the memory and legacy of communism, however, is still the responsibility of communism for the devastating wars and massacres of the twentieth century.

If we accept the point that, while the system change in the Soviet Union and in the countries of the Soviet bloc was due to many factors that made the communist system unmanageable, there existed aside from the dismantling of that system no clear programme for the future, then we could argue that the rebuttal of the communist past and the negation of communism gave a common identity to the very mixed group of agents involved in the transition period. Just as communist politicians and numerous communist ideologists wanted to 'sweep away' the past and praised their system for destroying the reactionary 'feudo-capitalist' regimes, so the rejection of communism was the 'constituting other'[61] for post-communist regimes.

Notes

1 In spite of its relative length, the chapter can only give a rough outline of these problems. Two recent books with extensive bibliographies can guide the interested reader further: James Mark, *The Unfinished Revolution. Making Sense of the Communist Past in Central-Eastern Europe* (London, 2010); and Stefan Troebst (ed.), *Politische Geschichtskulturen im Süden und Osten Europas. Bestandsaufnahme und Forschungsperspektiven* (Göttingen, 2010). Indispensable when dealing with the memory of communism in Eastern and Central Europe is an earlier book by Vladimir Tismaneanu, *Fantasies of Salvation. Democracy, Nationalism and Myth in Post-Communist Europe* (Princeton, 1998).

2 Such projects included *European Historical Consciousness*, a cooperation between the Körber Stiftung in Hamburg and the Institute for Advanced Study in the Humanitites (KWI), Essen, under the direction of Jörn Rüsen (1998 to 2000), and the European Science Foundation Project *Representations of the Past: The Writing of National Histories in Nineteenth and Twentieth Century Europe (NHIST)* from 2003 to 2008. My involvement in such projects was as a Hungarian coordinator of *the European Network of Remembrance and Solidarity* (www.enrs.eu), and as a member of both the curatorium of the Willy Brandt Institut in Wroclaw, and the advisory council of the *Imre Kertész Kolleg* in Jena.

3   A very special, most original piece in the literature of my subject is István Rév, *Retroactive Justice. Prehistory of Post Communism. Cultural Memory in the Present* (Stanford, 2005), an imagined prehistory of the collapse of communism using literary methods.

4   I was born in 1950. Cf. the website: www.single-generation.de/kohorten/68er. htm (accessed 3 March 2013) that gives a list of some better known members of this generation and hosts a debate on their achievements.

5   Here is the root of the frequently referenced statement by the most creative and influential Marxist philosopher of the twentieth century, György Lukács: 'the worst socialism is better than the best capitalism' (first stated in *Népszabadság*, the Hungarian party daily, on 24 December 1967).

6   Professor Georg Iggers gave a most succinct summary of the two axioms of the Marxist interpretation of history in a paper prepared for the 2010 Amsterdam World Congress of Historians. The one is the economic interpretation of history, the other the interpretation of class struggle as the driving force of history. (The paper was sent to the author of this essay as a manuscript.)

7   A typical formulation from a standard manual of Marxist philosophy ran: 'the positivists lead a crusade against scientific abstractions that helps us to define the essence of things, under the banner of a struggle against "abstraction" and "pure speculation" for positive (factual) knowledge.' In *A marxista filozófia alapjai* (*The Basics of Marxist Philosophy*) (Kossuth, 1959), p. 352.

8   For a contemporary appraisal, see M. B. Mitin, M. D. Kammari, and M. D. Aleksandrov, 'The Contribution of J. V. Stalin to Marxism-Leninism', in *The Seventieth Anniversary of Joseph Vissarionovich Stalin*, published in Izvestia Akademii Nauk SSSR, Seria Istorii i Filosofii, Tom VII, Izdatelstvo Akademii Nauk SSSR (Moscow, 1950), pp. 3–30. See http://www.revolutionarydemocracy.org/rdv4n1/stalin70.htm (accessed 3 March 2013).

9   The best example for this approach is a comprehensive 10-volume 'History of the World' published by the Soviet Academy of Sciences during the 1950s.

10 Jenő Szűcs, *Nation und Geschichte* (Budapest, 1981).

11 Cf. the works by Zsigmond Pál Pach, Iván T. Berend, and György Ránki.

12 See Péter Hanák, 'Hungary in the Austro-Hungarian Monarchy: Preponderancy or Dependency?'. *Austrian History Yearbook* 3:1 (1967), 260–302.

13 Jerzy Tomaszewski, 'The Different Histories of Twentieth-Century Poland', in Erik Lönnroth, Karl Molin, Ranar Björk (eds), *Conceptions of National History. Proceedings of Nobel symposium* 78 (Berlin-New York, 1994), p. 233.

14 Piotr S. Wandycz, 'Historiography of the Countries of Eastern Europe: Poland'. *The American Historical Review* 97:4 (October 1992), 1011–25, here p. 1018.

15 Wandycz, 'Historiography of the Countries of Eastern Europe: Poland', p. 1021.

16 Jiri Koralka, 'Historiography of the Countries of Eastern Europe: Czechoslovakia'. *American Historical Review* 97:4 (October 1992), 1026–40, here p. 1028.

17 Keith Hitchins, 'Historiography of the Countries of Eastern Europe: Romania'. *American Historical Review* 97:4 (October 1992), 1064–83, here p. 1081.

18   Maria Todorova, 'Historiography of the Countries of Eastern Europe:
     Bulgaria'. *American Historical Review* 97:4 (October 1992), 1105–17,
     here p. 1108.

19   Todorova, 'Historiography of the Countries of Eastern Europe: Bulgaria',
     p. 1117.

20   Ivo Banac, 'Historiography of the Countries of Eastern Europe: Yugoslavia'.
     American Historical Review 97:4 (October 1992), 1084–104, here p. 1101.

21   Vasilije Krestic, 'O genezi genocida nad Srbima u NDH', *Knijezewne novine*,
     15 September 1986, 5. Quoted by Ivo Banac, 'Historiography of the Countries
     of Eastern Europe: Yugoslavia', p. 1101. Krestic also organized a successful
     campaign against a nationally moderate colleague of his, Drago Roksandic.
     Roksandic was fired from the University of Belgrade in 1989. See the protest
     letter of a number of foreign collegues in *The New York Review of Books* 37:5
     (29 March 1990).

22   For the most recent and comprehensive survey, see Mark, *The Unfinished
     Revolution.*

23   http.//www.haon.hu/china-and-hungary-form-new-major-alliance,
     25 June 2011.

24   Adrian Cioflanca, 'Politics of Oblivion in Post-Communist Romania'. *The
     Romanian Journal of Political Science* 2 (2002), 85–93, here p. 90 (cited by
     Mark, *The Unfinished Revolution*, p. 35). A good insight into the theoretical-
     methodological approach to communism represented by the commission is
     offered in a presentation by its prestigious chairman, Vladimir Tismaneanu,
     educated in Bucharest, but living in the West since 1981. See http://www.
     wilsoncenter.org/publication/241-understanding-radical-evil-communism-
     fascism-and-the-lessons-the-20th-century (accessed 3 March 2013).

25   Mark, *The Unfinished Revolution*, p. 40.

26   Ibid., p. 46.

27   Cf. Stéphane Courtois, Nicolas Werth, Jean-Louis Panné, Karel Bartosek, Jean-
     Louis Margolin, Andrzej Paczkowski (eds), *Le livre noir du communism* (Paris,
     1997). I have used the English version: Stéphane Courtois et al. (eds), *The
     Black Book of Communism: Crimes, Terror, Repression* (Cambridge, 1999).
     The book has been translated into nearly 20 languages and is well known in
     post-communist countries.

28   The most comprehensive book on the origins of the myth is by Adolf
     Armbruster, *Romanitatea Romanilor. Istoria unei idei* (Bucharest, 1993). For a
     review, see Ambrus Miskolczy, 'Historical Verities'. *Budapest Review of Books*
     1 (1997), 18–22.

29   József Bayer, 'A rendszerváltásról két évtized múltán', in József Bayer
     and Boda Zsolt, (eds), *A rendszerváltás húsz éve:változások és válaszok*
     (Budapest, 2009), p. 13. The difference between the perspective of
     contemporaries and that of later historians is, of course, an old problem
     of historical theory and methodology. See especially the works of Reinhart
     Koselleck. For an excellent selection in English of some of his most important
     essays, see *The Practice of Conceptual History: Timing History, Spacing
     Concepts* (Stanford, 2002).

30 Ralf Dahrendorf, *Universities after Communism* (Hamburg, 2000). 11. For the Michnik quotation, see *Lettre Internaionale* 25:2 (1994), p. 11.

31 Bayer, 'A rendszerváltásról két évtized múltán', p. 14.

32 On 30 July 1990, the 90-year-old Kálmán Kéri, a high-ranking anti-Nazi officer of the Hungarian army during World War II and the oldest member of the new, freely elected Hungarian parliament argued that although it was unfortunate that the Hungarian army got to the Don river, the army's struggle was just; it was fighting communism. In the ensuing debate, the historian Prime Minister, József Antall, pointed out the great dilemma of Hungarian military and political leaders during World War II: the anti-fascist political forces allied for overthrowing Hitler's Germany included Stalin's Soviet Union as well. For Hungary, fighting on the side of Germany meant fighting against communism, a justified cause in this interpretation, and at the same time against the anti-Hitler allies, a wrong cause from this perspective. Antall was trying to explain that, far from justifying Hungary's participation in World War II on the 'wrong' side, the old officer was defending the honour of his fellow soldiers who carry no responsibility for being sent to the front. See http://www.antalljozsef.hu/node/72 (accessed 3 March 2013).

33 Jozef Jelacic (1801–59), the Croatian national leader who, in 1848–49, had a decisive role in crushing the Hungarian anti-Habsburg war of independence, became a symbolic figure of Croatian national identity and sovereignty.

34 Iskra Iveljic, 'Cum ira et studio. Geschichte und Gesellschaft Kroatiens in den 1990er Jahren', in Helmut Altrichter (ed.), *GegenErinnerung. Geschichte als politiches Argument* (Munich, 2006), p. 197.

35 Carl Bethke and Holm Sundhaussen, 'Zurück zur alten Übersichtlichkeit? Geschichte in den jugoslawischen Nachfolgekriegen 1991–2000', in Altrichter (ed.), *GegenErinnerung*, p. 207.

36 *taz*, 13 April 1999 (cited by Bethke and Sundhausen, 'Zurück zur alten Übersichtlichkeit?', p. 217).

37 Bethke and Sundhausen, 'Zurück zur alten Übersichtlichkeit?', p. 211.

38 Ibid.

39 Markus Wien, 'Die bulgarische Monarchie', in Altrichter, *GegenErinnerung*, pp. 219–36.

40 The most recent and most detailed description of this process has been provided by Iskra Baeva, Evgenija Kalinova and Nikolaj Poppetrov, 'Die kommunistische Ära im kollektiven Gedächtnis der Bulgaren', in Stefan Troebst (ed.), *Postdiktatorische Geschichtskulturen im Süden und Osten Europas. Bestandsaufnahme und Forschungsperspektiven* (Göttingen, 2010), pp. 405–501.

41 Mark, *The Unfinished Revolution*, p. 67.

42 See http://www.muzeum-pribram.cz/jaziky/anglicky/vojnamemorial/vojnamemorial.html (accessed 3 March 2013). The museum opened in 2005.

43 Mark, *The Unfinished Revolution*, p. 70.

44 In addition to translations of *The Black Book of Communism* and Anne Applebaum's *GULAG. A History of the Camps* (New York, 2003), numerous

local research projects deal with the issue. Much has been published about the Hungarian victims in particular. See the rich bibliography in Steven Béla Várdy and Agnes Várdy, *Stalin's Gulag. The Hungarian Experience* (Naples, 2007).

45 For a general survey of the problem, cf. István Deák, Jan T. Gross and Tony Judt (eds), *The Politics of Retribution in Europe. World War Two and Its Aftermath* (Princeton, 2001).

46 Tamás Csapody, 'Felmagasztosult keretlegények. Öt sír nyomában a Rákoskeresztúri új köztemető 298-as parcellájában', *Népszabadság, Hétvége*, 24 November 2007, pp. 2–3. During the spring of 2008, a five-member historians' commission examined the graves and especially the large marble plaques where names of common criminals and murderers appear together with those of victims of communist terror. Their research proved that 40 per cent of the 315 names on the plaque referred to common criminals. As a result, in June 2008 the plaque was taken down; but the corpses were not identified and were not removed.

47 Deák, Gross and Judt, *The Politics of Retribution*, p. 31.

48 Daniel Jonah Goldhagen, *Worse than War. Genocide, Eliminationism, and the Ongoing Assault on Humanity* (New York, 2009).

49 Theodor W. Adorno, Else Frenkel-Brunswik, Daniel Levinson, and Nevitt Sanford, *The Authoritarian Personality* (New York, 1950).

50 Richárd László, 'Posztkommunista társadalom és kollektív emlékezet'. *Valóság* 2 (February 1999), 1–18.

51 For a comprehensive theoretical approach to this problem with examples from the first half of the 1990s, see Jason Wittenberg, 'Rethinking Political Continuity in East Central Europe', in John S. Micgiel (ed.), *Perspectives on Political and Economic Transitions after Communism* (New York, 1997).

52 Mária Székelyi (with György-Örkény Csepeli and Ildikó Antal-Barna), 'Blindness to success. Social-psychological objectives along the way to a market economy in Eastern Europe', in János Kornai, Bo Rothstein and Susan Rose-Ackeman (eds), *Creating Social Trust in Post-Socialist Transition* (New York, 2004), pp. 213–40.

53 The most well known scholars here are Jerzy Jedlicky, Iván T. Berend, GyörgyRánki, Pál Zsigmond Pach, Miroslav Hroch, and Emil Niederhauser.

54 Jenő Szűcs, 'The Three Historical Regions of Europe: An Outline'. *Acta Historica Academiae Scientiarum Hungaricae* 29 (1983), 133.

55 For a concise and lucid summary of the key issues of this debate, see Andrew C. Janos, *East Central Europe in the Modern World. The Politics of the Borderlands from Pre- to Postcommunism* (Stanford, 2000), especially pp. 11–124.

56 The first uses of the concept date back to the first half of the nineteenth century, but an impetus for this research was provided by the famous writer Miloslav Kundera in his famous 1984 article 'The Tragedy of Central Europe'. *New York Review of Books* 31:7 (26 April 1984). For a short but thorough survey of these debates, see the wide-ranging article by the young Czech historian Michal Kopecek, 'From Kundera to Visegrad', at

http://www.visegrad.info/?q=hu/node/78frk (published July 2004, and accessed 3 March 2013).

57 Pál Zsigmond Pach, Die ungarische Agrarentwicklung im 16.-17. Jahrhundert. Abbiegung vom westeuropäischen Entwicklungsgang (Budapest, 1964); idem., Hungary and the European Economy in Early Modern Times (Aldershot, 1994). For a critical approach, see Gábor Gyáni, 'Történészviták hazánk Európán belüli hovatartozásáról', Valóság 1988, p. 4; and Gábor Gyáni, 'Hol tart ma a történészek régióvitája?'. Limes 3–4 (1999), 51–65.

58 Ferenc Miszlivetz, A világrendszer ingája és a Jövőegyetem. Beszélgetések Immanuel Wallersteinnel (Szombathely, 2010), pp. 10–11; and Ivan T. Berend, From the Soviet Bloc to the European Union: the Economic and Social Transformation of Central and Eastern Europe since 1973 (Cambridge, 2009).

59 Ivan T. Berend, Central and Eastern Europe 1944–1993. Detour from the Periphery to the Periphery (Cambridge, 1996), pp. 367–71.

60 Stefan Berger and Chris Lorenz, 'Introduction: National History Writing in Europe in a Global Age', in Stefan Berger and Chris Lorenz (eds), The Contested Nation. Ethnicity, Class, Religion and Gender in National Histories (Basingstoke, 2008), pp. 1–23, here p. 1.

61 For more on this concept, see Iver B. Neumann, 'Russia as Central Europe's Constituting Other'. East European Politics and Societies 7:2 (Spring 1993), 349–69. For a discussion of identity construction by negation, see Chris Lorenz, 'Representations of Identity: Ethnicity, Race, Class, Gender and Religion. An Introduction to Conceptual History', in Berger and Lorenz (eds), The Contested Nation, pp. 24–59, here 25–6.

Further reading

Ivan T. Berend, Central and Eastern Europe 1944–1993. Detour from the Periphery to the Periphery (Cambridge, 1996).

Stéphane Courtois, Nicolas Werth, Jean-Louis Panne, Andrzej Paczkowski, Karel Bartosek and Jean-Louis Margolin, The Black Book of Communism: Crimes, Terror, Repression (Cambridge, 1999).

István Deák, Jan T. Gross, Tony Judt (eds), The Politics of Retribution in Europe. World War Two and Its Aftermath (Princeton, 2001).

Maciej Górny, 'Die Wahrheit ist auf unserer Seite'. Nation, Marxismus und Geschichte im Ostblock (Cologne, Weimar and Vienna, 2011).

Historiography of the Countries of Eastern Europe, special edition of American Historical Review 97:4 (1992).

History of Communism in Europe (Review published by the Institute for the Investigation of Communist Crimes in Bucharest) Volume 1 (2010): Politics of Memory in Post-Communist Europe.

Andrew C. Janos, East Central Europe in the Modern World. The Politics of the Borderlands from Pre- to Postcommunism (Stanford, 2000).

James Mark, The Unfinished Revolution. Making Sense of the Communist Past in Central-Eastern Europe (London, 2010).

John S. Micgiel (ed.), *Perspectives on Political and Economic Transitions after Communism* (New York, 1997).

István Rév, *Retroactive Justice. Prehistory of Post Communism. Cultural Memory in the Present* (Stanford, 2005).

Vladimir Tismaneanu, *Fantasies of Salvation. Democracy, Nationalism and Myth in Post-Communist Europe* (Princeton, 1998).

Jerzy Tomaszewski, 'The Different Histories of Twentieth-Century Poland', in Erik Lönnroth, Karl Molin, Ranar Björk (eds), *Conceptions of National History. Proceedings of Nobel Symposium 78* (Berlin-New York, 1994).

Stefan Troebst (ed.), *Postdiktatorische Geschichtskulturen im Süden und Osten Europas. Bestandsaufnahme und Forschungsperspektiven* (Göttingen, 2010).

CHAPTER NINE

Holocaust memoriography and the impact of memory on the historiography of the Holocaust

Peter Carrier

Few events in contemporary history have inspired as many works about memory as the Holocaust.[*] These works testify to such creativity and innovation that, collectively, they merit being defined as a category of historiography in its own right as Holocaust 'memoriography', a body of professional historical writings which deals with the way in which this event is recalled and understood in the present. A glance at some of the major titles in this field reveals that, in practical terms, most works of Holocaust memoriography are not works of memory, but primarily works *about* memory. In other words, they reflect theoretically about techniques of representing memory, about historians' complex relation to their own and other people's memories and about ethics, gender, ideology and law. In practice, although memory tops the bill as one of the favourite topics of contemporary Holocaust historiography, historians generally shirk discussion of the genuinely subjective aspect of memory, with all its contradictions and flaws, because it cannot be encapsulated in a clearly structured narrative. Those historians who do address such evidence as diaries, witness accounts, art or music, for example, operate on the periphery of the discipline, while classic works of Holocaust memoriography, such as Lawrence Langer's *Holocaust Testimonies* or Sybil Milton's *In Fitting*

Memory, do not fit squarely into the historiographical canon. Many historians are either sceptical towards or dismissive of memory. Annette Wieviorka and Dominique Mehl, for example, claim that the evidence contained in witness reports is prone to instrumentalization, subject to the limited subjective knowledge of authors, and gives priority to feelings over reflection. Mehl even concludes that the enhanced status of the witness reflects 'a crisis of expert discourse and a calling into question of the pedagogical authority of the historian'.[1] Peter Novick calls testimony a 'not very useful historical source'.[2] Or else memory is subsumed to history, as in the case of Konrad Jarausch's index reference to 'Memory, burden of', which advises readers to 'See history, burden of'![3]

At the present time, Holocaust memoriography is largely a *meta*genre, one which reflects upon the relation between memory and history. At least since the 1980s, historians have taken a keen interest in the memorial distortions of knowledge of the Holocaust, the political and social implications of evocations of this event, as well as the impact of memory on their own writings. By necessity, the study of memory compels historians to deal with questions concerning epistemology, politics, religion, ethics and language. Conversely, it also compels specialists of these disciplines to address the significance of the past, and has led to a blossoming of interdisciplinary encounters and writings which have enriched the field of contemporary history. In short, the Holocaust has acted as a catalyst by opening the historical discipline to other disciplines, and vice versa. Where barriers between hitherto distinct disciplines and their institutional administration have weakened, new questions have been applied to new (or old) sources, and audiences have encountered and appropriated unfamiliar concepts. Unlike the topics dealt with in the first volume of *Writing History*, Holocaust memoriography can be circumscribed neither by its theme (as in economic history) nor by its method (as in oral history). Instead, it proposes an alternative genre based on *interdisciplinarity* and focused on socially practicable *constructions* of historical understanding.

In this short survey of the issues and debates arising from the preoccupation with memory in writings about the Holocaust, I will argue that the study of memory began well before the catchword 'memory' entered the vocabulary of academic speech and writing. Moreover, although recollections of the Holocaust are typically addressed in terms of their political utility (to specific groups at specific times in specific places), they have also elicited a number of epistemological issues which cut across social, temporal and spatial boundaries. The examples from English, French and German writings about the Holocaust examined in this chapter reveal how issues relevant to specific groups at specific times and places are contiguous, and raise questions which are echoed in the memoriographies of events other than the Holocaust, and should thus provide guidance to students who approach the field of memory in their own writings.

1 Memoriography of the Holocaust before the memory boom

In *The Destruction of the European Jews* (1961), one of the first thorough and perhaps most enduring works of history about the Holocaust, Raul Hilberg wrote that,

> As time passes on, the destruction of the European Jews will recede into the background. Its most immediate consequences are almost over, and whatever developments may henceforth be traced to the catastrophe will be consequences of consequences, more and more remote. Already the Nazi outburst has become historical. But this is a strange page in history. Few events of modern times were so filled with unpredicted action and unsuspected death. A primordial impulse had suddenly surfaced among the Western nations; it had been unfettered through their machines. From this moment, fundamental assumptions about our civilization have no longer stood unchallenged, for while the occurrence is past, the phenomenon remains.[4]

At least 20 years before the word 'memory' pervaded the minds and works of academic enquiry,[5] Hilberg effectively anticipated a topic which was to increasingly preoccupy historians, sociologists, political and social scientists and philosophers who attempted to understand and explain the Holocaust. Moreover, Hilberg indicates not only why the Holocaust was to remain one of the most prolific objects of historiography well into the twenty-first century, but also why the number of articles and books about this topic has *increased* over time.

In broad terms, without referring explicitly to 'memory', Hilberg explains the continuing interest in the Holocaust not as a result of the extraordinarily high numbers of people who were killed, or how and why they were killed, but in terms of (a) the shock resulting from the fact that this event had not been predicted and that its consequences had been inadequately recognized, and (b) the challenge, represented by this event, to values acquired in the course of humanist Enlightenment tradition in the west. Though formulated in highly metaphorical spatial, temporal and kinetic terms, Hilberg's account of an event which 'recedes' into the past while its traces transcend the period of the event itself and cause 'consequences of consequences' is a succinct definition of the otherwise elusive concept of 'memory', which is not an arbitrary analytical concept (as critics of memory studies frequently claim) but a necessary response to an event whose scale was unprecedented, and whose consequences cast doubt on the viability of humanist tradition itself. This is why Hilberg's deceptively simple suggestion that 'while the occurrence is past, the phenomenon remains' effectively heralds the subsequent preoccupation with memory among multiple academic disciplines, and among professional historians and museum workers alike.

It was over 20 years after Hilberg's precursory statements about the way in which the past (in this case, National Socialism and the Holocaust) would be remembered and understood in the future that Saul Friedländer, an equally authoritative historian of the Holocaust, boldly addressed (and largely ushered in study of) the memory of National Socialism and the Holocaust in psychoanalytical terms, as an 'obsession' with the past based on 'fears' and 'hidden desires':

> Nazism has disappeared, but the obsession which it represents for contemporary imagination along with the appearance of a new discourse which ceaselessly elaborates on this past and reinterprets it forces us to respond to the ultimate question: with one's attention turned towards the past, is this obsession in fact nothing more than gratuitous reverie, the attraction of spectacle, a necessary exorcism and a constant need to understand, or is it rather, now as it always was, the expression of profound fears and, for some people, of hidden desires?[6]

Whereas Hilberg had tentatively predicted the process by which the past event would recede in time while its consequences continued to preoccupy us in the present, Friedländer argues retrospectively that this historical 'spectacle' colours people's dreams and drives their emotions in the face of (if not because of) ongoing incomprehension. Friedländer further explains the lingering fascination with National Socialism and the Holocaust beyond the event itself (which is perhaps the very condition of memory) in terms of its emotional impact, and metaphorically in terms of an 'after-image', as when a bright light leaves an impression on the brain well after the source of light has been removed.[7]

The significance of these remarks is that they enable us to locate the impulse for studies about memory of the Holocaust as a necessary consequence of the Holocaust. Holocaust memoriography is not, as some sceptics claim, an academic fashion, but an expedient and compelling response to the event itself. Indeed, it is the sense of urgency that the *effects* of the Holocaust or 'consequences of consequences' need to be acknowledged and analysed which underpins Holocaust memoriography. Moreover, both Hilberg's and Friedländer's recognition that the Holocaust represented a shock, in the form of a caesura in humanist tradition and radical challenge to existing methods of historical explanation, suggests that historical writing may adequately account for this event only if it combines factual evidence with evidence of recollections, representations and modes of understanding on the basis of a partnership between historians, historians of ideas, philosophers, sociologists, linguists and psychoanalysts. The study of memory should not, therefore, be conceived as an *alternative* to the study of historiography (as popular polemic would have us believe), but as its *complement*. For the very beginnings of professional Holocaust historiography contain in germ the shift from explanations of the event itself (the relation between actions and their motives) to explanations of the effects of the event (the relation between actions and their consequences today) and the challenge it poses to our understanding. When writing about memory in relation to the Holocaust, it is important to acknowledge this shift, which constitutes one of the origins of contemporary Holocaust 'memoriography', because it shows that Holocaust memoriography *evolved* from Holocaust historiography.

Whereas the Holocaust memoriography we know today mostly refers to the éffects of the Holocaust on people and politics after the event, the first works about the relation between history and memory strove to explain the Holocaust in relation to the appeal of authoritarian regimes to what Friedländer calls the 'subconscious foundations of a "collective mentality"'.[8] Works from the social sciences such as *The Authoritarian Personality* (1950) likewise conceived of memory not as *retrospection* (which reveals how our identities are determined by past experience), but as *prospection*, that is, as a determiner of future action; an individual's degree of 'susceptibility' to (fascist or anti-Semitic) ideologies from the 1930s onwards was thought to be governed by 'psychological needs' rooted in the individual's previous experience.[9] According to Friedländer, the historian's work on the interaction of events over time therefore correlates with the psychoanalyst's work on the interaction of events in the lives of individuals: 'for the historian, the place and interaction of events over time form the very content of his discipline; for the psychoanalyst, the place and interaction of events during the course of stages in the development of personality constitute the essential foundation of his enquiry; for both of them, the evolution of people is determined by the past'.[10]

This analogy between psychoanalysis and history, in which debates about the relation between memory and history originated, is interesting precisely because it contrasts starkly with current preoccupations. Instead of considering personality as something which is determined by past experience and determines future events, Holocaust memoriography today is generally devoted to the deconstruction of modes of representing the past. A shift has taken place from the relation between *personality* and *ideology* to the relation between *identity* and *representations*. In other words, the present memory boom is driven by the urge to understand the mechanisms of identity formation today rather than the influence of personality on causes of the event. In both cases, the understanding of memory is conceived as a step towards emancipation from the enduring 'after-images' to which Friedländer refers, and which influence unconscious motivations.

Whatever the focus of memory studies – be it the role of memory in the motivation and behaviour of those involved in the event, or the role of memory in the behaviour of those who reflect retrospectively on the event – we must acknowledge the pioneering work on the relation between history and psychoanalysis because it has bequeathed us with the three thematic pillars which underpin memoriography today: personality (or identity), institutions (or frameworks of memory formation) and symbols (or representations). However, while Holocaust scholars in the fields of social psychology, literary studies and sociology have recourse to psychoanalytical interpretations of representations of the Holocaust and its human toll on witnesses, psychoanalytical interpretations have remained marginal in historiography.[11] There is, in short, a disciplinary imbalance. More prevalent has been the application of *psychoanalytical metaphors* to historical interpretations of memories of the Holocaust. One example of this practice is the work of the French historian Henry Rousso, who frames chronologically successive phases of the postwar social memory of the Vichy regime in France in terms habitually applied to explain the psychological development of an individual. The expressive titles of chapters in Rousso's book *The Vichy Syndrome* include 'Unfinished mourning (1944–1954)', 'Repressions (1954–1971)', 'The Broken Mirror (1971–1974)' and 'Obsession (after 1974)'. However, Rousso does not apply psychological theory, but borrows psychoanalytical concepts, claiming that symbolic manifestations or 'symptoms' of collective memory like films, speeches, commemorations and historiography operate 'a little like the subconscious in Freudian theory',[12] that is, as responses to collective traumatism. Moreover, the psychoanalytically defined narrative structure of this book conveys an image of the nation as an organic unit with a collective memory akin to an individual's memory – a topos favoured by romantic historians of the nineteenth century such as Jules Michelet in his *Tableau de France* (1861).[13]

2 The 'politics of memory'

By far the largest number of memoriographical writings about the Holocaust is devoted to the 'politics of memory', and address political interests underlying linguistic, symbolic and ritual representations of the past. These works typically claim to debunk the political 'instrumentalisation' of the past, with the aim of deconstructing manipulative representations, or rather exposing their mechanisms so that we may be able to understand and respond to them, or at least not be duped by them.

Henry Rousso, one of the pioneers of contemporary Holocaust memoriography, exposes the political function of popular representations such as films, press reports, monuments, speeches and commemorations in France since the 1940s. His goal is to write the 'history of memory, that is, the study of the evolution of different social practices, their form and their content, whose object or effect (whether explicitly or not) is the representation of the past and the preservation of its memory, either within a given group or throughout society'.[14] These memorial practices, he claims, occurred in response to 'profound crises which have beset French unity and identity' and to the resulting tensions between 'rival social groups which jealously guard their respective reconstructions [of the past]'.[15] However lucid Rousso's analyses of the politically motivated construction and reception of memories of Vichy and its role in the Holocaust are, his context remains national and his narrative linear, as he focuses on the central role of heads of state such as Charles de Gaulle, and adopts the perspective of 'the French' and 'France' as a personified historical agent.

A more recent example of political memoriography, Peter Novick's *The Holocaust in American Life* (1999), adopts a similarly chronological and national perspective. However, there is a significant difference between the approaches adopted by Rousso and Novick. While they are both historians by trade, Rousso's approach is more historical and descriptive, Novick's more that of a political scientist and his analytical categories more narrow. While Rousso seeks primarily to identify 'stages'[16] in the unfolding of national memory on the basis of its public representations, Novick focuses on the *agents* of national memory, whose central representatives he names from the outset as 'American gentiles and Jews'.[17] Novick's Holocaust is the tool of mechanistic political agency within an 'American agenda'[18] in which American Jewry, the right, conservatives and liberals each utilize the Holocaust to provide sustenance for American identity. Novick has his sights on 'liberals', who warn against restrictions on immigration, for example, on the 'political centre', which evokes the Holocaust as a European event in order to celebrate the 'American way of life', and on 'the right' which, he claims, evokes the Holocaust in order to underpin an American Jewish identity in place of a weakened common religious bond, to criticize communism as a totalitarian system akin to National Socialism and to lament the breakdown of family values and religion in Germany during the 1930s.[19] According to Berel Lang, Novick's theses are partial and commonplace, since no memories of historical events today escape political instrumentalization.[20] More significantly, Novick's theses are founded on questionable analytical concepts which suggest that social cohesion is secured on the basis of shared memories which are confined to national and ethnic groups, and which are therefore closed, mutually exclusive and do not allow for overlaps.

Existing works on the politics of memory remind us that our categories of analysis extend beyond mere party political interests. However, is there truly an (ethnically grounded) 'Jewish' or 'German', a (nationally grounded) American or Israeli, or even a (linguistically grounded) English, German and French memory of the Holocaust, each of which presupposes a cohesive group memory? And should historians themselves and their audiences be included among the agents of social memory? In a pioneering essay of 1980, John Conway claimed that 'the impact of the Holocaust has been interpreted by historians largely according to the present needs of their audiences'. However, Conway's definition of 'rival schools'[21] of Jewish, German and Christian historians falsely assumes that both historians and their audiences belong exclusively to one or another of these schools, that is, that historians only write in the interest of their own clan. Conway does not consider whether these are valid categories of analysis, that some historians and their audiences may belong to none of these categories, or that overlap occurs between one category and another. As Holocaust 'memoriographers', we should therefore use politically, religiously and ethnically connoted categories of analysis with caution, especially when they retain the ideological ballast of the political systems which are the object of our analyses. The lesson of works by Novick, Conway (or even Norman Finkelstein)[22] is that, when writing about the history of memory, we should beware of categorizing *too* clearly, or rather applying labels to the agents of memory, including historians themselves.

The fact that Holocaust memoriography dealing with the 'politics of memory' is so profuse should not be imputed exclusively to group interests or to domestic political motives, as Rousso and Novick suggest. The motive underlying this memoriographical abundance, which distinguishes the specificity of the Holocaust as a field of memory research, is rather the fact that, on all sides, only losers emerged from this event. Societies in which the past is taken for granted are ones in which issues are settled, defined by what John Barnes calls 'structural amnesia'.[23] Memoriography, by contrast, thrives on reflection about past issues which are *not* settled. This is perhaps the crucial specificity of the Holocaust today.

3 Integrating memory and history

The destruction of European Jewry represents a radical caesura which has highlighted the discrepancy between history and memory as categories of thought and analysis. Memory is widely conceived of as a form of counter-history, of which there are three guiding principles. First, in the wake of Walter Benjamin's 'Theses on History',[24] the 'new history' in France or oral history, memory invokes the voices of those people who had previously not been heard in the public sphere. The historian's job then consists in reconstructing the past where little or even no physical trace has been left behind, and often consists in *creating* new traces of the past by listening to and recording living people who remember events they witnessed. Second, it follows that the reconstruction of the past on the basis of such tenuous memorial sources requires a non-linear narrative form which does not conform to the norms of national historiography.[25] Third, the radical intrusion of history represented by the Holocaust, and the subsequent creation of the state of Israel, has accentuated our awareness of different *temporalities* of history and memory, where historical time (of Jews living in the state of Israel, or the diaspora assimilated in various nation-states) is largely linear and secular, while memorial (ritual, religious, metahistorical) time is largely non-linear (circular or anarchic) and spiritual.[26] One of the first historians to write about the relation between the history and memory of the Holocaust was Yosef Yerushalmi, who sought to lend meaning to this event in the context of Jewish tradition. History, writes Yerushalmi, is opposed to tradition, as secularism is opposed to spirituality, knowledge to ritual and historicity to 'eternal contemporaneity' as performed in daily religious ritual.[27]

A further, more prosaic, methodological dichotomy between history and memory stems from the fact that, though each generally makes use of these sources (state archives, images, diaries, everyday objects, monuments, interviews), they use the same sources to seek answers to different questions. Historical questions typically pertain either to facts of the event, while memorial questions pertain to constructions of meanings of the past in the present. In the words of James Young, the difference between history and memory is a distinction between events in themselves and the subjective meanings attached to them retrospectively. '[H]istory as that which happened; memory as that which is remembered of what happened.'[28] Likewise, the difference between historiography and memoriography involves a shift in focus from *what* happened to *how* what happened has been rendered meaningful in words, images and ritual action. What is at stake here is essentially a shift in causality, from a quest to explain the event to a quest to explain the meaning and effects of the event for those who look back on it. This shift is, however, one of degree. Historiography neither binds historians to writing exclusively about causes of events, just as memoriography does not bind students of memory to writing exclusively about causes of the consequences of events. While historiography seeks to establish meaning of the event in its own context, memoriography focuses on seeking meaning for members of present-day societies. Moreover, memoriography exposes the *relative positions* of those involved in the process of knowledge production, and encourages both reflection about the process of making meaning about the past, as well as about the role of protagonists (politicians, lawyers, artists and, of course, historians themselves) in this process.

However, this epistemological dichotomy is often mistakenly used to dismiss Holocaust memoriography as something that should remain on the periphery of more 'serious' historical writing. Georges Bensoussan typically claims that 'collective memory . . . mythicises history. It does not help to tell the truth since it is too closely tied up in its highly emotional and ideological surroundings'.[29] Of course, the historical discipline may be justifiably employed as a corrective of social memory (as myth), when the latter is used to distort factual evidence. Holocaust denial or revision, whereby spurious arguments are backed up with allegedly new statistical calculations of the numbers of victims (which largely claim considerably lower numbers of Jewish victims) is one obvious example of this. Indeed, the Holocaust makes specific demands on historians, whose job is to define the truth or limits of what may be legitimately said about the past or depicted. Perhaps more than other violent historical events, the Holocaust is prone to incite disbelief, motivated either by professional Holocaust deniers who deny aspects of the Holocaust such as the existence of the gas chambers or argue that the numbers of victims was significantly lower than previously proven, but also by the limits of the human imagination to grasp extreme degrees of brutality,[30] or because much evidence of the Holocaust was either deliberately destroyed towards the end of World War II or has crumbled over time.

Perhaps the most monumental event in Holocaust memoriography, which spurred numerous works in Europe and North America, was the debate between Martin Broszat and Saul Friedländer over the historicization of National Socialism and the Holocaust. In essence, Martin Broszat called on historians to 'historicise'[31] National Socialism and the Holocaust by focusing less on criminality and ideology (such as anti-Jewish and anti-Roma legislation) and more on everyday history, revealing 'normal' aspects of the period such that it would not be 'bracketed'[32] out of previous and subsequent events and therefore approached in a less moralistic way, which had previously impeded people from acquiring knowledge of the period precisely because they tended to reject the event rather than trying to understand it.[33]

What is the significance of the debate between Broszat and Friedländer for the study of Holocaust memory? Like the examples above, Broszat sets up an antithesis between memory and history. By claiming that the passage of time should facilitate greater objectivity and a less moralistic approach to the Holocaust, he presupposes that 'remembrance' and the existential involvement of contemporary historians in the periods about which they write will give way (over time) to 'scientific knowledge'.[34] In response, Broszat's interlocutor Friedländer argued vehemently that this antithesis (between objective, value-free, detached history and subjective, moralistic, involved memory) is untenable, that 'this past is still much too present for present-day historians',[35] such that there is a 'constitutive link'[36] between history and memory. In short, Friedländer bemoaned the 'defence mechanism' or 'dissociation'[37] in contemporary historiography of the National Socialist period. This involved, first, the tendency to exclude Auschwitz from historiography and thereby marginalize the experience and memories of victims, second, the fragmentation of historiography into 'single, specialised and disconnected topics' and, third, the separate treatment of the background to the Holocaust and the actual events.[38] Friedländer wrote his monumental two-volume historical work *Nazi Germany and the Jews* (*The Years of Persecution*, 1997, and *The Years of Extermination*, 2007)[39] in direct response to the theoretical issues raised during the dispute with Broszat, such that this work is a fitting example of the cross-fertilization of historiographical theory and practice.

The most vivid illustration of Friedländer's proposed *integrated* historiography, in which memory and history and stories of victims and perpetrators are to be depicted in relation to one another, can be found in the introduction to *The Years of Extermination*, in which he radically defends the historian's use of everyday subjective accounts of the past by eyewitnesses. 'By its very nature, by dint of its humanness and freedom, an individual voice suddenly arising in the course of an ordinary historical narrative of events such as those presented here can tear through seamless interpretation and pierce the (mostly involuntary) smugness of scholarly detachment and "objectivity".' Friedländer goes on to justify the 'disruptive function' of witnesses' voices on the grounds that it is 'essential to the historical representation of mass extermination and other sequences of mass suffering that "business as usual historiography" necessarily domesticates and "flattens". . . . The immediacy of a witness's cry of terror, of despair, or of unfounded hope may trigger our own emotional reaction and shake our prior and well-protected representation of extreme historical events'.[40] Friedländer here defies in principle the ingrained dichotomy between history and memory and between historiography and memoriography. At the same time, however, his use of emotive, highly metaphorical and moralistic language, to decry the disparity between detachment and involvement, effectively entrenches the very dichotomy he is resolved to overcome.

Paying homage to Friedländer's 'integrated' memory and history of·the Holocaust, James Young appeals to historians not 'to forget the present as they recount the past', but to explore 'what happened' and 'how it is remembered'[41] in combination. According to Young, past realities are accessible only if those who lived through and remembered them are included in the analysis of the past, that is, if factual knowledge about the past is complemented by information about where and how this knowledge was acquired. In practice, however, Friedländer does not appear to do this. His references to victims' experiences and memories are, according to Tony Kushner, '*tacked onto* what is the essence of the narrative structure – one created and driven by the Nazis', such that textual sources from diaries and testimonies are used 'to *illustrate* the nature of Nazism' and such that 'there is no way that victim testimony is allowed to disrupt the harmony of the narrative flow'.[42] In short, Kushner argues that Friedländer does not put his principles (of integrated historiography) into practice. Indeed, in both volumes, Friedländer profusely quotes testimonies from diaries, letters and speeches by both perpetrators and victims, in order to demonstrate the facts of the event in detail, but all of these quotes are fragments which Friedländer fits into his factual and chronological logic rather than approaching them as texts in their own right with respect to their specific historical contexts and idiosyncratic narrative logic.[43]

What principles and practices does Kushner propose instead? Building on Friedländer's responses to Broszat, Kushner criticizes the treatment of memory in existing Holocaust historiography on the grounds that it poses an exaggerated demand of factual accuracy on memorial sources, coerces them into a chronological narrative form which is incommensurate with the subjective 'complexity' or 'chaos' of victims' life stories,[44] which should rather be taken 'seriously' on their own terms, such that they reveal their 'own internal dynamics'.[45] Kushner is clearly pushing the historical discipline to its limits. The account of 'internal dynamics' he is calling for has, in many respects, already been achieved by literary specialists such as Lawrence Langer or social psychologists like Dan Bar-On. Nonetheless, an integrated account of the memory and history of the Holocaust, one which gives equal voice to ideology and to life stories, has yet to be written.

4 The ambivalent position of the historian

Until now we have been looking at the works of historians *about* memories of the Holocaust, that is, works which address such memory as an object of inquiry. However, there are other ways in which historians work with memory, insofar as memory also influences and is influenced by historical writings. Historical writings influence memory, for example, when they are read, and when the ideas they contain or their narrative structure impinges upon the way in which readers imagine, and explain to themselves, the past. Although it is difficult to measure the impact of a work of history on memory, some canonical works such as Christopher Browning's *Ordinary Men* (1993),[46] or even notorious works like Andreas Hillgruber's *Zweierlei Untergang* (1986),[47] have provoked such intense public response that one could say that these works are memory *makers*.

As well as being makers of historical memory, the works of historians are also, to a degree, *made* by memory, insofar as the personal memories of historians, and dominant representations of the past in the media, affect their approaches to the past. However much they may strive to achieve personal detachment and abide by the rules of empirical research, they too are involved in the world about which they write, however far back into the past this world reaches. Again, Holocaust historiography has brought notice to the ambivalent position of historians as both agents and recipients of memory.[48] This ambivalence is particularly prevalent in Holocaust historiography, and in contemporary historiography more generally, because first- and second-generation historians who lived during or in the shadow of the event possess experience and are therefore involved in the event despite their pledge to professional detachment.[49] This does not mean that we can calculate the degree of involvement or detachment of historians from their dates of birth alone. It does, however, force historians to ask themselves to what *degree* and by what *media* their own memories are 'made', and how they propose to 'make' future memories, as 'consequences of consequences'.[50]

In practice, it is not the age of historians or even their personal experience which determines the relative involvement or detachment of either their person or their writing, but the practical way in which they *position* themselves within their writing as agents who create for their readers meaningful links between the past and present, whether these links are legal (in analyses of attempts to repair injury caused during the Holocaust),[51] political (in analyses of strategies for using history to foster legitimation in the present)[52] or moral (where the Holocaust is identified as a measure of bad or even good actions).[53] There is no cogent logic or compelling biographical reason, for example, why such works as Richard Evans' *The Coming of the Third Reich*, Peter Reichel's *Politik mit der Erinnerung* (Politics with Memory), Norbert Frei's *Adenauer's Germany and the Nazi Past*, Jörg Friedrich's *Der Brand* (The Fire), Pierre Vidal-Naquet's *Assassins of Memory* or Annette Wieviorka's *Déportation et genocide* (Deportation and Genocide) all avoid auctorial positioning. One must assume, therefore, that these authors make a choice *not* to position themselves in their texts in order to arouse the impression that their writing speaks for itself, without complicating the task of readers by expecting them to contextualize the text in relation to the author's biography or to show deference towards the authority of an author who may have gained personal insight as an eyewitness.

When authors do preface their works with biographical information about their own connection with the event, such statements are rarely confessional, but rather offer readers an opportunity to contextualize and relativize the statements of the authors, and in turn protect the authors by qualifying their statements, pointing out that they are not omniscient, but take a stance relative to the subject position from which they construct their analyses. This technique not only enhances the authenticity of the writing, but also encourages critical reflection on the part of readers.

However, few authors can today afford the luxury of auctorial authority demonstrated by such authors as Friedländer, who opens the introduction to the first volume of his magnum opus by saying that 'most historians of my generation, born on the eve of the Nazi era, recognize either explicitly or implicitly that plowing through the events of those years entails not only excavating and interpreting a collective past like any other, but also recovery and confronting decisive elements of our own lives'.[54] Rather, an increasing number of authors explicate their positions in terms of their roles as secondary witnesses or 'witnesses of witnesses', an issue admirably demonstrated by Jackie Feldman in his work *Above the Death Pits*.[55] Yet, while authorial positioning may be a welcome invitation to foster reflexivity among readers, *too much* positioning can raise questions which detract from historical analysis itself, and may even be misused as a means to legitimate the plausibility of an argument. Conway's suggestion that there are *essential* differences between the approaches of German, Jewish and Christian authors is one example of this. A further manifestation of the legitimacy ascribed to historians' work on the basis of their national or religious identity is reflected in the recruitment patterns of universities and research establishments to posts in the field of Holocaust studies, where candidates who are neither manifestly German nor Jewish are at a disadvantage. One author who resists this trend by justifying his subject position as a non-Jewish non-German specialist in this field, for example, is Jacques Sémelin, who claims that the Holocaust is of such significance to understanding and maintaining humanist traditions that its historiography should not and cannot be appropriated by presumed national, religious or ethnic identities.[56]

In short, as an object of historiography and memoriography, the Holocaust accentuates our awareness of the tension between the knowing subject's dual involvement in and detachment from the event about which he or she writes. It also accentuates our sensitivity to the 'dual belongingness'[57] of historians, that is, to their ambivalent role as 'travellers' between the past and the present, between their roles as 'witnesses' of and 'exiles' from the past.

5 The language of memory in Holocaust memoriography

I would like to conclude this chapter by sketching some examples of the ways in which language impinges on the memory of the Holocaust in historical writings, and how language opens a window onto historians' relation to their objects of study in this field. Twofold caution is called for when writing about memory and the Holocaust because both these concepts are controversial. Indeed, analytical concepts used by historians are themselves historical, and the legitimacy which they acquire for each generation of scholars by dint of repetition and the legitimizing institutions (in the fields of education, publishing and even politics) which use them is neither permanent nor self-evident. The attraction of 'memory' as a field of study, for example, is heightened by dint of its polysemous character, for it lends itself to almost all humanities disciplines from history to literary studies, anthropology, sociology and art history. It is therefore the responsibility of all those who write in this field to beware of the trap posed by this conceptual hotchpotch, and of historians in particular to be aware of (and warn others of) the conditionality of the concept 'memory' and conceptual language used in relation to it.

The languages of memory in Holocaust memoriography take three forms. First, language *inscribes* our memories of the Holocaust with meaning. The very debate over the terms with which we should refer to this event is a manifestation of concern for semantic distinctions and emphases to be placed on the event and, by extension, for the manner in which it will be remembered and interpreted in the future. Common alternatives to the term Holocaust (derived from the Greek, meaning burnt offering or sacrifice) are 'Shoah' (Hebrew, catastrophe) or 'Churban' (Yiddish and Hebrew, referring to the destruction of the Temple in Jerusalem), none of which convey the full meaning of what happened. Since the United Nations' Convention on the Prevention and Punishment of the Crime of Genocide of 1948, there has been an increased tendency to refer to 'genocide' as a generic term defining, according to the convention, the killing or harming of people 'with intent to destroy, in whole or in part, a national, ethnical, racial or religious group'. However, since the term genocide has been used to define successive mass killings which have taken place in different parts of the world since the mass murders carried out by the National Socialists and their allies in the 1940s, it has partially dehistoricized mass murder. This legal term has, as a memorial sign, created a direct link between the genocide of the 1940s in Europe with previous and successive genocides. At the same time, it lends itself to comparisons which are made on the basis of criteria which are less historical than humanitarian (when international aid is summoned), legal (when perpetrators are sought for trial under the convention of 1948) or political (when governments are accused of, or hold others responsible for, excessive violence). However, as Jacques Sémelin has pointed out, the use of this term has been inflationary, especially since the 1990s in the wake of genocides in Bosnia, Rwanda and Sudan. Sémelin does not claim that these events, in which hundreds of thousands of innocent people were murdered, are not genocides, but warns against the risk that indiscriminate use of this term can detract from the gravity and the specificity of each these events. Moreover, in order to circumvent the etymologically ethnic conception of a social group contained in the term 'genocide' (meaning, literally, the killing of a race), alternative terms have come into use such as 'democide' or 'politicide' and, during the 1990s, 'mass crime' (Dieter Pohl), 'extreme violence' (Sémelin) or 'massacre' (Sémelin).

There is widespread reluctance today to apply the term 'genocide' to events such as the conflict in Darfur because, according to Sémelin, this term is a 'symbolic shield designed to assert one's identity as a victim people',[58] and it opens the way to judicial measures. In Sémelin's words, 'the term aims to strike people's imaginations, to arouse their consciences, and to incite people to rally in favour of the victims'.[59] Not that it is wrong to support victims, but such political action diverts attention from understanding the situation in all its complexity and seeking diplomatic intervention by negotiation, for example. In short, the politics of genocide prevention and punishment is limited in scope because it presupposes *morally motivated judicial intervention and punishment* in line with the United Nations' convention of 1948. Moreover, when non-governmental organizations describe Darfur as a 'crime against humanity' or a 'war crime',[60] the use of these terms destabilizes their users, and 'involves' them. 'Morality,' according to Sémelin, 'seems to be always on the side of those who denounce an ongoing genocide'.[61] In light of Sémelin's work on the language of the Holocaust and genocide, we should not remember the Holocaust as a genocide, but more generally in terms of a 'massacre'.

A second manifestation of the way in which language impinges upon the memory of the Holocaust is reflected in the way in which historians *define* memory in their writings about the Holocaust. Peter Novick, for example, tends to avoid the sweeping notion of 'Holocaust memory'. Inspired by Maurice Halbwachs' exploration of 'the ways in which present concerns determine what of the past we remember and how we remember it',[62] Novick effectively translates the notion of memory, preferring instead various definitions of the object of his bestselling book as (according to its title) 'the Holocaust in American life' or 'in the American mind',[63] 'the centrality [of the Holocaust] in consciousness',[64] as an event which 'has come to loom so large in our culture' and which plays a 'prominent role' in 'both American and Jewish discourse'.[65] These everyday circumlocutions confirm the versatility of the concept of memory but also its inherent ambiguity.

Finally, it is curious to observe how historians *describe* memory in their writings about the Holocaust, for historians who address memory – either as the history *of* memory or as the impingement of memory on history and historiography – face the difficult task of describing precisely the relation between history and memory. One historian of memory who does this admirably is Christoph Cornelißen. In an essay about 'Generations of Historians in West Germany since 1945', Cornelißen distinguishes between 'memory of history' (*Erinnerung an die Geschichte*) when referring to the event as a whole, 'memories of occurrences' (*Erinnerungen an die Vorgänge*) when referring to specific details, and 'historiographical memory' (*historiographische Erinnerung*) as the representation of an event as it is found in historical writings.[66] Although he largely maintains the duality between history as rational, scientific and driven by interests, versus memory as emotional, moral and driven by political and existential needs,[67] his formulations testify to the search for a language for memoriography which focuses not on essentialist distinctions but on the complex *relationship* between memory and history – to the 'relation between the lived past and historical-scientific interest in contemporary history' and to the 'political and existential implications of scientifically informed memories'.[68]

Notes

*   The author would like to thank Kobi Kabalek for his comments on the draft of this chapter.

1   Quoted in Annette Wieviorka, *The Era of the Witness*, trans by Jared Stark (Ithaca, 2006), p. 142.

2   Peter Novick, *The Holocaust in American Life* (Boston and New York, 1999), p. 275, quoted in Tony Kushner, 'Holocaust Testimony, Ethics, and the Problem of Representation'. *Poetics Today* 2:27, 275–95, here pp. 280–1, p. 286.

3   Konrad Jarausch (ed.), *After Unity. Reconfiguring German Identities* (Providence, Oxford, 1997), p. 215.

4   Raul Hilberg, *The Destruction of the European Jews* (Chicago, 1961), p. 760.

5   Among the first historical works about memory and the Holocaust were Lawrence Langer's *Holocaust Testimonies. The Ruins of Memory* (New Haven and London, 1991), Sybil Milton's *In Fitting Memory. The Art and Politics of Holocaust Memorials* (Detroit, 1991), and Pierre Vidal-Naquet's 'Les assassins de la mémoire' (1987), in *Les assassins de la mémoire. 'Un Eichmann de papier' et autres essays sur le révisionnisme* (Paris, 1991).

6   Saul Friedländer, *Reflets du nazisme* (Paris, 1982), p. 17 (this and subsequent translations are by the author, unless otherwise indicated).

7   Friedländer, *Reflets du nazisme*, p. 13.

8   Saul Friedländer, *Histoire et Psychoanalyse. Essai sur les possibilitiés et les limites de la psychohistoire* (Seuil, 1975), p. 205.

9   Theodor W. Adorno, Else Frenkel-Brunswik, Daniel Levinson and Nevitt Sanford (eds), *The Authoritarian Personality* (New York, 1950), p. 3.

10   Friedländer, *Histoire et psychoanalyse*, p. 26.

11   A notable exception is Dominick LaCapra's *History and Memory after Auschwitz* (Ithaca, 1998).

12   Henry Rousso, *Le syndrome de Vichy 1944–198 . . .* (Paris, 1987), p. 20 (English edition *The Vichy Syndrome 1944–198 . . .*, trans. by Arthur Goldhammer (Cambridge, 1991)).

13   Jules Michelet, *Tableau de France. Géographie physique, politique et morale* (Paris, 1962) (1861).

14   Rousso, *The Vichy Syndrome*, p. 13.

15   Ibid., p. 14.

16   Ibid., p. 25.

17   Novick, *The Holocaust*, p. 19.

18   Ibid., p. 226.

19   Ibid., pp. 12–13.

20   Berel Lang (ed.), 'Lachrymose without Tears. Misreading the Holocaust in American Life', in *Post-Holocaust. Interpretation, Misinterpretation, and the Claims of History* (Bloomington & Indianapolis, 2005), pp. 128–36, p. 129.

21   John Conway, 'The Holocaust and the Historians'. *Annals of the American Academy of Political and Social Science* 450 (1980), 153–64, p. 153.

22   Norman Finkelstein, *The Holocaust Industry. Reflections on the Exploitation of Jewish Suffering,* (London, 2000).

23   Quoted in Peter Burke, 'History as Social Memory', in Thomas Butler (ed.), *Memory, History, Culture and Mind* (Oxford, 1989), pp. 97–113.

24   Walter Benjamin, *Illuminations*, trans. by Harry Zohn (New York, 1969).

25   Amos Funkenstein, *Perceptions of Jewish History* (Oxford, 1993), p. 349f.

26   This distinction derives from the attempts by philosophers like Franz Rosenzweig and Gershom Scholem to explain the Holocaust in terms of Jewish tradition. See Stéphane Mosès, *L'Ange de l'histoire. Rosenzweig, Benjamin, Scholem* (Paris, 1992), p. 191ff.

27 Yosef Yerushalmi, *Zakhor. Jewish History and Jewish Memory* (Seattle and London, 1982), p. 96.

28 James Young, 'Between History and Memory: The Uncanny Voices of Historian and Survivor'. *History and Memory* 9:1/2 (1997), 47–58, p. 50.

29 Georges Bensoussan, *Auschwitz en héritage? D'un bon usage de la mémoire* (Paris, 1998), p. 45.

30 Arthur Koestler (ed.), 'On Disbelieving Atrocities', in *Yogi and the Commissar and Other Essays* (London, 1945).

31 Martin Broszat, 'A Plea for the Historicization of National Socialism', in Peter Baldwin (ed.), *Reworking the Past. Hitler, the Holocaust, and the Historians' Debate* (Boston, 1990), pp. 77–87, p. 82.

32 Ian Kershaw, *The Nazi Dictatorship. Problems and Perspectives of Interpretation* (London, 2000), p. 220.

33 See Jörn Rüsen, 'Historicizing Nazi-time: Metahistorical Reflections on the Debate between Friedländer and Broszat', in Rüsen (ed.), *History. Narration, Interpretation, Orientation* (Oxford and New York, 2005), pp. 163–87, here p. 165.

34 Rüsen, 'Historicizing Nazi-time', p. 166.

35 Saul Friedländer, 'Some Reflections on the Historicization of National Socialism', in Baldwin, (ed.), *Reworking the Past*, pp. 88–101, here p. 98.

36 Rüsen, 'Historicizing Nazi-time', p. 166.

37 Saul Friedländer, 'Trauma, Erinnerung und Übertragung in der historischen Darstellung des Nationalsozialismus und des Holocaust', in Wolfgang Beck (ed.), *Die Juden in der europäischen Geschichte* (Munich, 1992), pp. 136–51, here p. 142.

38 Friedländer, 'Trauma, Erinnerung und Übertragung', pp. 142–5.

39 Saul Friedländer, *Nazi Germany and the Jews. The Years of Persecution, 1933–1939* (New York, 1997), and *The Years of Extermination. Nazi Germany and the Jews, 1939–1945* (New York, 2007).

40 Friedländer, *The Years of Extermination*, xxv–xxvi.

41 Young, 'Between History and Memory', p. 57.

42 Kushner, 'Holocaust Testimony, Ethics', pp. 280–1.

43 One example of how Friedländer decontextualizes textual sources and recontextualises them within his own narrative is his quotation of Etty Hillesum in Friedländer, *The Years of Extermination*, p. 407.

44 Kushner, 'Holocaust Testimony, Ethics', p. 291.

45 Ibid., p. 283, p. 289.

46 Christopher Browning, *Ordinary Men. Reserve Batallion 101 and the Final Solution in Poland* (New York, 1993). Browning innovatively postulates several possible motivations behind the brutality of a single battalion of order police, who were neither trained to be nor possessed personalities prone to brutality.

47 Andreas Hillgruber, *Zweierlei Untergang. Die Zerschlagung des dritten Reiches und das Ende des europäischen Judentums* (Berlin, 1986). Hillgruber compares

the fate of Jews during World War II to that of displaced German people at the end of the war.

48 See Rousso, *Le syndrome de Vichy*, p. 14, and Friedländer, *Nazi Germany and the Jews*, p. 11.

49 For a detailed study of the dual involvement and detachment of academic workers, see Norbert Elias, *Involvement and Detachment* (Oxford, 1987).

50 See Hilberg, *The Destruction of the European Jews*.

51 E.g. Norbert Frei, *Adenauer's Germany and the Nazi Past: The Politics of Amnesty and Integration* (New York, 2002).

52 E.g. Peter Reichel, *Politik mit der Erinnerung. Gedächtnisorte im Streit um die nationalsozialistische Vergangenheit* (Munich, 1995).

53 E.g. Tzvetan Todorov, *Les abus de la mémoire* (Paris, 1995).

54 Friedländer, *Nazi Germany and the Jews*, p. 1.

55 Jackie Feldman, *Above the Death Pits, beneath the Flag. Youth Voyages to Poland and the Performance of Israeli National Identity* (New York and Oxford, 2008).

56 See the preface to: Jacques Sémelin, *Purifier et détruire. Usages politiques des massacres et génocides* (Paris, 2005).

57 Enzo Traverso, *La pensée dispersée. Figures de l'exil judéo-allemand* (Paris, 2004), p. 201.

58 Sémelin, *Purifier et détruire*, p. 371.

59 Ibid., p. 369.

60 Ibid.

61 Ibid., pp. 369–70.

62 Novick, *The Holocaust*, p. 3.

63 Ibid., p. 20.

64 Ibid., p. 19.

65 Ibid., p. 1.

66 Christoph Cornelißen, 'Historikergenerationen in Westdeutschland seit 1945', in Christoph Cornelißen et al. (eds), *Erinnerungskulturen. Deutschland, Italien und Japan seit 1945* (Frankfurt am Main, 2003), pp. 139–52, 142–3.

67 See Cornelißen, 'Historikergenerationen in Westdeutschland', pp. 145–9.

68 In German: 'zum Verhältnis von gelebter Vergangenheit und historisch-wissenschaftlichem Interesse an der Zeitgeschichte' (Cornelißen, 'Historikergenerationen in Westdeutschland', p. 145); 'die politisch-existentiellen Bezüge wissenschaftlich angeleiteter Erinnerungen' (Cornelißen, 'Historikergenerationen in Westdeutschland', p. 149).

Further reading

Gulie Ne'eman Arad (ed.), *Passing into History: Nazism and the Holocaust beyond Memory*. special issue of *History and Memory* 1/2:9 (1997).

Peter Baldwin (ed.), *Reworking the Past. Hitler, the Holocaust, and the Historians' Debate* (Boston, 1990).

Peter Hayes (ed.), *Lessons and Legacies,* vol. III: *Memory, Memorialization and Denial,* (Evanston, 1999).

Dominick LaCapra, *History and Memory after Auschwitz* (Ithaca, 1998).

Lawrence Langer, *Holocaust Testimonies. The Ruins of Memory* (New Haven and London, 1991).

Sybil Milton, *In Fitting Memory. The Art and Politics of Holocaust Memorials* (Detroit, 1991).

Philippe Petit, *La Hantise du passé* (interview with Henry Rousso) (Paris, 1998).

Peter Reichel, *Politik mit der Erinnerung. Gedächtnisorte im Streit um die nationalsozialistische Vergangenheit* (Munich, 1995).

Pierre Vidal-Naquet, *Assassins of Memory. Essays on the Denial of the Holocaust,* trans. by Jeffrey Mehlman (New York, 1992).

Annette Wieviorka, *Déportation et génocide: entre la mémoire et l'oubli* (Paris, 1992).

CHAPTER TEN

History and memorialization

Richard Crownshaw

Memorialization is an act of remembrance: the commemoration of historical losses as opposed to the celebration of historical events. In topographical terms, memorialization imposes sites of memory on sites of historic activity or geographically distanced from them. Whether by building museums or monuments, preserving archaeological ruins, or just describing what happened at a now unmarked place, national, group and communal organizations and institutions, as well as individuals, have all sponsored memorials. Whatever the scale of memorialization, and whoever the sponsor (official or unofficial), the memorial (architectural or ritualistic) is not complete without those who visit it, in whom memory is invoked. This chapter outlines the ways in which memorials shape the past, the significance of memorials in academic discourses that centre on questions of historical representation and how memorials might be historicized. Given the necessary limitations on a chapter like this, the following focuses in particular on what would be described under a subset of memorials and monuments. As James E. Young notes:

> there are memorial books, memorial activities, memorial days, memorial festivals and memorial sculptures. Some of these are mournful, some celebratory: but all are memorials in a larger sense. Monuments, on the other hand, will refer to a subset of memorials: the material objects, sculptures, and installations used to memorialize a person or a thing.[1]

To further that definition, monuments are the objects in and around which an individual's or, for the purposes of our discussion, a group's or society's memories collect, and where past events represented by those objects can be remembered by those who witnessed the events directly or who have no direct experience of them. These objects inevitably become the focus of remembrance for those who have no such direct experience of witnessing, as, with passing of time, witnesses die off, leaving monuments as the focal point for 'second-order' memory.[2]

Memorials, like other cultural expressions of a group's or society's memory, are never of course just mediated by the forms they take and the shape they give to the past – their designers' and architects' intentions made manifest – but also by ideological and political discourses that authorize their creation or which create the right ideological and political conditions for their conception and the eventual inception.[3] The politics of memorial memory are particularly visible where monuments have been created in the name of national identity. Eric Hobsbawm would describe this material expression of a national identity as the 'invention of tradition'. As Hobsbawm explains '"Invented tradition" is taken to mean a set of practices, normally governed by overtly or tacitly accepted rules and of a ritual or symbolic nature, which seek to inculcate certain values and norms of behaviour by repetition, which automatically implies continuity with the past.... In short, they are responses to novel situations which take the form of reference to old situations, or which establish their own past by quasi-obligatory repetition.'[4] 'Tradition', as Hobsbawm defines it, was 'invented' in the West after the industrial revolution when modernization radically changed patterns and conditions of living and existence, irreversibly altering the social fabric. Tradition was invented to regenerate a sense social belonging in light of change, by at least appearing to bridge the gap between the old and the new. However, it was the rise of the nation state during the course of the long nineteenth century that emphasized that sense of belonging in terms of an identification with the nation and citizenship.[5] Just as the memorial materials of state focused a sense of belonging, or at least intended to, repairing the social fabric rent by discontinuities between past and present, so they also rooted the relatively modern and novel phenomena of the nation state in the past, thereby naturalizing it.[6]

Hobsbawm finds tradition invented at different levels of society and by and for different social groups, particularly those defined by class, but the invention of tradition in relation to national identity is of particular interest to historians given the relatively recent historical 'innovation' of 'the nation, its associated phenomena: nationalism, the nation-state, national symbols, histories', and the political power exercised through them.[7] Reflection on the invention of tradition also affords historians the opportunity to reflect on the way in which societies interpret and remember their own pasts, an activity echoed in the historian's own 'craft', as her activities contribute to this collective memory and what it finds significant. Attention paid to the invented traditions of nation, though, should not concede political power as something that is exercised in a purely top-down fashion, especially through the memorial or monumental materialization of that power.

Problematizing the conception of tradition (and its monumental materialization) affords the opportunity to consider in more complex terms how historical writing might better conceptualize monumentality and the memories it materializes. Alon Confino has argued that the history of memory often concentrates on how the past is represented but not why its representations were received or rejected. Without an understanding of reception, social and political context would be deemed to inhere in historical representation, or in this case, the monument, and that form of representation would be transparent to its context. A more sophisticated history of memory would understand historical representation in relation to the full spectrum of representations available in a given culture and the relations between them, 'analyzing the ideas, values, and practices embedded in and symbolized by . . . particular imagery'. In other words, by attending to the textual specificity of historical representation, the relationship between representations, the mechanisms and systems by which representations circulate in a given culture, and the discourses, institutions and agencies that mediate their circulation and reception, a better understanding is reached about how representations gain significance (or not as the case may be), no matter their intended significance.[8] Wulf Kansteiner adds to Confino's reconceptualization of how historical writing might regard memory, with a methodological critique of memory studies that reminds us that the objects of memory, no matter the intentions that motivate their cultural circulation – the intentions of the discourses and institutions of the public sphere that authorize their meaningful dissemination, as well as the intentions of the makers of those objects – may not be received as memoratively pertinent or significant. The focus of memory studies for Kansteiner should be on the hermeneutical triangle of object, maker and consumer.[9] Taking these correctives into consideration, what emerges in the history of memory is a much more dynamic model of memory, in which historical representations are not isolated, nor are their politics viewed as immanent to their material presence. As Confino puts it, the cultural is not sacrificed to the political, in which the political significance of representation is not taken for granted, arbitrarily identified, over other representations, in advance of a systematic study of the different historical representations and their materialization of memory's transmission and reception.[10]

In considering the notion of reception, the history of memory is better placed to conceptualize a more dynamic and cultural version of memory as it is focused and materialized in monumental form. Indeed, it is reception that is at the heart of James Young's redefinition of collective memory in his cultural history of Holocaust memorials. First, as Young reminds us, when considering the collective memories that are focused by memorials and more specifically monuments, it may be more accurate to speak of collected memories rather than collective memories. The former describes 'the many discrete memories that are gathered into common memorial spaces and assigned common meaning';[11] the latter assumes some kind of an essential memory shared in the same way by all those who remember. In reality

> [a] society's memory, in this context, might be regarded as an aggregate collection of its members' many, often competing memories. If societies remember, it is only in so far as their institutions and rituals organize, shape, even inspire their constituents' memories. For a society's memory cannot exist outside of those people who do the remembering – even if such memory happens to be at the society's bidding, in its name.[12]

Without a constituency of visitors, who react to monuments, project meanings onto them (not necessarily intended by the monuments' makers or those who authorized its creation), the monument would lose social significance. In that sense, the monument's meaning is a process of dialogue between its intended meaning and those who visit it.

Indeed, Jay Winter makes the interesting point that studies of memorials and monuments to the Great War tend to overlook their ritual functions. The symbolism of memorials to the Great War may mostly articulate the effects of war in terms of tragedy and sacrifice, often religiously inflected and, occasionally, a more existential questioning of the meaning of life and loss in relation to war. Such symbolism is more often than not governed or framed by a nationalist understanding of the meaning of war – a necessary sacrifice for the nation, citizenship affirmed through sacrifice and so on. It is those symbols that may survive to the present day – for the attention of historians – but during the war and its immediate aftermath 'communal commemorative art provided first and foremost a framework for and legitimation of individual and family grief'.[13] Ceremonies at which monuments were unveiled, annual, official commemorations at monuments and private, unofficial visits to them by those related or known to the fallen marked the life of monuments. Moments of official commemorative ritual 'are rarely the reflection of a simple text, a script rigidly prepared by political leaders determined to fortify their position of power' given the myriad responses of those who participate – a situation amplified in the scenario of unofficial ritual.[14] The political framework may mediate responses to memorials but at the same time cannot contain them. Ritualized expressions of individual and familial grief may render such memorial sites and spaces both public and private, national and particular, 'macrohistorical' and 'microhistorical', but such spaces and sites can also foster politically motivated behaviour that deliberately goes against the grain of nationalist intentions given form by memorials and monuments. For example, on Armistice Day, 11 November, Great War monuments have become the focal point of demonstrations of pacifist *and* militarist values.

Monuments are not, then, just to be understood in a functionalist manner, as may be implied in the concept of invented tradition, but rather as the focal point of a 'chorus' of commemorative voices and practices, locally accented, even if some may at times be 'louder than others', and which change over time as the political culture and state of collective memory of the events memorialized changes.[15] Accordingly, national identity, reflected in monuments, is not a discrete natural object or fact waiting to be discovered by historians but rather a shifting construct belied by a myriad of responses to the past.[16]

What historical writing should conceptualize, given the dynamism captured by or reflected in, monumental forms, is *cultural* memory. Building on the classic definition of 'collective memory' articulated by Maurice Halbwachs in which individual remembrance always takes place in social, collective frameworks of the present moment – the individual always remembers in groups, but the group also remembers in the individual[17] – Jan and Aleida Assmann, respectively, theorize 'cultural memory' as that which bridges the individual and the collective. Cultural memory describes the artefacts (texts, objects and symbols) by which memory is socialized, or, rather, by which memory is further socialized and mobilized. When individual memory, social by nature, is represented artefactually, it has the potential to be unmoored from social groups and is no longer necessarily identifiable with or affiliated to those groups, their values, ideas and temporal horizons. This could be described as a transformation of 'episodic' or 'communicative' memory into 'semantic' memory, from an embodied to disembodied transmission of the past. (Embodied transmission would be, for example, familial and intergenerational; the disembodiment of memory and its materialization would allow transgenerational transmission, but memory may be re-embodied through participatory rites and rituals organized around the materials of memory, such as monuments – although this is not the same kind of embodied experience found in communicative and episodic memory and its transmission.) The dynamism of cultural memory and its artefacts makes it potentially centrifugal, as well as centripetal, available for wider participation and negotiation as well as instrumental to 'political' memory that seeks homogeneity (a 'unity of consciousness of the past') rather than heterogeneity.[18] For Ann Rigney, no matter the political instrumentality of remembrance, 'cultural memory' foregrounds the construction of the past via the distribution and reception of memorative materials.[19] As Alon Confino and Peter Fritzsche argue, memory is a process 'embedded in social networks' rather than solely and statically in institutions, sites, objects, texts or people.[20] To sum up, the cultural memory is not as static as the monumental materials that represent it.

In considering what might be remembered at monuments, and more generally sites of memorialization, it is important to anchor acts of memory historically, or rather to recognize that memory itself has a history. This idea can be better understood with reference to the wider context of the boom in memory studies over the last 20 years, as well as to the sceptical reactions to memory studies by the discipline of history. Debates in and over memory studies pivot around the relation of history and memory.

Pierre Nora's multivolume *Les Lieux de Mémoire* has played a seminal if not unproblematic part in the memory boom.[21] Nora's project was essentially to catalogue memorial sites and objects of French national memory, and in doing so to confirm their status as inauthentic, artificial and, what is more, historical. For Nora, the changes brought about by modernity meant that there was no longer a living memory culture, a *milieu de mémoire*, only historical markers to the past in its place.[22] Nora's work has attracted widespread criticism, not only for its nostalgic nationalism, but also for its opposition of history to memory: 'history is perpetually suspicious of memory, and its true mission is to suppress and destroy it.'[23] Dominick LaCapra has argued that history is neither identical to memory nor its opposite: memory is crucial to understanding the way in which history approaches its object of enquiry, as well as a vital source of history. Given memory's 'falsifications, repressions, displacements and denials of the past',[24] 'left to itself', memory would render 'history, a documented account of the past, impossible'.[25] Yet the documentation of the past, by individuals, groups and institutions is grounded in what is remembered by individuals, groups and within cultures. So, memory foregrounds the way in which history approaches the past and indeed the way that approach is mediated by memory. 'Moreover, a critically informed memory is crucial in the attempt to determine what in history deserves preservation in living traditions, either as something to be criticized and avoided, or as something to be respected and emulated. Conversely, history serves to question and test memory in critical fashion and to specify what in it is empirically accurate or has a different, but still possibly significant, status. Indeed once history loses contact with memory, it tends to address dead issues that no longer elicit evaluative and emotional interest or investment.' History, then, functions to adjudicate 'the truth-claims and the transmissions of critically tested memory'.[26] With this entanglement of memory and history – a mutual inclusiveness in which acts of historical representation are informed by the ways in which individuals, cultures and social groups remember; and the fact that memories are informed by the histories written within and by a particular group – the dividing line between history and memory is permeable and the traffic between the two discourses considerable.[27] Winter argues that the imbrication of history and memory is best articulated by the term 'historical remembrance', which describes what happens at sites of memorialization, and which avoids charging 'memory' with vagueness and 'history' with a putative objectivity.[28] Therefore, monuments demonstrate that the self-fashioning of group, particularly national history is a matter of memory, while such materializations of memory need, where necessary, to be subject to corrective critical histories of the event remembered and of the remembrance of the event. Acts of memory, from the construction of a monument to the responses to it, need to be placed in historical context – a history of memory.

However, the 'emergence of memory in historical discourse', as Kerwin Lee Klein puts it, has raised concerns in recent years. As Susannah Radstone explains, the turn to memory is part of a broader, postmodern movement that saw the problematization of the idea of the grand narrative, of 'History' and its claims to universality, totality and objectivity, and its substitution by lived experience, the local, subjective and partial, which are all embodied by memory and materialized by memorial forms.[29] The turn to memory, though, has not only reinscribed a binary opposition in which memory is validated over history, it has eclipsed history altogether. The 'inner world and its very processes has become predominant, and has been taken as "the" world'.[30] Under this academic regime, the memory in memory studies can become over-personalized at the expense of a wider historical context and, without historical specificity, any object, discourse or practice can be taken as memory.[31] Given its new-found authority, and indeed autonomy, memory seems to have a life, or agency, of its own, freed from historical context and specificity.[32] Under the auspices of memory studies, memorials and monuments could then be considered as free-floating objects, their meaning and significance wholly determined by the memories brought to them by and that they provoke in their visitors, and not informed by the histories that brought them into being. So, although invented tradition and national identity might be regarded as master narratives that overshadow if not subsume what is actually remembered at monuments, a history of monuments must not lose sight of the historical conditions that allow that remembrance to take place.

To that end, the most recent interesting work on monuments has tracked the histories of their conception, inception and reception – in other words, from the idea of a memorial, to its materialization, to its usage.[33] As Jennifer Jordan states, 'new memorials are generated in part by public discussion, and often by arduous bureaucratic processes. But they tend to hide their origins in the smooth surface of the finished memorial. There is rarely any sign in the bronze, stone, or glass of the political wrangling or budgetary back-and-forth that ultimately gave rise to these memorial sites.'[34] Jordan's investigation of the post-1989 topography of Berlin's memorial and monumental terrain seeks to unearth that discursive history and is particularly innovative for its tracking of memorial projects through the work of memory activists or 'entrepreneurs' who lobby for the construction of monuments, their negotiations with institutions of local, regional and state government until such projects have political approval, at least in principle, and local and national resonance, recognition and financing, and the ways memorial projects have to fit into the existing grid of land-use (private and state-owned property, civic-, state- and commercially planned urban development). 'Memory thus shapes the landscapes through the day-to-day practices of memorial construction, which range from international debates about art and history to the bureaucracies of local parks departments, historic preservation offices or property registries'.[35] Of course, these myriad and fraught intersections do not fit neatly with the lifespan of political and ideological regimes (for example, pre- and post-1989, in the Federal and

Democratic Republics) but often messily overlap them, leading to a complex layering of memorial activities and processes that do not sit easily with each other. Memory, then, can be found in the mundane, the bureaucratic, but this is all part of the history of memorials and monuments.

The history of memorials should not stop with content but must be sensitive to monumental form as well. Although abstraction can be found in monuments to the victims of the Great War, as in the Cenotaph in London's Whitehall designed by Edwin Lutyens, this aspect of form and design was often intended to contribute to the redemption of loss and its translation into a set of transcendent meanings. However, it would be a mistake to suggest that such monuments did not gesture towards the problematization of historical representation. As Mike Rowlands puts it, 'material images take the place of verbal images precisely at those points where naming things becomes impossible'.[36] Implicit in the monument's very material presence is a failure to articulate fully the events memorialized. What is more, the inscribed lists of names common to most if not all World War I monuments may, on the one hand, de-individuate and dehistoricize the fallen – all that the dead have in common is the fact of their death – making them malleable figures in the service of nationalist narratives of war. Yet, naming also foregrounds that incompleteness of reference suggested by Rowlands: the monument can never fully remember individual losses and therefore can never fully conscript the dead for services to nation.

While World War I monuments introduce notions of the limits of representation, the extremes of modernity experienced in World War II and the Holocaust have informed a wave of what Young has described as 'anti-redemptive' or 'counter-monumental' architecture.[37] Since the 1980s in Germany in particular, 'anti-redemptive' architecture has been considered the only appropriate form by which to memorialize the Holocaust. Since then, German architectural memorialization of the Holocaust has taken a counter-monumental turn. Counter-monuments are designed to avoid the perceived fascistic connotations of monumentalism (the imposition on the public of a monolithic version of the past). Consequently, they do not remember the victims in the final and redemptive terms of the perpetrators. Necessarily open-ended, the counter-monument does not turn the absence of the Holocaust's victims into a presence through their complete memorial (monumental) representation. It is not just the absence of the Holocaust's victims that is conveyed by a monumental form that cannot substitute for that absence, but the rupture or wound as they were torn from the social and cultural fabric. This idea of a rupture or wound, then, describes the society without those who became its victims and the trauma of those who suffered a radical decontextualization. The consequent incompleteness of these monuments – their architectural articulation of the wound and their refusal to complete the representation of those they remember – creates space for the visitor's continuation of the memory-work that cannot be concluded by the monument. In fact, it is the traumatic structure of the architecture that is designed to provoke remembrance or at least the attempt to remember. Architecture ruptured by loss – or designed around a series of voids – suggests the belated intrusion of the past (and its affectiveness) upon the present. It is the present generation, the monument's visitors, then, who act as vicarious witnesses to what was beyond witnessing when it occurred.

A seminal example of the counter-monument can be found in Jochen and Esther Shalev Gerz's 'Monument against Fascism, War and Violence – and for Peace and Human Rights'. In a shopping centre of Harburg (a working class and guest-worker suburb of Hamburg), the Gerzes built a self-effacing monument. It was unveiled on 10 October 1986 as a 12-metre high, 1-metre square, pillar, covered with a layer of soft lead. An inscription near its base reads in German, French, English, Russian, Hebrew, Arabic and Turkish:

> We invite the citizens of Harburg, and visitors to the town, to add their names here to ours. In doing so we commit ourselves to remain vigilant. As more and more names cover this 12-meter tall lead column, it will be gradually lowered into the ground. One day it will have disappeared completely, and site of the Harburg monument against fascism will be empty. In the end, it is only we ourselves who can rise up against injustice.

Using steel-pointed styli attached to the monument, visitors made their own inscriptions. One-and-a-half metres at a time, the monument was lowered into a chamber beneath it (as deep as the monument was high). On 10 November 1993, lowered for the eighth time, the monument disappeared (except for its top surface now at ground level), and the burden of memory was, hopefully, fully divested to those who visited and will visit the site. As Jochen Gerz puts it, 'we will one day reach the point of where anti-Fascist memorials will no longer be necessary, when vigilance will be kept alive by the invisible pictures of resemblance'.[38] As Young adds, '"invisible pictures", in this case, would correspond to our internalized images of the memorial itself, now locked into the mind's eye as a source of perpetual memory. All that remains, then, is the memory of the monument, an after-image projected onto the landscape by the rememberer. The best monument, in Gerz's view, may be no monument at all, but only the memory of an absent monument'.[39]

The monument was conceived in opposition to a perceived association of monumentality and fascism, or rather fascism's exploitation of monumentality. In other words, the fascistic counterpart imposes a version of the past on its visitors: it is the materialization of a master narrative. The invited interaction between spectator and the Gerzes' monument encourages memory-work that would have been discouraged under its projected fascistic counterpart. As Jochen Gerz put it: 'the point is finding the form in which to publicise something, a form that isn't denunciative, that exerts only the slightest pressure, that doesn't point any fingers at anyone, but instead – by removing and withdrawing all the means of pressure you have – brings what has been repressed to light in the midst of the square.'[40] Visitors to the monument literally co-author its meaning, and this meaning changed over time with each new inscription and lowering, reflecting the impermanent and ever-changing nature of memory itself. 'In its conceptual self-destruction, the counter-monument refers not only to its physical impermanence, but also to the contingency of all meaning and memory – especially that embodied in a form that insists on its eternal fixity.'[41]

The counter-monument presents an absence to be filled by the memory work of those who visit it – an absence the emptiness of which is resonant with the traumatic effect of historic loss that memorialization cannot redeem – and suggests a disruptive form of historical representation that finds its corollary in recent innovations in the writing of Holocaust history. For example, Saul Friedländer has incorporated elements of Holocaust testimony, diary, chronicle and memoir – what might be described as the inscriptions of memory – into Holocaust history. Friedländer terms memory, so inscribed, as a form of 'commentary' on the linear narrative drive common to much if not all forms of historiography:

> The commentary should disrupt the facile linear progression of the narration, introduce alternative interpretations, question any partial conclusion, withstand the need for closure. Because of the necessity of some form of narrative sequence in the writing of history, such commentary may introduce splintered or constantly recurring refractions of a traumatic past . . . . [and] puncture such normality.[42]

Commentary, then, holds the claims of history in check, prevents the narrative organization of the past and its momentum from over-determining conclusions about that past. Conversely, the vagaries of inscribed memory, its disrupted and disruptive representation of the past, is given coherence and anchorage by the conventions of historical narrative. The dialectical exchange between history and (inscribed) memory is practised in Friedländer's historiography, namely *The Years of Persecution: Nazi Germany and the Jews, 1933–1939* (2007) and *The Years of Extermination: Nazi Germany and the Jews, 1939–1945* (2008).[43]

There are other, related ways to consider the materialization of anti-redemptive memorialization in terms of narrative irresolution and its corollaries in historical writing. What the following will argue is that counter-monumentalism may be thought of as an intransitive form of historical narration. For Hayden White, this form of narration counters the redemptive modes by which the Holocaust is emplotted. Historical narratives are rendered meaningful by the modes by which they are emplotted, producing tonal characteristics and narrative expectations of the genres into which they are inscribed. In fact, it is this mode of emplotment that illuminates the inextricability of historical facticity – in terms of the significance accorded past phenomena – and narrativization: facts are not found intact and unmediated by narrative and then presented as such; they are made by their narration. Modes of emplotment can be utilized in the argument that some historical phenomena or happenings lend themselves to particular genres, such as tragedy, which also means that some genres are inherently inappropriate considering the nature of the historical phenomena they represent. While such claims foreclose the possibility of ironic modes of representation, they more problematically naturalize particular modes of emplotment, subsuming the ideological and political contexts and motivations that mediate the production of history. In turn, that naturalization produces narrative competition between emplotted phenomena.[44]

What is more, the tonal qualities lent by genre to historical narrative make some historical participants available for identification and others not. White takes the example of Andreas Hillgruber's *Zweierlei Untergang: Die Zerschlangung des Deutchen Reiches und das Ende des europäischen Judentums* (*Two Kinds of Ruin: the Shattering of the German Reich and the End of the European Jewry*).[45] Hillgruber's historical narrative confers a tragic heroism on the Wehrmacht's defence of Germany's Eastern Front in 1944–45. To focus on and ennoble, in sympathetic fashion, the actions of the Wehrmacht overlooks, as many historians have pointed out, the fact that it was the actions of the Wehrmacht in the East that facilitated the Final Solution, and that those prolonged actions (and delayed surrender) allowed many more Jews to die. Furthermore, the 'tragedy' of the Wehrmacht's actions raises the answered question as to what type of plot is reserved for the 'end of European Jewry', if not tragedy, in this hierarchization of historical narratives. As White summarizes: 'Hillgruber's suggestion for the emplotment of history of the eastern front during the winter of 1944–45 indicates the ways in which a specific plot type (tragedy) can simultaneously determine the kinds of events to be featured in any story that can be told about them and provide a pattern for the assignment of roles that can possibly be played by the agents and agencies inhabiting the scene thus constituted. At the same time, Hillgruber's suggestion also indicates how the choice of a mode of emplotment can justify ignoring certain kinds of events, agents, actions, agencies and patients that may inhabit a given historical scene or its context.'[46]

So, how can historical narration avoid what Eric Santner would describe as 'narrative fetishism' – the orchestration of a narrative of trauma (the 'end of European of Jewry') in such a way as to expunge it, or the fetishization of one trauma (the Wehrmacht's war) over another (the Holocaust)?[47] Or put another way: how can historical narrative avoid redeeming the violence that is its subject matter. Borrowing from the work of Jacques Derrida and Roland Barthes, White argues for a form of intransitive writing, or as he puts it, the articulation of the 'middle voice': 'whereas in the active and passive voices, the subject of the verb is presumed to be external to the action, as either agent or patient, in the middle voice the subject is presumed to be *interior* to the action.' In the activity of writing, the historian, the writing subject, is 'constituted as immediately contemporary with the writing, being effected and affected by it'.[48] Not only does the middle voice, which for Barthes characterizes modernist writing, articulate a challenge to the nineteenth-century mode of realist historical writing that claims objective and disinterested distance on what it represents, it can also work against the redemptive modes of emplotment deployed by twentieth-century historians (and exemplified by Hillgruber) that have the same totalizing effects.

White argues that the modernism of the middle voice is commensurate with the realist intentions of post-1945 historiography but also with the impediments to historical representation engendered by totalitarianism and genocide, with the frustration, disruption and deferral of a total explanation of the experience of those events if not of their actuality.[49] Dominick LaCapra further explains how, taking a disruptive and disrupted form of representation, the middle voice can offer fidelity to the victim's voice without claiming it. The middle voice is empathetic rather than over-identificatory, where identification is the 'unmediated fusion of self and other in which the otherness or alterity of the other is not recognized and respected'; whereas with empathy 'one does not feel compelled or authorized to speak in the other's voice or take the other's place, for example, as surrogate victim or perpetrator', and this is fundamental to an ethical stance towards the other. The middle voice therefore allows proximity to and distance from the other, its subjective stance anchored by a faith in some degree of objective history. 'Empathetic unsettlement' ensues in LaCapra's terms – and this is certainly commensurate with the perception of loss that counter-monumental architecture is designed to provoke – but of equal significance to this relation of the concept of historical writing and the concept of memorialization is the way in which in both forms of representation the subjectivities of those who remember are foregrounded. Where in Hillgruber's revisionism, the historian's line of identification is naturalized by the emplotment of tragedy – the tragedy seems to inhere in the fate of the Wehrmacht, not in the representation of the fate – for LaCapra the resonance of the middle voice generates space around representation in which one's subject position in relation to the past and past actors is illuminated, where, to put it differently, one's 'transferential' relations with the object of remembrance are revealed.[50] After all, the defining concept of the counter-monument is its illumination of the fact that the meaning of memorials is co-authored by those who visit them and occupy their spaces.

Counter-monumental architecture not only corresponds with an ethically appropriate form of writing Holocaust history, it also suggests the antithesis of the invention of traditions that consolidated relatively new national identities and senses of belonging. Yet, a history of memorials should not lose sight of national history – a history of the national uses of Holocaust memorials – while paying attention to the aesthetic and experiential dimension of monuments. The recently built national memorial in Berlin, the

Memorial for the Murdered Jews of Europe, designed by Peter Eisenman, an example of counter-monumental architecture writ large, is a case in point. The memorial, which opened on 10 May 2005, is located east of the Tiergarten and on the western edge of the historic district and between the federal district and the Potsdamer Platz business district. It consists of 2,700 concrete steles of different heights, from 1 and 1.5 to 10 feet tall, contouring an undulating field. (An 800 sq. m underground information centre is located in the southeast corner of the field.)

As Karen Till has argued, the experience of the field changes in relation to the body that navigates it and is unable to impose memory work (dictate a pathway) in a traditional monumental fashion.[51] In this way, Eisenman's architecture constitutes a *Denkmal*, which allows time for reflection, as opposed to a more traditional *Mahnmal*. In other words, Eisenman's architecture seems, at least ostensibly, to be counter-monumental in the sense discussed so far. The counter-monumentality was heightened by the original design (which was co-designed by Richard Serra, who left the project in 1998). The original design featured 4,000 tilted and jagged stone pillars, some up to 20 m high, giving the impression that they might topple. The effect was supposed to be labyrinthine, which, for Eisenman, figures the 'non-narrative, non-linear, non-anthropocentric' – a narrative that is without continuity, conclusion and uninhabitable.[52] The effect still remains with the revised and built design. The experience of the memorial has been described as disorientating, the 'inherent instability' of which allows 'the visitor to take part in a dialogue' with the past rather than experience its monumental imposition.[53] The site, then, is conceptually accessible *and* inaccessible; it cannot emplace memory and those who remember with any permanency, or so the theory goes, and its impermanence allows a dynamic and dialogic process of remembrance – in true counter-monumental fashion.

However, as some critics attest, belying the memorial's counter-monumentality is its monumental implications. Caroline Wiedmer, writing in 1999, was sceptical about the translation of the monumentality of Germany's crime into (counter-)monumental form.[54] Karen Till argues that the memorial overcomes its ostensible *Denkmal* nature to be more '*Mahnmal*, working within a monumental memorial culture of admonishment located in a highly visible public space. Its mandate that Germans show guilt and mourning reflects the culture of dismay and consternation (*Betroffenheit*), which are in turn defined by universal Western metaphysical categories of good and evil'.[55] That a national monument explicitly refers to a wider European context signals Germany's place in a new post-Cold War, international moral order.[56] (Indeed, as Jordan points out, debate over the memorial's evolution in local and national political forums, public meetings and symposia, international design competitions and newspaper articles received both national and international attention and commentary.)[57] This international display of shame marks a shift in the way in which nations fashion their own history. After 1989, national 'History' is not defined as 'triumphalist', something to emulate, but as something not to repeat. Negative events become points of orientation for national 'History', and the difference between past and present the measure of progress.[58] Yet, how much progress has been made? Interpreted positively, the monument's explicitly European coordinates are a reminder of the European dimensions of Germany's responsibility and German-inflicted loss, which will in turn prevent German remembrance from looking inwards – using memory in instrumental and nationalist ways.[59] However, a critique of the monument would highlight just that: the monument's instrumentalization of the Holocaust in the service of national identity rather than its reflection on past national crimes and the remembrance of the Holocaust's victims. So, the international moral stance materialized in the monument operates in terms of a simple binary opposition of good and evil, by which past evils can be circumscribed or made good by the 'hypervisible' display of shame and guilt.[60] The memorial thereby contributes to national identity by distancing the past, effectively rendering past mass violence, social injustice and the victims of the Holocaust invisible beneath this 'hypervisibility'.[61]

The idea of the hypervisible extends to the memorial's specific reference to Jewish victims, separates them from German perpetrators and makes it difficult to lump together all victims of World War II, National Socialism and the Holocaust, which had been a tendency of West German memory in particular. This disaggregation is at the expense of the exclusion of other victims of genocide, particularly the Roma and Sinti.[62] By creating a 'meta-Holocaust victim category, Germany will continue to define Jews as Other in the nation's contemporary society through the memorial and the culture of dismay and mourning'.[63] Remembering Jews becomes the very means of their re-exclusion from German society and culture – and this othering is instrumental in a series of other exclusions (the Roma and Sinti and other victims).

By way of conclusion, it is worth noting that critics have seen the Berlin monument as symptomatic of the globalization of Holocaust memory, in that its national centrality is associated with the trends of a global Holocaust memory industry with its easy-to-consume and popular representations of the Holocaust. That centralization in turn detracts attention away from a decentralized network of local memorial and monumental sites across Germany and Europe that represent the complex operations and reach of the Holocaust.[64] Yet the globalization of the Holocaust, and the idea of global historical memory in general, is something that a history of memorials and monuments should countenance in less dismissive terms. Recent directions in historiography have explored the structural continuities and discontinuities between modernity's extremes, particularly between episodes of colonial violence and the Holocaust, finding a wide-reaching genocidal logic or potential shared by events.[65] While historiography has laid down the conceptual grounds for comparing atrocities, memory studies has been ambivalent about the globalization of memory. Daniel Levy and Natan Sznaider advocate a cosmopolitanized Holocaust memory, which instituted internationally can be a measure of and spur to the institution of human rights across nations.[66] Put differently, an imported Holocaust memory becomes the paradigm by which local traumas can be represented and recognized. Aleida Assmann begs to differ.[67] What worries Assmann about the globalization of memory is its putative standardization as a top-down memory that rides roughshod over local landscapes, institutes, sites, places, spaces and textures of memory. Such a universalized memory may not resonate with multicultural constituencies of memory, for whom other traumas are prominent, nor with different generations of memory for whom recent events may be more defining, and such memory may displace indigenous traumas and so inform the erection of evasive screen memories. Her worst fear is that the Holocaust is reduced to a global icon disseminated and unscrutinized by the mass media, emptied of historical content and pressed into serving potentially any social cause. Assmann calls for a delimitation of the Holocaust's memory community and a distinction between memory and history: 'History is universal and memory particular' she writes.[68] It seems, then, that a future history of memorials and monuments needs to scrutinize the way in which intersecting histories are memorialized, historicizing local inflections of remembrance in the face of globalized memory while mindful of the cosmopolitan possibilities of a meeting of memories.

Notes

1 James E. Young, *The Texture of Meaning: Holocaust Memorials and Meaning* (New Haven and London, 1993), p. 3.

2 Jay Winter, 'Sites of Memory', in Susannah Radstone and Bill Schwarz (eds), *Memory: Histories, Theories, Debates* (New York, 2010), pp. 312–25 (here, p. 313).

3 Susannah S. Radstone, 'Reconceiving Binaries: The Limits of Memory'. *History Workshop Journal* 59 (2005), 134–50.

4 Eric Hobsbawm, 'Introduction: The Invention of Tradition', in Eric Hobsbawm and Terence Ranger (eds), *The Invention of Tradition* (Cambridge, 2010), pp. 1–14 (here, pp. 2–3).

5 Hobsbawm, 'Introduction: The Invention of Tradition', pp. 9–10, 12–13; Eric Hobsbawm, 'Mass-Producing Traditions: Europe, 1870–1914', in Hobsbawm and T. Ranger (eds), *The Invention of Tradition*, pp. 263–308 (here, pp. 263–5, 271–2, 275–6).

6 Hobsbawm, 'Introduction: The Invention of Tradition', p. 14.

7 Ibid., p. 13.

8 Alon Confino, 'Collective Memory and Cultural History'. *American Historical Review* 102:5 (1997), 1386–403 (here, pp. 1389–91).

9 Wulf Kansteiner, 'Finding Meaning in Memory: A Methodological Critique of Memory Studies'. *History and Theory* 41 (2002), 179–97 (here, p. 197).

10 Confino, 'Collective Memory and Cultural History', pp. 1395–7.

11 James Young, *The Texture of Meaning: Holocaust Memorials and Meaning* (New Haven and London, 1993), p. xi.

12 Young, *The Texture of Meaning*, p. xi.

13 Jay Winter, *Sites of Memory, Sites of Mourning: The Great War in European Cultural History* (Cambridge, 2009), pp. 93–8.

14 Jay Winter, 'Sites of Memory', in Radstone and Schwarz (eds), *Memory: Histories, Theories, Debates*, pp. 312–25 (here, p. 322).

15 Winter, 'Sites of Memory', pp. 316–17.

16 J. R. Gillis, 'Memory and Identity: The History of a Relationship', in J. R. Gillis (ed.), *Commemoration: The Politics of National Identity* (Princeton, 1996), pp. 3–26, (here, p. 6).

17 Maurice Halbwachs, *On Collective Memory*, ed. and trans. L. A. Coser (Chicago, 1992), pp. 40, 52–3.

18 Aleida Assmann, 'Four Formats of Memory: From Individual to Collective Constructions of the Past', in Christian Emden and David Midgley (eds), *Cultural Memory and Historical Consciousness in the German Speaking World Since 1500* (Bern, 2004), pp. 19–37 (here, pp. 22–36); Aleida Assmann, 'Memory, Individual and Collective', in Robert E. Goodin and Charles Tilly (eds), *The Oxford Handbook of Contextual Political Analysis* (Oxford, 2006), pp. 210–24 (here, pp. 211–23); Aleida Assmann, 'Transformations between History and Memory', *Social Research* 75:1 (2008), pp. 49–71 (esp. pp. 51–6); Jan Assmann, 'Collective Memory and Cultural Identity', trans. by J. Czaplicka. *New German Critique* 65 (1995), 125–33 (here, pp. 127–32).

19 Ann Rigney, 'Plenitude, Scarcity and the Circulation of Cultural Memory'. *Journal of European Studies* 35:1 (2000), 11–28; Ann Rigney, 'Portable Monuments: Literature, Cultural Memory, and the Case of Jeanie Deans'. *Poetics Today* 25:2 (2004), 361–96.

20 Alon Confino and Peter Fritzsche, 'Introduction: Noises of the Past', in Alon Confino and Peter Fritzsche (eds), *The Work of Memory: New Directions in the Study of German Society and Culture* (Urbana and Chicago, 2002), pp. 1–24.

21 See the chapter by Benoît Majerus in this volume.

22 Pierre Nora 'Between Memory and History: *Les Lieux de Memoire*', trans. by M. Roundebush. *Representations* 26 (1989), 7–25.

23 Nora, 'Between Memory and History', p. 9.

24 Dominick LaCapra, *History and Memory After Auschwitz* (Ithaca and London, 1998), pp. 19–20.

25 Winter, 'Sites of Memory', p. 314.

26 LaCapra, *History and Memory*, pp. 19–20.

27 Marita Sturken, *Tangled Memories: The Vietnam War, The AIDS Epidemic, and the Politics of Remembering* (Berkeley, 1997), pp. 1–17.

28 Winter, 'Sites of Memory', p. 314.

29 Susannah Radstone, 'Screening Trauma: *Forrest Gump*, Film and Memory', in Susannah Radstone (ed.), *Memory and Methodology* (Oxford, 2000), pp. 79–110 (here, p. 84).

30 Radstone, 'Reconceiving Binaries', p. 140.

31 Ibid.

32 Kerwin Lee Klein, 'On the Emergence of *Memory* in Historical Discourse'. *Representations* 69 (2000), 127–50.

33 See Peter Carrier, *Holocaust Monuments and National Memory Cultures in France and Germany since 1989* (New York and Oxford, 2005) and Caroline Wiedmer, *The Claims of Memory: Representations of the Holocaust in Contemporary Germany and France* (Ithaca and London, 1999).

34 Jennifer Jordan, *Structures of Memory: Understanding Urban Change in Berlin and Beyond* (Stanford, 2006), p. 132.

35 Jordan, *Structures of Memory*, pp. 1–2.

36 Mike Rowlands, 'Memory, Sacrifice and the Nation'. *New Formations* 30 (1996), 8–17 (here, pp. 8–10).

37 James E. Young, *At Memory's Edge: After-Images of the Holocaust in Contemporary Art and Architecture* (New Haven and London, 2000).

38 Quoted in Young, *At Memory's Edge*, p. 134.

39 Young, *At Memory's Edge*, p. 134.

40 Quoted in Noam Lupu, 'Memory Vanished, Absent, and Confined: The Countermemorial Project in 1980s and 1990s Germany'. *History and Memory* 15:2 (2003), 130–64 (here, p. 137).

41 Young, *The Texture of Memory*, p. 48.

42 Saul Friedländer, *History, Memory and the Extermination of the Jews* (Bloomington and Indianapolis, 1993), p. 132.

43 Saul Friedländer, *The Years of Persecution: Nazi Germany and the Jews, 1933–1939* (London, 2007) and Saul Friedländer, *The Years of Extermination: Nazi Germany and the Jews, 1939–1945* (London, 2008).

44 Hayden White, 'Historical Emplotment and the Problem of Truth', in Saul Friedlander (ed.), *Probing the Limits of Representation* (Cambridge, MA, 1992), pp. 37–53.

45 Andreas Hillgruber, *Zweierlei Untergang: Die Zerschlagung des Deutschen Reiches und das Ende des europäischen Judentums* (Berlin, 1986).

46 White, 'Historical Emplotment and the Problem of Truth', pp. 42–3.

47 Eric Santner, 'History Beyond the Pleasure Principle: Some Thoughts on the Representation of Trauma', in Saul Friedlander (ed.), *Probing the Limits of Representation*, pp. 143–54 (here, p. 144).

48 White, 'Historical Emplotment and the Problem of Truth', pp. 48–9.

49 Ibid., p. 52.

50 Dominick LaCapra, *Representing the Holocaust: History, Theory, Trauma* (London, 1996), p. 46; Dominick LaCapra, *Writing History, Writing Trauma* (Baltimore, 2001), pp. 27–8, 30, 35, 41, 198.

51 Karen E. Till, *The New Berlin: Memory, Politics, Place* (Minneapolis and London, 2005), p. 167.

52 Peter Eisenman, quoted in Brett Ashley Kaplan, *Unwanted Beauty: Aesthetic Pleasure in Holocaust Representation* (Urbana and Chicago, 2007), p. 158.

53   Bill Niven, *Facing the Nazi Past: United Germany and the Legacy of the Third Reich* (London and New York, 2002), p. 232.

54   Wiedmer, *The Claims of Memory*, p. 151.

55   Till, *The New Berlin*, p. 187.

56   Ibid., pp. 21–2.

57   Jordan, *Structures of Memory*, pp. 124–5.

58   Niven, *Facing the Nazi Past*, p. 215.

59   Ibid., pp. 215, 218.

60   Till, *The New Berlin*, p. 202.

61   Ibid., p. 204.

62   Niven, *Facing the Nazi Past*, p. 218.

63   Till, *The New Berlin*, p. 188.

64   Wiedmer, *The Claims of Memory*, pp. 162–4.

65   See, for example, A. Dirk Moses (ed.), *Empire, Colony, Genocide* (New York and Oxford, 2008).

66   Daniel Levy and Natan Sznaider, *The Holocaust and Memory in the Global Age*, trans. by A. Oksiloff (Philadelphia, 2005).

67   Aleida Assmann, 'The Holocaust – a Global Memory? Extensions and Limits of a New Memory Community', in Aleida Assmann and Sebastian Conrad (eds), *Memory in a Global Age: Discourses, Practices, and Trajectories* (London, 2010), pp. 97–108.

68   Assmann, 'The Holocaust – a Global Memory?', p. 99.

Further reading

Aleida Assmann, 'The Holocaust – a Global Memory? Extensions and Limits of a New Memory Community', in Aleida Assmann and Sebastian Conrad (eds), *Memory in a Global Age: Discourses, Practices, and Trajectories* (London, 2010), pp. 97–118.

Peter Carrier, *Holocaust Monuments and National Memory Cultures in France and Germany since 1989* (New York and Oxford, 2005).

Jennifer Jordan, *Structures of Memory: Understanding Urban Change in Berlin and Beyond* (Stanford, 2006).

Saul Friedländer, *The Years of Persecution: Nazi Germany and the Jews, 1933–1939* (London, 2007).

—, *The Years of Extermination: Nazi Germany and the Jews, 1939–1945* (London, 2008).

John Gillis, 'Memory and Identity: The History of a Relationship', in John R. Gillis (ed.), *Commemoration: The Politics of National Identity* (Princeton, 1996), pp. 3–26.

Eric Hobsbawm, 'Introduction: The Invention of Tradition', in Eric Hobsbawm and Terence Ranger (eds), *The Invention of Tradition* (Cambridge, 2010a), pp. 1–14.

—, 'Mass-Producing Traditions: Europe, 1870–1914', in Eric Hobsbawm and Terence Ranger (eds), *The Invention of Tradition* (Cambridge, 2010b), pp. 263–308.

Wulf Kansteiner, 'Genealogy of Category Mistake: A Critical Intellectual History of the Cultural Trauma Metaphor'. *Rethinking History* 8.2 (2004), 193–221.

Kerwin L. Klein, 'On the Emergence of Memory in Historical Discourse'. *Representations* 69 (2000), 127–50.

Dominick LaCapra, *History and Memory After Auschwitz* (Ithaca and London, 1998).

Daniel Levy and Natan Sznaider, *The Holocaust and Memory in the Global Age*, trans. by A. Oksiloff (Philadelphia, 2005).

Noam Lupu, 'Memory Vanished, Absent, and Confined: The Countermemorial Project in 1980s and 1990s Germany'. *History and Memory* 15.2 (2003), 130–64.

Dirk Moses (ed.), *Empire, Colony, Genocide* (New York and Oxford, 2008).

Bill Niven, *Facing the Nazi Past: United Germany and the Legacy of the Third Reich* (London and New York, 2002).

Pierre Nora, 'Between Memory and History: Les Lieux de Memoire'. trans. M. Roundebush, *Representations* 26 (1989), 7–25.

Susannah Radstone, 'Screening Trauma: Forrest Gump, Film and Memory', in Susannah Radstone (ed.), *Memory and Methodology* (Oxford, 2000), pp. 79–110.

—, 'Reconceiving Binaries: The Limits of Memory'. *History Workshop Journal* 59 (2005), 134–50.

Michael Rowlands, 'Memory, Sacrifice and the Nation'. *New Formations* 30 (1996), 8–17.

Marita Sturken, *Tangled Memories: The Vietnam War, The AIDS Epidemic, and the Politics of Remembering* (Berkeley, 1997).

Karen E. Till, *The New Berlin: Memory, Politics, Place* (Minneapolis and London, 2005).

Caroline Wiedmer, *The Claims of Memory: Representations of the Holocaust in Contemporary Germany and France* (Ithaca and London, 1999).

Jay Winter, *Sites of Memory, Sites of Mourning: The Great War in European Cultural History* (Cambridge, 2009).

—, 'Sites of Memory', in Susannah Radstone and Bill Schwarz (eds), *Memory: Histories, Theories, Debates* (New York, 2010), pp. 312–25.

James E. Young, *The Texture of Meaning: Holocaust Memorials and Meaning* (New Haven and London, 1993).

—, *At Memory's Edge: After-Images of the Holocaust in Contemporary Art and Architecture* (New Haven and London, 2000).

INDEX